Applauding Thunder

Applauding Thunder

life, work and critics of Alexander Smith

Simon Berry

First published in Great Britain by FTRR Press 2013

1 3 5 7 9 10 8 6 4 2

Copyright (c) 2013 by Simon Berry

This book is copyright under the Berne Convention. No reproduction without permission. All rights reserved.
The right of Simon Berry to be identified as the author of this work has been asserted by him in accordance with the Copyright, Designs and Patents Act 1988.

All rights reserved. No part of this publication may be reproduced, stored in a retrieval system, or transmitted in any form or by any means, electronic, mechanical, photocopying, recording or otherwise, without the prior permission of the copyright owner.

A CIP catalogue record for this book is available from the British Library

ISBN: 978-1-905787-59-3

More background information on this book is available on
http://www.facebook.com/ApplaudingThunder

Printed by FTRR Press, 60 Grant Street,
Inverness IV3 8BN

Contents

Acknowledgments   vii

Narrative & Dramatis Personae   viii

1: (1829-41)   1
Kilmarnock & birthdate – move to Paisley – death of Katy – move to Glasgow: social conditions – Charlotte Street – schooling and "brain fever" – apprenticeship

2: (1841-47)   15
Weaving in Bridgeton – growth of cotton industry – embroidered muslins trade – early reading – designing at Robertsons' warehouse – Worker poets –Rev. George Gilfillan – the Disruption and Evangelicalism

3: (1847-50)   30
Culture in 1840s Glasgow – Glasgow Addisonians – influence of Thomas Brisbane – Hugh Macdonald and Pat Alexander – social conditions and 'Glasgow' – poet not preacher

4: (1850-52)   45
James Hedderwick and 'Lines to a Friend' – death of Barbara – contact with Gilfillan – Pringle Nichol and Glasgow College – serialisation in The Critic – contributions to the Scottish Athenaeum

5: (1853)   60
Poems published – the periodical press – 'A Life-Drama' and its reception – reaction to celebrity – London with John Nichol – application for Secretary post at Edinburgh College – The Glasgow Miscellany

6: (1854-56)   79
Scottish universities – the New College – Prof. Aytoun – *Firmilian* and the Spasmodic School – Sydney Dobell and *Sonnets on the War* – social cronies – Horatio McCulloch on Skye – Raleigh Club

7: (1857)   98
The Athenaeum – 'Z', Henry Chorley and plagiarism – Smith's defenders – 'Scottish Ballads' and Prof Blackie – Secretary's disciplinary duties – marriage to Flora MacDonald – reception of *City Poems* – the mid-Victorian critical temper

8: (1858-61) **121**
Married life – mid-Victorian Edinburgh literary scene – University Reform legislation – publication and reception of *Edwin of Deira* – Wardie – early essays in Blackwoods and Macmillan's – Kenneth McLeod of Gesto – student riots

9: (1861-64) **140**
Gesto Villa and a-musement – Secretary's drudgery – RSA reviewing – Alexander Strahan and Good Words – essays for NB Review – Montaigne and 'deceits' – publication and reception of *Dreamthorp* – 'A Lark's Flight'

10: (1864-65) **158**
Golden Treasury *Burns* – Alexander Nicolson and social vagabonds – *Alfred Hagart's Household* serialised – RSA reviewing – 'The Minister-Painter' – Gilfillan's 'Night'

11: (1865-67) **175**
A Summer in Skye published – Flora's family – 'An Essay on an Old Subject' – failing health – 'A Spring Chanson' – *Golden Leaves from the American Poets* – the Quiver and last poems – death

12: (1867-73) **193**
Obituaries and contemporary critical standing – former attempts at biographies – fate of siblings – Flora's last years

13: (postscript) **206**
City poet? – Scottish ? – Spasmodic? – writers influenced? – RLS's debt

Appendix: The Gestation of 'Glasgow' **214**

Notes 220

Bibliography 229

Index 235

Acknowledgements

I OWE A HUGE DEBT of thanks to Prof. Florence Boos of the University of Iowa English Department for the time she devoted to making invaluable suggestions based on her knowledge of the Victorian scene. This was when I was revising the original typescript whilst teaching in Cyprus. Many insights are largely thanks to her, but the oversights are entirely of my own making.

This book would also have been impossible without the continuous input of Hamish Whyte, formerly head of Rare Books and Manuscripts at the Mitchell Library, Glasgow. He read through numerous revisions without demur. I must also thank Elizabeth Sutherland for agreeing to read through the final MS. and Prof. Douglas Dunn for reading the original draft, making helpful comments and giving me useful contacts in the academic world.

Parts of the revised MS has been read and commented upon by the following, again to my great benefit in new information and informed comment: John P. McCaffrey, Prof. Robert Crawford, Prof. Richard Cronin, the late Edwin Morgan, Prof. Ian Campbell. Once again all failings are my own. Parts of this work have already appeared in issues of *Scottish Book Collector* and my thanks go to Jennie Renton for her encouragement.

Facilities were afforded to me for research by the following institutions: University of Glasgow Library and Special Collections department; the National Library of Scotland manuscripts department; the Dick Institute, Kilmarnock; Paisley Museum & Art Gallery; The British Library newspaper collection, Colindale; University of Edinburgh Library special collections department and also their press office. Martha Sachs of the Penn State Harrisburg Library (Special Collections) also provided me with valuable material on the US sales of Smith's work.

I was delighted to be able to correspond with and eventually meet Smith's two grand-daughters Dorothea and Marian (both now deceased). For the Skye portions I am indebted to feedback and encouragement from Prof. James Hunter, Ruaraidh Maclean and Derek Cooper.

Thanks should go to the Scottish Arts Council for a research grant more than twenty years ago and to the then Literature Director Walter Cairns. Finally thanks are due to my long-suffering colleagues at FTRR, Kevin Swanson and Stewart Forbes who coped with everything.

Dingwall, Scotland
March 2013

Narrative & Dramatis Personae

Alexander Smith worked as a pattern-designer in a Glasgow muslin warehouse for 12 years before being discovered and hailed as a second Keats. At the age of 23 he became famous overnight through the publication of 'A Life-Drama'. It received rave notices, but some reviewers sneered at his lack of a formal education.

His friend **Hugh MacDonald**, a journalist and versifier who habitually wore a plumed Glengarry bonnet, had trained as a blockmaker in the Bridgeton area of the city. MacDonald encouraged the apprentice to send off his verses, initially written furtively on scraps of paper at his work.

They were read by **Rev. George Gilfillan**, an influential literary talent scout and Free Church minister in Dundee. Gilfillan championed a new breed of poets who aimed to dispel the mid-Victorian mellowness typified by Tennyson and Arnold. Typically the new poets were from modest backgrounds with radical views and wrote to gain attention. Gilfillan advised him to create a long dramatic poem, thereby claiming for himself some of the credit for Smith's success.

He was invited to London to meet assorted editors and literati, accompanied on the journey south by **John Nichol** (the son of Prof. Pringle Nichol at Glasgow College) also a poet and academic in the making. He later took the English chair at Glasgow and defended Smith from repeated critical attacks.

Thanks to **James Hedderwick**, who had already championed Smith in the Glasgow Evening Citizen, he was in 1854 offered the job of Secretary to the College (later University) of Edinburgh. This involved a 10 to 4 daily round of administrative chores but it allowed him a long annual holiday in August and September.

Smith had been greatly influenced by the poet **Sydney Dobell**, already lauded for his long epic *The Roman*. Dobell had just moved to Edinburgh, he and his wife both prizing the medical treatment available there. They, along with two or three other younger poets, became known as The Spasmodic School.

Son-in-law of Prof. John Wilson (Christopher North), **W.E. Aytoun** was one of the Blackwoods set and held the chair of Rhetoric and

Belles-Lettres at Edinburgh. Shortly after Smith's arrival to take up the Secretary post, Aytoun published his Spasmodic spoof, entitled *Firmilian* (by 'T.Percy Jones') which ridiculed stylistic excess and by implication undermined any attempt to counter the literary elitism of the times. Despite the devastating effect of *Firmilian* (which destroyed Gilfillan completely) Smith and Aytoun over the next decade seem to have developed a mutual respect.

Another of the Edinburgh professors Smith grew to like was **John Stuart Blackie**, an eccentric but brilliant linguist who was responsible for promoting both Scottish University Reform and Home Rule. He held the Chair of Greek for more than thirty years and made his subject more accessible. They disagreed over the role of contemporary poetry since Blackie supported re-inventing the ballad form.

Another Edinburgh friend was the landscape painter **Horatio McCulloch** who regularly threw late dinners in his Danube Street studio. Married to a Macdonald from Skye, McCulloch always spent a summer break on the island for initial sketches which were later worked up into his giant canvases. He took Smith along and it was on the Sleat peninsula he met **Flora Macdonald**, an indirect descendant of the Jacobite heroine and possessor of a locket containing Bonnie Prince Charlie's hair.

Smith's second collection *City Poems* (containing his best-known poem 'Glasgow') was published just after he returned from his honeymoon. Quite different stylistically from his first book it was savaged by the critics. Earlier that year (1857) Smith had been the target of a plagiarism campaign which began with an anonymous letter in the highbrow weekly The Athenaeum. The writer was a rival poet **William Allingham** whose publications had been overshadowed by Smith's. The charges, on slender evidence, were fortified by the literary editor **Henry Chorley**, another thwarted writer.

Kenneth McLeod was Flora's uncle who had made a fortune from indigo manufacture in Bengal. He returned to Skye and bought large swathes of the Macleod estates to introduce new approaches to crofting. Thanks to Kenneth's generosity the newly-weds were able to move into a large house in Wardie but this soon proved a financial burden. Now destroyed as a poet, Smith had to turn to prose to supplement the Secretary's modest salary.

Encouraged by Gaelic scholar **Alexander Nicolson,** he wrote *A Summer in Skye,* utilising material he had already written for several monthly periodicals. **Alexander Strahan**, who made and lost a fortune from periodical publishing, brought out the book in 1865 with great success and it has rarely been out of print since. Strahan also published his Montaigne-inspired book of essays *Dreamthorp* and an autobiographical novel which he had written in monthly instalments for serialisation.

On the death of Aytoun, Smith stood for the Professorship but was let down by his lack of academic credentials, plus he was a poor public speaker. **David Masson,** one of his supporters during the Spasmodic days, took the Chair. Smith now had well-placed friends in both Glasgow and Edinburgh but London critics never accepted him on merit. Aware that his health was failing he wrote furiously, mainly journalistic essays, to leave some kind of a legacy for his growing family whilst still continuing with his university job. A few days after his 37th birthday he died of typhus.

James Hannay, a native Scot who made his name as an editor in London, had come up to edit the Edinburgh Courant. He was one of a small group who used to meet at Smith's house for A-musement evenings (i.e. without any muse). They were in the main non-practising lawyers, freelance *Britannica* contributors, grubbing writers and other aimless individuals known as Vagabonds. Smith was far more at home with these more down-to-earth characters than the Edinburgh *beau monde.*

The only biography of Smith is *The Early Years* by Rev. **Thomas Brisbane** who knew Smith during the years before 'A Life-Drama' was published in 1853. Brisbane misleadingly tries to make Smith into a saintly figure diverted from a career in the ministry through his scandalous success as a poet. However, it is thanks to Brisbane that we still have the minute book of the Glasgow Addisonian Literary Society (with entries in Smith's hand) and a series of heartbreaking letters written by Flora after his death.

To Colleen

In memory of those Easters at Ord

Chapter 1:
1829-41

Merciful God!
It comes – that face again, that white, white face
Set in a night of hair; reproachful eyes
That make me mad. Oh, save me from those eyes!
('A Life-Drama' sc.10)

IT WAS A FAMILY JOKE that baby Aleck had first-footed his mother by being born either late on December 31st or early on January 1st[1]. This became a custom he apparently kept up throughout his life even when he had a family of his own. His adult personality showed traces of both parents. The semi-autobiographical novel *Alfred Hagart's Household* emphasises the difference between his father's excitable artistic nature and the more practical attitude of his mother, usually pictured at the needlework which formed a necessary extra source of family income. A Glasgow newspaper article[2] revealed the close fit between the fictional characters and the originals. John Smith, Aleck's father, was born in 1803 in Ayrshire, in the Burns country. Nothing is known of his early life, but he seems to have deserted his agricultural background to study art in London. Here he met Christina Murray, who was a year younger. When the reminiscence was originally written both parents were in their sixties. John was credited with "a delightful and quiet manner" and "he spoke in a clear, slow, distinct manner that was more like Edinburgh than the West of Scotland where he had lived so long."

Whether it was through lack of ambition or opportunity, John never succeeded as a watercolour painter. Back in Scotland he turned to pattern designing for the booming muslin shawl industry based chiefly in Paisley and Glasgow. By moving from one warehouse to another he seems to have brought in a steady income. One senses the writer was more impressed by Christina who, although she came from Paisley, had Highland gentry connections:

The mother was a gifted woman, intelligent, industrious, full of courage and resource, quiet in manner with Scottish pride that made her always remember that she was one of the Highland Murrays, and yet [possessing] a commonsense that never deserted her. She had many troubles and disappointments, but she bore all burdens bravely, and I never found her manner change in all the years I knew her.[3]

John and Christina lived to see a daughter die in early childhood and three sons dead before the age of forty. The two surviving daughters both married: young Christina went to America, while of Marion nothing is known. The parents' early life before marriage seems to have been plagued by misfortune too. In the novel Alfred (John) gives painting lessons at a girls school and makes the classic mistake of eloping with Margaret (Christina), one of his pupils. Margaret's aged father reacts to type and cuts her off without a penny:

> Old port and bad temper in a year or two assisted the irate old gentleman into the other world; and then his money – and report said he cut up well – was divided equally between his children by his first marriage – Kate, a spinster lady living at Hawkhead, and Hector, sheep-farmer and married man, in the remotest Hebrides – leaving not a stiver to his youngest daughter and, up till the period of her disgraceful marriage, his best beloved.[4]

Margaret's small savings are soon dissipated by Alfred playing the stock market. They have to return to the West of Scotland where they are soon blessed with a first child named John after the poet Milton. Within fifteen months a daughter Catherine was born. In reality Alexander (known as Aleck, and possibly named after Dumas père) and Catherine (known as Katy) were born in a new 2-storey thatched cottage in Kilmarnock, one of a row in Douglas (now Bentinck) Street, a short cul-de-sac running between the main Glasgow road and the Kilmarnock burn. A nearby footbridge led west to extensive cow-pastures flanked to the north by the Troon railroad. It was used by two prototype steam engines taking coal, timber and slates to the Ayrshire coast.

With a population of around 15,000 (in 1831) Kilmarnock was a rapidly growing industrial centre. The Second Statistical Account of Scotland noted that 1,400 people were employed in weaving and printing shawls made of worsted. Interestingly the writer, a local minister, after commenting favourably on the "vigorous proportions" of the local peasantry (contrasted with the dissolute town-dwellers) criticises both communities for their "neglect to have their children's names inserted in the parish register." Clearly John and Christina adopted the local custom, presumably to avoid paying a gratuity.

In the summer of 1832 cholera reached Kilmarnock. Around the middle of December John Smith decided to leave and go to Paisley, eighteen miles to the north. The appointed time of departure was the afternoon of Christmas day, a normal working day in Scotland. The means of travel was Petrie's caravan and remarkably there was a witness to the journey. This was 12-year-old Allan Andrews, about to become John Smith's apprentice drawer (or designer). As he was to live with the family in Paisley he accompanied them in the covered wagon along with the furniture and other worldly possessions. They started off on a dull dirty afternoon at four o'clock. Mrs Smith, the poet's mother; Little Aleck, as the future poet was called, at that time a little over three years of age; and his sister Kate, aged about eighteen months, were already stowed away in the caravan amongst boxes, bales and parcels, and I tumbled in amongst them in the best way I could. The journey to Paisley was dreary in the extreme. It was nearly dark when I got into the caravan and of course continued dark the whole way. What with the slow pace of the horse, the numerous stoppings on the road to deliver letters, parcels &c., it was 3 o'clock next morning when we arrived at Petrie's quarters in Causeyside Street, Paisley. The recollections of that journey will never be effaced from my memory. The 11 mortal hours occupied in the journey, the total darkness the whole way, the squalling of the children, the discomfort of the accommodation for passengers, were such that I have often thought that if the horrors of the Middle Passage could beat them they must be very bad indeed.[5]

In Paisley they found their new home "down a narrow, dirty close off Water Wynd, up two flights of stairs into a house occupied by two maiden sisters of Mrs Smith." Later they moved from the Misses Murrays' dilapidated property to 21 Gauze Street, near the Renfrewshire Tontine building. Surviving photos of this weaver's cottage, showing the ground floor workshop converted into a grocer's shop, reveal that the early years of Aleck's childhood were spent in pretty grim conditions. Paisley was to be the Smith family's home for the next six years, although they may have made a short move in the mid 1830s either back to Kilmarnock or to Glasgow. The poet's recollections (in the 1853 note to Hugh Macdonald) are again far from clear, but he clearly retained an afffection for the town where most of his short childhood was spent. In *Alfred Hagart's Household* Greysley is depicted as an urban Arcadia, relatively immune to industrial progress. Hawkhead (Glasgow) was, by contrast, a dynamic and disturbing place where nothing stayed the same for long:

Thirty years ago, before it had become enmeshed in a network of railways, Greysley was a second-rate Scotch town of considerable picturesqueness and individuality. In those days Greysley was self-sustained and had an existence of its own. It sat at its looms and drove its shuttles all day. The inhabitants had their peculiarities of dress and *patois*, and one of them walking the streets of the neighbouring city of Hawkhead – of which Greysley is now a kind of outlying suburb – could be detected at once by a sharp eye. Hawkhead was an energetic place, and was distinguished by the most varied industrial activity. It worked in iron, it built ships, it was continually deepening its river, for on the river its prosperity mainly depended; the glare of its furnaces hung nightly over it; and it was skilful besides in more nice and delicate arts. It hummed with cotton mills, it printed cloths and its muslins were embroidered by the girls of Ulster as they sat before their cottage doors, in sight of their plots of ripening flax, in the summer evenings.

As a consequence of these industrial means and appliances, Hawkhead could keep its pot boiling in tolerable comfort, for while one branch of industry suffered, another was certain to be in respect. Printed cloths and embroidered muslins fluctuated terribly at times, but coal and iron and ships were in constant demand. Greysley, on the other hand, had no variety of occupation. It was to all intents and purposes a weaving town. During the entire day, in the old-fashioned, crooked side streets, the monotonous click of the loom and the sharp whirr of the shuttle were continually heard. While trade was brisk Greysley stuck to its work and lived well; when depressed, it stood in groups about the market-place and the corners of the streets, and in the evenings read and argued over the fiercest political newspapers. Thirty years ago trade was good, and in the spring and summer evenings the weaver, having comfortably dined, bird-nested or botanised, and later still discussed European and local politics in cozy taverns, went to bed with the idea that he was the most intelligent of human beings, and that Greysley generally was the axis on which the world revolved.[6]

The semi-rural atmosphere clearly imprinted itself in the mind of Wee Aleck (he was considered small for his age). The handloom weavers, many working on the famous Paisley Pattern shawls designed by his father, lived in adjoining villages or in cottages on the outskirts. Steam-powered Jacquard looms in purpose-built mills were still almost a decade away. Despite the huge demand for Paisley shawls, providing work for around 700 handloom weavers in the town, there was no attempt until then to centralise the various production stages. By the 1870s the handloom weaver would be virtually extinct, certain parts of the town still characterised by the thatched two-storey cottages that held living space and loom-shed under the same roof. Wee Aleck saw the pre-industrial twilight of Paisley. Already beginning to swallow up adjacent weavers' villages, the town lost much of its picturesque appearance and began to replicate the wide, regimented streets already being built in Glasgow's mid-Victorian inner city.

"Paisley about a couple of years – school-teacher a Mr Graham" is the only reference to his schooling there. The PO Directory mentions a Reverend James Graham, minister of the North Church in Love Street, so the school could well have been church-funded. Five-year-old Aleck's daily walk to school would have taken him beside the river Cart to where it was crossed by a stone aqueduct carrying the Glasgow-Johnston canal. In *Alfred Hagart's Household* the horse-drawn passenger boats are vividly depicted, manned by canal staff in their scarlet jackets. In total contrast to the railway, which (when it opened in 1842) reached Glasgow in less than 20 minutes, the ride by canal boat was quiet, smooth and relatively peaceful. But it occupied nearer two hours.

John Smith soon discovered that, even in the birthplace of the shawl trade, freelance designing was an unpredictable business. He still had artistic pretensions, and maybe the latest Paris designs didn't go down so well in Renfrewshire. The best Paisley shawls, made of fine muslin or silk, were luxury items with price tags of up to £20 (around £500 by equivalent value) and demand fluctuated dramatically according to the state of the Scottish economy. 1837 seems to have been a bad year, but losses were more than recovered in subsequent years. Then shawl merchants would have been more willing to take a gamble on new designs and John would have been making real money maybe for the first time. Aleck's younger brother David, the third child, was born during this time.

Wee Aleck continued at the parish school where "he got his first flogging which he remembers to this day". The incident is again used in *Alfred Hagart's Household* where young Jack Hagart is beaten by the dominie for fighting in the schoolyard with a boy called Thomson. He had tried to cheat at marbles and witness to these events is Jack's younger sister Katy. As already mentioned, the Smiths' second child was called Katy. She died at the age of three or four. Clearly the death of a younger sibling leaves deep scars and almost three chapters in the novel are devoted to her death scene and funeral. Popular Victorian fiction routinely demanded a child sacrifice but now we tend to be less comfortable with extravagant celebration of premature extinction. Such scenes are reminiscent of the plaster statuettes of "sleeping" sisters or brothers displayed each under a glass dome in well-to-do households. The description of Katy's death is done obliquely and probably better stands the test of time. The first picture of Katy, however, freely mixes realistic detail and fictional stereotype:

The solitary occupant of the playground – the girl who cried while the battle was proceeding, the sister of one of the combatants, and from the fact that he was "keepit in" apparently the most blameworthy – was a mere windflower of a thing, with auburn hair, blue eyes, and a colourless face or a face that seemed colourless when compared with the red and white of her ruder companions. Amongst them she seemed delicate, but it was not so much the delicacy of weakness as of breeding. Grace and paleness belong to the lily. As she sat there patiently, her eyes fixed on the school door, which seemed as if it would never again open, her face had its own beauty, but it was a beauty of an oversensitive kind; especially there was a tremulousness about the slight, mobile mouth which was indicative of an unusual capacity for joy or sorrow. To a little thing with such a face and mouth, a harsh word would come like a blow, a kiss of forgiveness melt like a reproach... And while she sat on the playground seat, and when the better part of an hour had passed, the little tender mouth began to grow piteous in expression, and the blue eyes to fill.[7]

Some time after the birth of David in 1838 the family left the cottage in Gauze Street, just a few yards from the picturesque ruins of the Abbey. In a recent grave lay Katy, his first companion. By the age of eight Wee Aleck was still probably small for his age; however, within a few years he would be expected to help support a growing family in a large industrial city. For John Smith's plans had taken yet another restless turn. The family must uproot themselves again as he sought a new market for his artistic talent. Semi-pastoral Paisley was left behind as the Smiths again were uprooted to head towards the sight and sound of clattering mills and roaring furnaces.

By the 1830s the city of Glasgow was poised for its most radical transformation. Approached from the south the skyline would still have boasted the spires and towers of the old mercantile port where sailing ships had brought goods from the colonies up the Clyde to wharves and warehouses right in the town centre. This source of wealth had dwindled with the outbreak of the American Civil War, and tobacco, sugar and linen had never fully recovered their former dominance. Sixty years later it was increasingly a city economy driven by steam production, with a basis of manufacturing rather than trading and exchanges. Massive amounts of labour were needed for the new mills and factories, the population climbing by more than 40% over the decade to 1840 despite regular outbreaks of cholera and typhus.

As the Smiths crossed the Stockwell Street bridge and headed along Customhouse quay to their new home near Glasgow Green they might well have shared the initial impressions of a London visitor five years previously:

Although a great part of the city is little inferior in architecture to the New Town of Edinburgh, while it is infinitely more lively and animated, yet there is something connected with the forges, the furnaces, the foundries and the factories – the steamers and the steam-engines – the tar and the hemp – the cables and the anchors – the warehouses, casks, cotton bales, packing-cases, rum-puncheons, tobacco hogsheads, and all the protean forms and denominations which manufacturers and merchandise assume – that damped or annihilated my picturesque ideas and almost indeed induced me to put a quill behind my ear and look as thoughtful as the crowds whom I met in the streets.[8]

The area of the city to which the four Smiths now made their way was indeed lively and animated. Glasgow Cross, a meeting of broad and dignified thoroughfares in the 18th century city, was by now the centre of an unimaginable congeries of squalor and petty criminality. The merchants' houses, once gracious residences within easy reach of the Tontine building (originally the Tobacco Exchange), were now subdivided into small apartments utilised by the first wave of industrialised migrants. Further east new tenements were rapidly being put up in areas such as Bridgeton and Dalmarnock, flanking Glasgow Green. To the west (and to some extent across the Clyde in the parish of Gorbals) neo-Classical townhouses were arising to house the new managers and factory owners.

Charlotte Street is situated just to the north of St Andrew's Square with its imposing parish church resembling London's St Martin-in-the-Fields. In the original 17th-century cobbled wynds that snaked away either side of the Trongate were also authentic reminders of the merchant town. Timber-fronted houses with projecting upper floors that had somehow escaped the great fire of 1677 had been recorded by the deft pencil and brush of William Simpson, at this time an apprentice lithographer in Glasgow but later to become a famous war artist in the Crimea. To the rear of the Smiths' tenement (at number 12) was an old sugar-house or refinery, hemmed in between two rows of five-storey tenements, its crow-stepped gables projecting over the rooftops. Like many other landmarks and streetscapes captured by Simpson, it was to disappear during the 1840s, a victim of the pressure for new housing in the east end of the city and also of the railway companies seeking routes to their terminus stations. Large areas between Trongate and the north bank of the river, providing makeshift accommodation for thousands of incomers from surrounding areas and also from the Highlands and increasingly from Ireland, was swept away under the City Improvement act in the 1880s.

For those forced to live here, of course, the antique aspects would have had little attraction. They breathed the foulest air, at ground level saw little sunlight, lived and died in squalor. The results were evidenced in stunted growth and appalling child mortality rates (only one in three reaching the age of five) as well as many incidental side-effects of poverty and malnutrition. The 1851 City Chamberlain's report commented on "the forbidding aspect of a large portion of the dwellings in the older part of the town, engendering as they do an absence of due self-respect, followed by low and debasing habits in their inhabitants." Drunkenness topped the list with licensed premises provided for every 200 of the population, children included. The most punished street offences were wantonly injuring a lamp or lamp post, recklessly or furiously riding an animal, and wilfully and indecently exposing the person. They were strictly dealt with: an automatic fine of £5 or thirty days in prison. By comparison to stay "decently tipsy", according to a street hawker, would cost only fifteen pence a day.

There had been some improvements during the previous forty years. In 1790 a new Infirmary (now the Royal Infirmary) was built to a design by Robert Adam near the cathedral. A rudimentary police force patrolled the streets with staves and rattles. In the 1820s the Green was avenued with trees and laid out with carriageways. A lying-in hospital was also provided to reduce the risks from home confinements. A large poorhouse was also built during the 1840s. These were the result of the changes in social attitudes that led to the 1832 Reform Act. Although this widened the franchise in Glasgow it was still only around 5% who had the vote. The idea of full adult suffrage was soon being taken up by the Chartists. Their six demands, which included annual parliaments, were published in 1838, at a time when many anticipated imminent insurrection. The poor and dispossessed flocked to a huge Chartist meeting on the Green, but rioting was avoided. The spectre of "Kentucky violence" had arisen in 1837, leading to the murder of a man who had continued working at a cotton-mill in Anderston during a six-week strike by the spinners over a 25% reduction in wages.

Organised labour for many commentators meant nothing less than the roots of lawlessness. For Thomas De Quincey (in Tait's Magazine, December 1835) it represented "a Titan strength of purpose, imperturbable and remorseless". The Glasgow press, with the exception of the avowedly establishment papers such as the Glasgow Herald, were hot for more reform. More newsprint spewed from the presses to be consumed by the newly literate masses. The Scottish Times advocated "the rights of labour" and also free trade. In 1850 Robert Buchanan returned to Glasgow to start the Sentinel. He took on as his assistant the writer Hugh Macdonald , a strong supporter of the Chartist movement, who would later become a close friend and mentor of young Aleck.

The Smith family now occupied what would have been known locally as a "hoose". In fact it was a four-room apartment, probably the attic floor of 12 Charlotte Street. It was a good address. The southern end of Charlotte Street, nearest to the Green, was laid out in the 1780s, consisting of elegant town houses with pedimented facades designed by the Adam brothers. Named after George III's queen, it was the fashionable place to live for the next thirty years or so. Self-made mill-owner and philanthropist David Dale (Scott's original for Bailie Nicol Jarvie in *Rob Roy*) had built a house at the south-west corner, shielded by a high wall. This was not sufficient to prevent the Clyde in flood sweeping across the low-lying Green and pouring into Dale's kitchen and wine cellar. This happened on the evening he was entertaining a party of Edinburgh bankers. Fortunately neighbours further up the street, unaffected by the flood, came to his rescue by providing one course each. This striking proof of imperturbability persuaded the directors to award him the first branch of the Royal Bank of Scotland in the city.

By the 1830s the Green's defences had been improved and flooding was rare. But it was still an area jealously guarded as a place of recreation and other fashionable or not so fashionable activities. Linen bleaching took place there on sunny days. At weekends a variety of sports, including cricket, was played and the *beau monde* still promenaded across to the river. But this idyllic picture needs to be contrasted with the weekday picture when clouds of industrial smoke billowed across the pastures. Hugh Macdonald's *Rambles Round Glasgow* predicts a grim future for the trees that had been planted in the previous century:

Our ever-extending manufactures threaten indeed their speedy extinction. The westling winds bring suffocation to them from the Nursery mills; the orient blasts come laden with death from the Bridgeton factories; while the stormy north sweeps down upon their devoted heads with the congregated vapours of the city's ten thousand chimneys.[9]

A watercolour by John Small shows the southern fashionable end of Charlotte Street on a clear spring evening. In the foreground a girl makes her way to the Green with a large wicker basket full of washing. Beyond her, just visible behind the trellised ironwork of a gate that closed off the street, the city bustles in its smoke. Beyond the London Road crossing, there is a sudden change as the four-storey sandstone tenements predominate. The "close" (common stairway) occupied by the Smiths was at the furthest end, almost on the Gallowgate corner. This was a different social milieu. Although recently built, it was hardly a desirable place to live. The semi-basement was occupied by an inn with a separate entry from the street. The close entrance was reached by steps which led by a passageway to a brick-built circular stair or turnpike at the rear of the building, giving access to all four upper floors.

Between number 12 and the Gallowgate there was an area of waste ground which, unaccountably, was not built on until much later in the century. However, a photo of the corner of Charlotte Street and London Road in the Mitchell Library shows that their tenement survived until after the First World War. Before that a wall plaque was put up by a group of the poet's admirers, only to be consigned to the rubbish tip some twenty years later. A greater loss to the city's heritage was the destruction of the whole of the southern half of Charlotte Street, culminating in the decision to pull down David Dale's house in the 1960s to make a temporary school playground. There still is one surviving example of the Adam style saved by the National Trust for Scotland. The last example of a turnpike tenement in Charlotte Street, which finished its 170-year existence as a knitwear factory, was pulled down several years ago. The attic of this building, surprisingly spacious and used for storage, still showed the outlines of where the original dormer windows would have been. The subdivision of the space must have provided fairly cramped bedrooms for the growing family, but with wonderful views out over the roof tops to the crown of the Tolbooth steeple with its musical chimes, the crowded breadth of Trongate, and (by craning your head to one side) over the Green to the meandering Clyde.

From this high vantage point, twenty metres or so above pavement level, Aleck was to get his first views of the city which would shape him into manhood. In teeming, dynamic, multifarious Glasgow, ever-expanding and perpetually locked into a fierce technological struggle with progress, he was to discover "another beauty sad and stern" quite different from the subject matter which had previously inspired poets. But that inspiration accompanied pitiful suffering alongside brutish exploitation and suppuration of the spirit. Ten years later he was ready to write about it in his most frequently anthologised poem 'Glasgow':

> Draw thy fierce streams of blinding ore,
> Smite on a thousand anvils, roar
> > Down to the harbour bars;
> Smoulder in smoky sunsets, flare
> On rainy nights, with street and square
> > Lie empty to the stars.
> From terrace proud to alley base
> I know thee as my mother's face.[10]

"St David's School, High John Street, teacher Mr Livingston" is the next note written down by Hugh Macdonald as part of an 'obituary pact' in 1853. On Martin's 1842 map of Glasgow there are two adjacent schools on Stirling's Road (this runs into present-day Cathedral Street on the east side of the city centre) at the foot of a bare hillside near Bell's Brae quarry. It is approximately where the former Allan Glen's school now stands. The Post Office Directory states the teacher was David Millar; possibly Mr Livingston was the teacher for the infant school. A parish school had the advantage over a private venture school that teaching was done by an ordained or trainee minister of religion. A college education did not necessarily make him an effective teacher, of course, nor was the syllabus in such schools likely to have been wide-ranging or very pupil-centred. Macdonald's notes give a tongue-in-cheek idea: "Education – reading, writing, arithmetic never could learn, and English grammar imperfectly, with a slight knowledge of Geography and a considerable stock of Biblical

History". By the age of eleven he would almost certainly have mastered the basics of English composition.

A few years of schooling were an immense advantage to any child living in the years before the 1872 Education Acts. For many social reformers it was the key to improving the lot of future generations of the urban poor. At the upper end of the scale the High School of Glasgow's syllabus included the three Rs, languages both ancient and modern, writing and book-keeping as well as composition, logic and rhetoric. For nine-year-old Aleck Smith there was a less digestible diet of rote-learning seasoned with regular applications of the strap or "tawse". In Kingsley's *The Water Babies* (published in 1863) who can forget the unfortunate Root Vegetable Children on the Isle of Tomtoddies, living in perpetual fear of a visit from the schools inspector? However, Aleck seems to have shone at his lessons, possibly through natural shrewdness or even by discovering some personal affinity with tales from the Bible. A career as a minister of the church was confidently predicted, according to an early biographer (Thomas Brisbane, himself a man of the cloth), but this meant entry to the Glasgow College at the age of twelve. After five years of schooling, even had his parents been able to afford this, it was not to be.

A journey of ¾ mile took him every day from Charlotte Street west along Gallowgate past the Tontine steeple into Trongate, then north up Hutcheson Street past the new courthouse in Wilson Street, crossing Cochrane Street to reach John Street. This part of the street (now straddled by the Municipal Chambers) was relatively flat, whereas Upper John Street climbed steeply to the junction at Stirling's Road. Here there was an old sugar-house on one side and Dunn's brass foundry on the other. Some distance behind the school buildings but clearly visible was the dominant feature of the Glasgow skyline, the smokestacks of Tennant's chemical works built where Sighthill housing scheme now stands, close to the canal basin at Port Dundas. A memorable word picture of this part of the city occurs in his essay 'A Lark's Flight', utilising the event of a public hanging which took place in 1841. Two Irish navvies Doolan and Redding worked on the new Glasgow to Edinburgh railway line; they bludgeoned to death their English overseer because of a perceived slight; they were hunted down and subsequently appeared at the Spring Assizes where they received the death sentence for murder.

Wee Aleck was playing with his friends one evening in the Villafield area, a northern suburb now called Townhead. Escorted by dragoons from Duke Street barracks, the cart bearing the wooden gallows passed close by, heading out to Bishopbriggs near the canal cutting. By holding the execution near the scene of the crime the authorities hoped to send out a salutary warning to other Irish navvies and troublemakers. The trial had been given sensational press coverage the week before, so everyone knew the execution was due to take place, even children like Aleck. There is an extraordinary vividness in the account, suggesting the scene was deeply implanted in his eleven-year-old mind (the hanging itself he was to witness the next day):

The evening before the execution has arrived, and the reader has now to imagine the early May sunset falling pleasantly on the outskirts of the city. The houses looking out upon an open square or space, have little plots of garden-ground in their fronts, in which mahogany-coloured wallflowers and mealy auriculas are growing. The side of this square, along which the City Road stretches northward, is occupied by a blind asylum, a brick building, the bricks painted red and picked out with white, after the tidy English fashion, and a high white cemetery wall, over which peers the spire of the Gothic Cathedral; and beyond that on the other side of the ravine, rising out of a populous city of the dead, a stone John Knox looks down on the Cathedral, a Bible clutched in his outstretched and menacing hand. On all this the May sunset is striking, dressing everything in its warm, pleasant pink, lingering in the tufts of foliage that nestle around the asylum, and dipping the building itself one half in light one half in tender shade. This open space or square is an excellent place for the games of us boys, and "Prisoners Base" is being carried out with as much earnestness as the business of life now by those of us who are left. The girls, too, have their games of a quiet kind, which we hold in huge scorn and contempt. In two files, linked arm-in-arm, they alternately dance towards each other and then retire, singing the while, in their clear girlish treble, verses, the meaning and pertinence of which time has worn away-
   "The Campsie Duke's a-riding, a-riding, a-riding,"
being the oft-recurring "owercome" or refrain. All this is going on in the pleasant sunset light, when by the apparition of certain wagons coming up from the city, piled high with blocks and beams, and guarded by a dozen dragoons, on whose brazen helmets the sunset danced, every game is dismembered, and we are in a moment a mere mixed mob of boys and girls, flocking around to stare and wonder. Just at this place something went wrong with one of the wagon wheels, and the procession came to a stop. A crowd collected, and we heard some of the grown-up people say, that the scaffold was being carried out for the ceremony of to-morrow. Then, more intensely than ever, one realised the condition of the doomed men. We were all at our happy games in the sunset, they were entering on their last night on earth. After hammering and delay the wheel was put to rights, the sunset died out; wagons and dragoons got into motion and disappeared; and all the night through, whether awake or asleep I saw the torches burning and heard the hammers clinking, and witnessed as clearly as if I had been an onlooker, the horrid structure rising, till it stood complete, with a huge cross-beam from which two empty halters hung, in the early morning light.[11]

It was to be his last year of schooling and this is what the obituary pact note says: "Took brain fever on Christmas of 1840 (brain supposed not to be right since, fact not to be noticed), left school that day and never returned." The events leading up to the attack are described in some detail but with a degree of poetic licence in the semi-autobiographical 'A Boy's Poem', written around 1854. Set "in a large and crowded school" where "the murmuring forms [benches] were torture and the ringing playground hell", he "shrank from crowds of loud and boisterous boys". Selected as a regular victim, perhaps because of his size, he realises that he can retaliate with words. Using his gifts as a storyteller he casts a spell over his companions when they meet by a forge on autumn evenings – "I felt them grow towards me, drank the looks They cast round to the dark and frowning night That stood back from the glare."[12]

The immediate cause of the brain fever seems to have been a fight with a group of bullies. The "boy" strikes out, draws blood, then "I burst the broken ring and darted off With my blood boiling and my pulses mad." The fever strikes the same night:

And then, as if my limbs were touched by death,
A shudder shook me, all the rage that sprang
Like sudden fire in a deserted house
Making the windows fierce, had passed away;
The winds went through me.
                              At the dead of night
Fever beset me with a troop of fiends,
They hid in every crevice of the house
And called me with the voices of my mates,
And mocked me when I came. They made me blind,
And led me out to stumble among pits,
And smoke me in my blackness. Oft they hung
Me o'er the edges of the dizzy steeps,
And laughed to see me swinging in the wind;
And then a blast would whirl me like a leaf,
From my frail hold out to the peopled air,
Where dark hands plucked at me and dragged me down.
I lay in darkness 'neath a weight of chains, -
A burst of day and lo! A mighty sea
Of upturned faces murmured, heaved, and swayed
Around to see me die. Methought I fled
Along the road of death.[13]

The attack appears to have developed into coma, lasting for several weeks. The "boy" was left feeling that some judgment had been made upon him, although he remained confused over its significance. Whatever cerebral disorder he suffered (and as an adult Smith always played down its severity) the most obvious after-effect was a severe squint in his right eye. This remained with him for the rest of his life. The long days of convalescence were spent reading up in the attic, an ideal space well away from the noise and nuisance of the street, with pleasing echoes of the iconic Thomas Chatterton and countless other lesser-known poets and artists living low-rent early Victorian existences. Amongst the authors he read, Bunyan ("the Glorious Dreamer") looms large. By the late summer he was considered sufficiently recovered to work beside his father, helping to copy out shawl and dress designs. He was paid one shilling a week in recognition that he had, at the age of twelve, become part of the adult world.

Early in 1842 he was offered an apprenticeship as a pattern-drawer with Andrew Fulton in Wilson Street at two shillings and sixpence a week, moving later to Scotts's, a printer of lace and muslin in Argyle Arcade, where his pay rose to four shillings. And for the next eleven years his life was devoted to the long acquisition of a craft, taking up five and a half days of every week in the year save one, the annual trades holiday known as The Fair. Although not hard physical labour, it must have been taxing to the concentration of one so young. Reading and increasingly writing were his refuge. Privation is often cited by the self-made as the motivator that brought success, but that leaves out the role of self-belief. Where did young Sandie Smith find the belief that one day he would become a famous poet? About this time he began to nurture such beliefs. "First committed the sin of rhyme at about the age of eleven" says the Hugh Macdonald note, echoing Burns. Within ten years the apprentice pattern-designer was to turn (apparently overnight) into a master poet with an extraordinary assurance to his voice. Thomas Carlyle considered that "poverty and hard toil" strengthened character and made judgment sounder. In his review of Ebeneezer Elliot's *Corn-Law Rhymes* he even questioned whether conventional education had much influence.[14] As a self-made man, Carlyle clearly believed he had valuable insights. He concluded that the greater the advantages conferred in early life the more difficult it was for latent potential to emerge. In Aleck's case, as he grew into manhood, he must have been increasingly aware that others had many advantages over him in terms of education, health, means and connections. He was therefore, in Carlyle's terms, blessed many times over. And the poetry, when it came, was surely the living proof of it.

Chapter 2:
1841-47

More music! Music! Music! Maid divine!
My hungry senses, like a finch's brood,
Are all a-gape. O feed them, maid divine!
Feed, feed my hungry soul with melodies!
('A Life-Drama' sc.3)

FOR THE NEXT NINE YEARS he was to serve an apprenticeship as a designer or 'drawer' in various warehouses connected with the production and distribution of embroidered muslin. Almost from the start he would be working a 55-hour week, earning £2.50 (£500 equivalent) annually. To his new workmates and friends the 12-year-old became known as Young (sometimes Daft) Sandie.

John and Christina were not able to finance him through college, but they did the next best thing by finding Sandie work that was well away from the mills and manufacturing works of Bridgeton. The east end of Glasgow now reveals little of its former character. At the dawn of the 19th century the population of Bridgeton and Dalmarnock (some three thousand people) was predominantly involved in handloom weaving. The inhabitants lived in semi-rural conditions in small cottages with outhouses and gardens, and whole families were involved in producing the finished length of woollen cloth. In 1805 Henry Monteith's cotton-spinning mills at Barrowfield, and the nearby dye-works, were an early indication of the forest of smoke-stacks that would soon predominate. In the next twenty-five years Glasgow became by far the largest cotton town in Britain. Within a decade the space contained in one snaking loop of the Clyde would be overwhelmed first with booming cotton mills and dyeworks then joined by foundries for making the more efficient power-looms. In between there grew up densely-packed areas of stone tenements to house thousands of 'hands' and their families.

To the south-west, cushioning the Clyde from some of the more acrid by-products of this new technology, were the sixty acres of Glasgow Green, an open area of grass, trees and walks held under trusteeship by the Town Council, therefore protected from industrial development. By the 1840s the Green, although still "a verdant spot free to all", was effectively walled in on at least two sides by billowing chimneys both industrial and domestic. One observer likened Bridgeton to "the chimney-top of the neighbouring city". Another summed up the Green's attractions:

It is furnished with some delicious springs of water. It cannot at all times, however, be relied upon for the purity of its atmosphere.[15]

In the long summer evenings the Green was a favourite spot for recreation: once furnaces were damped down for the night healthy pursuits like cricket and gymnastics could be carried on. The local Volunteers (formed during the invasion-fever of the 1790s) drilled here with real muskets under Sam Hunter, the robustly Tory editor of the Glasgow Herald. During the day the Green served more utilitarian purposes. At the foot of William Street the Town Council had erected a public washing-house next to a stand of trees. A large area, known as Washing-house Green, was used for drying clothes by spreading them over the grass if weather permitted. Young Sandie, however, was more struck by its idyllic aspects. A typical late summer evening is conjured up in a Keatsian passage from his early poem 'A Life-Drama':

The park was loud with games: clear laughter, shrieks
Came from the rings of girls amid the trees:
The cricketers were eager at their play;
The stream was dotted with the swimmers' heads;
Gay boats flashed up and down. The level sun
Pour'd o'er the sward a farewell gush of light
And Sport transfigured stood! I hurried on,
Through all the mirth, to where the river ran
In the grey evening, 'tween the hanging woods,
With a soul-soothing murmur.[16]

Charlotte Street joined the Green at its southern end. In fact one of the carriageways which criss-crossed the whole area ended here at a pair of wrought-iron gates. These were closed after dark to discouraged ill-intentioned wanderers, adding to the exclusiveness of the southern end of the street with its matching neo-classical villas. In the 1840s a number of surgeons lived here and at number 35 the Misses Duff conducted a ladies' seminary. At the northern end, though, where the Smith family lived, the street became mainly four-storey tenements.

With his squinting right eye and delicate health, Sandie would surely have succumbed quickly to the harsh regime of factory work. Maybe through his father's connections he managed to land an apprenticeship at Alexander Buchanan's muslin warehouse in Queen Street. This was just around the corner from the imposing new Royal Exchange, fronted by Flaxman's statue of a mounted Duke of Wellington commissioned by public subscription in 1844. The Exchange's Corinthian-style portico projected to the outside world the impression of a temple, which in a sense it was, but one devoted to commodities and speculation. Astute traders in cotton could make rapid fortunes. They typified the boom time the city was entering. Sandie the poet was to call them men "with eyes of cold and cruel blue".

Cotton-related industries already provided employment to more than 200,000 people in the Glasgow and Paisley area.[17] Most of the red-brick mill buildings were either for spinning or weaving, although the largest sometimes combined both in the same complex. The weaving mills (or factories) were of two distinct types, equipped to produce either 'Gray' goods (later bleached, dyed or mercerised) or 'Coloured' (patterned cloth like ginghams, satteens, stripes or flannelettes). The Gray side of the industry included plain cloths like muslins, twills and calicoes as well as textiles with simple raised patterns (known as lappet-work). More fancy examples were brocades, quiltings and lace effects that could by now be produced on Jacquard looms. Coloureds consisted of various weights of self-coloured or patterned fabrics used by tailors and drapers. The *plain* end included zephyrs and oxfords, whilst *fancy-coloured* covered all the more elaborate patterns required for dressmaking and furnishings. The potential market for cotton goods was therefore diverse and expanding with the growth of empire. In the trade there was a watertight distinction between production for export ('the shipping trade') and goods for home distribution. Export orders were made up as large single runs of a particular cloth; there was therefore no need to keep stocks or to offer a variety of patterns. With 'the home trade', however, particularly on the fancy-coloured side which is where Sandie was employed, the cotton manufacturer employed designers to provide a new range of patterns each year for the wholesalers or 'merchants' who sent out their salesmen to the retail outlets. To ensure continuity of supply the merchants needed to build warehouses, often near the city centre, to hold stocks and act as a trade counter. Bales of cloth from the mill arrived daily on horse-drawn wagons at the warehouse; orders would be made up and despatched. Frederick Niven's *The Staff at Simsons* gives an inside view of a muslin warehouse in the 1880s and 1890s in many respects similar to the system in use 40 years before.

The staff required would not be anything like as large as that needed by the mills, and the other main difference was that the majority were women. It was here the twelve-year-old was to start his working life, grim enough to modern eyes, but when compared to Dickens in the blacking shop or to the dangers of working under the looms, Sandie probably had a lucky start. In *A Boy's Poem* he gives a darker picture of his initiation into the world of Victorian work:

> So, on a summer morning I was led
> Into a square of warehouses, and left

'Mong faces merciless as engine-wheels –
The right hand learns its cunning, and the feet
That tread upon the rough ways of the world
Grow mercifully callous.[18]

Alexander Buchanan, the owner, lived in a large villa called Slatefield on the outskirts of the city. A native of Paisley, he pioneered the handloom production of chenilles there in the 1820s. By the 1840s he had gone into hand-embroidered muslins. This was a new line that satisfied the need for middle-class wives and daughters to exhibit signs of taste and refinement. Now mainly associated with kitchen sieves, muslin was first produced in the 1780s as a light dress fabric for hot climates. Its lacy, semi-transparent qualities also accentuated the flowing lines of regency dresses. Embroidered muslin (generally known as 'sewed muslin') was a west of Scotland speciality which relied on home workers in adjoining rural districts of Ayrshire, Renfrewshire and the east coast of Ireland (only two or three hours away by steamer). By the 1840s machine-made muslin was in demand mainly for dress collars and cuffs as well as for christening robes and lappets. Its attractions were enhanced by hand-embroidering with floral motifs and leaf-sprays or sprigs, hence 'sprigged' muslin.[19]

This was an operation requiring the labour of thousands of women and girls who were paid from a penny ha'penny to fivepence (60p to £2) a day for working both in the warehouse and at home. Surviving examples of this intricate tambour work show what a phenomenal amount of sewing it entailed. A 4-metre dress length would contain about 3,500 motifs, sometimes embroidered in pale pink or lilac, but more often white or écru on a white background. In the Glasgow warehouses alone there were up to four thousand embroiderers earning eight shillings a week, executing especially complex patterns involving open-work on large swivelling frames or 'tambours'. These would sell through the haberdashery trade as high-priced fabric sold by the yard. This 'Scotch' or Ayrshire work has now become a collectors' item. Designs were especially elaborate on dress handkerchiefs which by the 1840s were replacing fans.

Collars, cuffs and kerchiefs were to employ Sandie's attention for the nine years of apprenticeship. Buchanan's was probably quite a congenial place to work. The pattern studio, where the designers worked, would have been on the top floor, and there were embroiderers and seamstresses nearby to take advantage of the natural light. On the ground floor would have been ceaseless activity as lengths of plain muslin, thread and patterns were packed up for distribution to the outworkers. Meanwhile packmen were bringing in the completed work from the country. It would have to be checked, finished and packaged for sending out to retailers. It was a strange mixture of old traditional skills with the new mass production of the steam-driven looms. And the warehouse where it was all taking place was only a few hundred metres from the main hotels and prime shopping streets of the city.

By 1856 the combined home and export sales of sewed muslins was recorded at around £1 million (nearer £150mn equivalent value). For many thousands of households it was a valuable supplement to meagre pickings. Within about five years, though, demand had died away completely. The manufacturers and merchants began to oversupply the market and sprigged muslin's exclusive label became less desirable as leaders of fashion looked to other types of fabric. Eventually prices tumbled and it came within the reach of the lower orders, a fatal marketing mistake. In the 1840s, though, demand was on the up and number 62 Queen Street must have been humming between eight and six. It was (and still is) reached by a 'pend' or archway between two shopfronts on Queen Street. There are four floors linked by a broad set of stone staircases and landings (the close) lit by windows on the courtyard side. By this means scores of packers and checkers, embroiderers and finishers came and went from their work, sending a babble of voices echoing up the close.

Breathless after climbing the stairs Sandie would arrive at 8am, in winter just as the sun was up. Here he passed his first two or three years wrestling with the correct way of making tasteful sprays, involving endless copying of the designs of others. According to Brisbane his first mastery was of 'penning', tracing sample designs with lithographic ink until they were indistinguishable from the originals. It must have been drudgery to a 12-year-old. The cast in his eye, though noticeable, clearly did not affect co-ordination between hand and eye. Unless there were other apprentices those he worked beside must have been older. It is difficult to imagine a young boy taking easily to this far from stimulating environment. On the open floors below was a different world. The gas jets burned all day to provide as much light as possible for the tambour-workers. Maybe Sandie went to spend time in this cosier environment when he wasn't needed in the studio. And by now he surely was reading whenever he could.

Although his education had not equipped him well in other ways, it would have taught Sandie how to read. Once sown, the flowering was inevitable. With some adolescents the power of the written word and the imaginative world it creates can become addictive. It is the means whereby the mind can grow and pace the process of physical growth: in a later poem he calls it "the idle key". So how and where did he get access to books to unlock? Probably there were some in Charlotte Street, but contemporary fiction would have been out of his reach.

More likely cheap reprints of the 'classics' would have been available as well as the kind of 'improving' books written to be read aloud in the family group. Prototype working men's libraries were certainly a feature of weaving areas. However obtained, Sandie read books in abundance. One of the few clues directly given is the reference in *A Boy's Poem* to Bunyan which he read during his period of recuperation:

> One night, when my weak limbs were drawing a strength
> From meats and drinks, and long delicious sleep,
> I raised a book to kill the tedious hours –
> The Glorious Dreamer's – he whose walls enclosed
> An emperor's state; upon whose lonely sleep
> The secret heavens opened, peopled thick
> With angels, as the beam with swirling motes.
> I was like one who at his girdle wears
> An idle key and with it, purposeless,
> In the mere impulse of a wayward mood,
> Opes a familiar door and stands amazed,
> Blind with the prisoned splendour which escapes
> Filling his dusky home.[20]

According to Thomas Brisbane, who met Sandie some five years later:

In novel reading, however, his natural literary taste made him eclectic. From his earliest days, Scott was his favourite in this department of literature, and after Scott came Cooper. Several of the American tales of the latter, which he read at a very early age, made a deep impression on his imagination, and constrained him to seek fuller knowledge of the scenery, history and literature of that country. Among the first books of travels which he consequently read was Stephens' Travels in South America; and it, together with Cooper's novels, so excited his mind that the first poem of any length which he composed was an American tale of love and war entitled 'Black Eagle' from the name of the hero of the piece who was an Indian warrior.[21]

There was little of what we now call teenage fiction, addressing immediate adolescent issues. The Victorians, whilst they idolised and sentimentalised childhood, terminated it pretty abruptly. By the age of nine or ten adulthood loomed large. Those with a nanny in the nursery might delay the moment a year or two, but the awakening from dream days was sudden, whether it was working with adults or going off to boarding school to join a tribe of one's peers. Girls would be faced by hours of needlework and drilling in social accomplishments. Romances for adults did emerge in the 1840s, alongside the growth in rail travel, but were often treated with suspicion. W.H.Smith was founded and prospered on the concession to operate bookstalls (and even lending libraries) on station platforms. Only in the 1860s would the price of most books, including reprints of the classics, fall dramatically with greater mechanisation of production and a voracious market created by near universal literacy.

The 1840s were a fertile time for the contemporary publishing trade. Carlyle's *Heroes and Hero-Worship*, Tennyson's *Morte d'Arthur* and Disraeli's *Coningsby*, an early 'silver-fork' novel, all appeared. Edward Lear's *Book of Nonsense* was also popular for quite different reasons, while the publication in 1845 Engels' *The Condition of the Working Classes in England* was a factor in leading to a more socio-documentary trend in fiction. *David Copperfield* was serialised and then sold in volume form, while Mrs Gaskell was launched with *Mary Barton*. 1847 was the amazing year when *Jane Eyre*, *Wuthering Heights* and *Vanity Fair* (serialised 1847-8) all appeared. At the end of the 1840s poetry reasserted its claims with *Sonnets from the Portuguese* and *In Memoriam*.

How much of all this contemporary literature could a young apprentice realistically have accessed? According to Pat Alexander, Sandie was voracious and had read widely among the classics: "With a fair round of general information, taken on his own special topics of English Poetry and the belles lettres – English literature, I may say, in extenso – he was always to be held, as it seemed to me, an unusually well-read man, even among men professedly literary."[22] Brisbane's account of these warehouse years indicates that Sandie was giving himself a knowledge of literature that might have characterised only a very exceptional humanities student:

It was his custom about this time to confine his reading and study for a period principally to one author till he had mastered him, and then devote himself similarly to another. Thus, for a considerable time he read all he could lay his hands on of the works of Byron, with critiques on these or whatever had been written by others relating to the life and writings of that extraordinary genius. Shelley next for a while engaged his leisure hours; then Coleridge or Wordsworth, or Keats, Tennyson, Campbell, Thomson, Burns, Shakespeare, Spenser, Chaucer, had each a season of study given specially to him.... His reading in other departments of literature, however, was of the most desultory and fortuitous nature. He had then a great partiality for editions of the poets in small volumes, seemingly because he could carry them in his pocket to read in his rambles, or consult and refresh his memory with at any spare moment. Indeed, he was never to be found without some favourite book on his person.[23]

Most who knew him later in life testify to an ability to quote at length from Shakespeare, Milton and the Romantics. He must have been gifted with an extraordinarily retentive memory that needed to recreate the lines in his own mind so that they felt as if they belonged to him. For a fledgling poet we shall see this was to be a curse as well as a blessing.

In 1844 *Woodnotes of A Wanderer* was issued by Fleet Street publisher David Bogue, a man with the knack of discovering new poetic talent. In fact the poet, John Ramsay, a Kilmarnock carpet-weaver, had been publishing satirical verses for the previous decade and had built up a local reputation. Many of the new verses show an impressive facility with rhyme and metre. Ramsay had self-published his first collection in the late 1830s and was inevitably hailed as a second Burns. Now the handsomely bound new collection was coolly received by the metropolitan critics ("emanating from a person moving in humble life but endowed with a gifted mind") but it still sold well. John (Sandie's father) might have known of Ramsay from their Kilmarnock days. He might have read 'On Being Asked What Figure Was Most Descriptive of a Poet' which makes creative use of Halley's comet as the "fair phantom" that symbolises the poet's innate vision..

> When long, long shadows of the midnight fall
> From the rent towers of yonder ruined wall,
> And the bright sentinels of heaven are seen
> Each in his post around their peerless queen;
> The winds are pillowed on the mountain's breast,
> And woods and waters are in waveless rest;
> Hast thou not seen the meteor on its way
> Diffusing round a secondary day,
> But scarce upon the eye its beams had shone
> When the fair phantom was for ever gone?

This elegant conceit-making could have served as an attractive model for an impressionable apprentice. There were some other worker poets (both men and women) who became a feature of the mid-Victorian industrialised north. With higher rates of literacy, already a distinctive feature of Scottish education, and the lessening restraints on freedom to publish in the wake of the Reform Act, there was a growth in writing by those who were in a similar situation to Sandie (ie working a long day as well as writing). Many of those who wrote poetry were also involved in organisations agitating for further reform. Their verse was intended to rouse and recruit. Others took a more personal standpoint, using writing as a way of searching for solace and consolation, finding some status in the role of worker poet. Much of this material, probably intended to be ephemeral, has disappeared. But some made its way from periodicals into hard covers and was therefore preserved in libraries and private collections. It is now the subject of a growing field of Victorian literature research, throwing a new and revealing light on the underclass of writers who may well have rivaled the elite poets in the numbers of readers who sampled their work. The work these worker poets produced was extremely diverse, as we shall see. Scholars have only recently attempted to categorise what has so far been discovered. One of those most actively involved, Prof Florence Boos of the University of Iowa, provides this overview:

> We have ranged briefly through some of the verse poor Britons wrote and sang in the nineteenth century, religious, anti-clerical, inspirational, instructive, humorous, meditative, reflective and reflexive poems in almost all their registers – 'traditional' and narrative ballads, urban broadsides, regional satires and political protests. Not all working-class literature was 'anti-establishment', of course or 'self-improving', or oral and traditional in character, or composed in quatrains, couplets or Spenserian stanzas. But its allusions were 'political' in a wider sense as well as 'literary', and many of the registers and tonalities they found would resonate deeply if they could be seen and understood by writers in 'the third world' today…
>
> In their thematic choices and affiliations, these works blended protest, reformist politics, self-assertion and moral reflection in complex ways. The ideals and aspirations which animated them could be integrated, up to a point, with generalized appeals to traditional faith, on the one hand, and with autodidactic variants of a classical or 'polite' education (as in Thomas Cooper's *Purgatory*) on the other. But the imaginative possibilities they sought were fundamentally opposed to many 'elite' traditions, and their oral, musical and affective roots neither heeded nor would have been likely to bear an extensive admixture of artistic framing, textual ambiguity and high-cultural allusions.[24]

Another category of proletarian verse writing was dialect poetry, continuing a tradition that started with broadsides hawked in the street, typically at large public gatherings like political hustings, open-air preaching, and public hangings. Hawkie was a well-known balladmonger in Glasgow who would have ready ballad-style accounts of those about to be hanged, using a medley of fact taken from newspaper accounts of the trial mixed up with pure sensation. Hawkie had one leg missing which may have helped his sales pitch. He also had a deep antipathy to the Irish immigrants to the city. Brandishing a crutch to attract attention he did good business at hangings. As the noose was tightened about the neck of the condemned man he would cry out "Thae infernal Eerish, thae infernal Eerish, they'll no' allow us to hae the honest use o' oor ain gallows!" This was gallows humour indeed.

One of those whose work has survived and who wrote in Scots was Janet Hamilton who made a living as an embroiderer or 'tambourer' in Coatbridge, south of Glasgow. Since she could not write until the age of fifty (when she taught herself) she had to compose, remember and recite all her works until her eldest son was old enough to take them down on paper. Although later she turned to writing in a form of urban Doric, her early poems and essays were in standard English. Perhaps they had to be since they were first published in the short-lived London-based The People's Journal. Meantime John Cassell had launched his penny weekly The Working Man's Friend and Family Instructor which had a clear reformist agenda. These were later collected in special supplements collectively entitled 'The Literature of Working Men' even though the most frequent contributor was Janet Hamilton. In December 1850 her essay 'The Uses and Pleasures of Poetry to the Working Classes' appeared, containing examples of uplifting verses and closing with the rallying cry:

> It is truly consoling for working men and women to know, aye, and feel, that on them, amidst all the toils, privations and hardships incidental to their position in life, the gifts of God, of Nature, and of the Muses are as impartially and profusely bestowed as on that portion of the community whose highest distinctions are too often found to consist only in the accidents of birth and fortune.[25]

Around 1846 Sandie changed employers and went to work for John Robertson & Sons, another warehouse barely fifty metres further up Queen Street from Buchanan's, situated again in an enclosed courtyard on the opposite side of the street. Queen's Court (now South Exchange Court, marked by a bronze plaque at the pend entrance) has three separate porticoed doorways. Presumably here the pay or working conditions were better, or maybe he had previously got to know some of the Robertsons' apprentices. It is unlikely to have had anything to do with promotion prospects. Brisbane's *Early Years* makes it clear Sandie had no intention of continuing with the pattern-drawing any longer than strictly necessary. Whatever the reason, he was to spend the next six years in Queen's Court engaged in similar activity. In that strange poem 'Horton' there are a number of semi-autobiographical passages (transposed, however, from Glasgow to the market towns of Kent) giving portraits of his workmates:

> With earnest faces bent above their tasks
> Some ten or twelve sat with me in the room.
> He at my right hand ever dwelt alone:
> A moat of dullness fenced him from the world.
> My left-hand neighbour was all flame and air,
> A restless spirit veering like the wind:
> And what a lover! And what an amorous heart!…
>   Among the rest

> Sat one with visage red with sun and wind
> As the last hip upon the frosted brier
> When the blithe huntsman snuffs the hoary morn.
> He poached at night in every stream for miles;
> Knew nests in every wood.....
>   A hand was laid
> Upon my shoulder; Harry's laughing face,
> Filled with his mischievous and merry eyes,
> Was thrust in mine. He slapped me, "Rouse thee, man!
> The hour is striking and your dinner waits.
> What is the precious subject of your thoughts?"
> "My thoughts?—the charitable snow which cools
> A hot volcano's lips; the nurse that takes
> Alike the crying and the crowing babe
> And stills them with a kiss." We all arose;
> The emptying warehouses had filled the street
> With a broad stream; from passage, lane and court
> Gushed tributary rills. We struggled out
> And soon were lost and mingled in the tide:
> Within an hour the streets again were brimmed
> With the returning flow.[26]

    It was at Robertsons' that he seems to have acquired the soubriquet 'Daft' Sandie. A silent, possibly at times morose creature, all wrapped up in his systematic reading scheme, spending any free time with his nose in a book rather than going on the town, it is not surprising that he would have stood out. Despite his squint, there was probably nothing malicious about the nickname. Any diversion to relieve the monotony of endless copying must have appeared welcome to the apprentices. And that was Sandie all over. Once you got him talking he would have plenty to tell you about the latest book or article he was reading. And there was one that particularly caught his attention.
    In 1845 Edinburgh printer James Hogg had issued the first number of Hogg's Weekly Instructor, a penny-ha'penny magazine for young men and women wanting to educate themselves. It had an avowedly religious agenda and Hogg had assembled a team of eloquent divines mostly from Scotland to form his band of contributors. Among them was the Reverend George Gilfillan of Dundee, a name that was to loom large in Sandie's development as a poet. In the July number of Hogg's Weekly Gilfillan kicked off with two extensive articles on 'Genius', apparently read with avidity by the 16-year-old apprentice. Gilfillan's prose style has dated, but the nub of what he had to say was quite original. Since the dawn of the Romantic era young genius-spotting had become a second string to the literary critic's bow. Clearly there was

cachet to be gained from being the first to announce a new poet, as Leigh Hunt had done successfully with Shelley and Keats. Gilfillan begins by distinguishing 'true' genius from the other subordinate characteristics that sometimes accompany it:

It has often ... been confounded with other powers, which bore to it a certain resemblance, and played under it a subordinate part; and frequently the glittering sheath has thus been mistaken for the flaming sword. Cleverness, talent, taste, mere imagination, passion and the fumes of physical excitement, have all at one time or other passed off for the genuine inspirations of this rare and fervent gift.[27]

The outpourings of the genius are always a cry from the heart ("sometimes rugged and wrathful") but equally often of a subdued nature: "Low sometimes as the sob of a dying deer, and loud sometimes as the crash and darkness of a thousand storms bursting their inaccessible abodes of crags and thunderclouds, it is ever a native and unborrowed and irresistible sound." Mere talent is no substitute; it is too tasteful. "Genius rushes forward wildly waving a torch, and casting broad and sudden illumination into the dark places of nature." In turn, imagination, passion and fumes of physical excitement ("any narcotic weed or liquorous distillation, or any such compound of 'fire and dirt' as oozes from the pierced poppy") are all dismissed as unnecessary concomitants:

What, then, is genius? It is, to recur to a former expression, the musical cry of a strong and loving soul. It is a voice from the depths of the human spirit. It is the utterance, native and irresistible, of one 'possessed' by an influence which, like the wind, bloweth where it listeth, comes he knows not whence and goes he knows not whither. It is a fainter degree of that prophetic inspiration which, to the rapt eye of the ancient seer, made the future present and the distant near. The man under its influence is a 'maker', working out ... certain creations of his own; he is a 'declarer', more or less distinctly, of the awful will of the unseen Lawgiver seated within his soul; he is a string to an invisible harper – a pen guided by a superhuman hand – a trumpet filled with a voice which is as the sound of many waters.

Clearly Gilfillan's writing struck a chord with Sandie. But Gilfillan was an inspirer rather than a creative spirit himself and, for better or worse, his influence on Sandie's early output was significant. Brisbane calls him a "herald" which somewhat understates his role. Certainly he heralded with the brassy trumpet of his prose quite a number of new poets. In the Everyman edition of Gilfillan's *A Gallery of Literary Portraits* (comprising twenty-five short critical assessments of leading figures in the Romantic movement, but also including Scottish-based writers such as De Quincey, Thomas Chalmers, John Wilson, and Thomas Campbell) editor W.R.Nicoll assessed his influence:

> For about five years (1849-54) George Gilfillan's position as a critic was one of very great influence. It may be doubted whether even Carlyle had more power over young minds. These years were the period of a Movement. There was a thrill in the air, a belief that the new world was at hand. This was felt beyond his immediate circle; it stirred in the books of the Brontes, the socialism of Kingsley, and the passionate preaching of Kossuth and Mazzini...[28]

Gilfillan himself came from humble beginnings before becoming a United Presbyterian minister in central Dundee. He was the youngest of eleven children born to a dissenting Free Church minister in Perthshire. There may not have been wealth in the home, but there were plenty of books and he devoured them. At the age of thirteen he walked to Glasgow and enrolled at the college, spending four hard years studying humanities and making useful literary contacts. He moved to Edinburgh in the hope of making a career from writing, but he almost died from the effects of poverty after failing to establish himself as a contributor to the periodicals published there. He ended up being accepted for a divinity course and took the first ministry offered to him. In 1847 he moved to a working-class area of Dundee and began a long and indefatigable career somehow combining his pastoral duties (which must have been unremitting) with writing on religious doctrine and producing critical firecrackers. From then on hardly a month passed without something of his appearing in the columns of the periodicals.

If Gilfillan's writing first lodged the idea in Sandie's head of becoming a published poet then posterity must thank him for it. Beneath the over-written pulpit-prose the young man discerned something that led him to recognise his own dawning powers. Possibly it made him admit to himself that he harboured the ambition. Certainly he was writing all the time, insofar as his occupational drudgery allowed, and colleagues in the pattern studio noticed that his mind often strayed from the designs on the table. Something would be briefly scribbled on an offcut of tracing paper that was lying handy and then be transferred speedily into his jacket pocket.

Religion was as palpably in the air during the 1840s as the feathery smuts that fell every day from the darkening skies. A youth with any intellectual pretensions could hardly have avoided being caught up in a spiritual crisis as nationwide the role of religious belief in everyday life was being put under the microscope. In Scotland the process was kick-started by the Disruption of the Church of Scotland. On 23 May 1843 at the annual Assembly the Church split into two implacable factions, ostensibly over the issue of 'patronage' and the freedom of congregations to choose their own minister. In fact the rift went deeper and division was largely along dogma and class lines: much has been written about this controversial period elsewhere. Many rural communities were affected with a suddenness and severity akin to a civil war. The immediate result was that nearly four hundred ministers (who now constituted the Free Church) signed "an act of separation and deed of demission" by which they renounced all claim to the benefices they had previously held. Besides splitting congregations the length and breadth of Scotland, the seceding ministers surrendered a combined income of some £100,000. They also, of course, abandoned their churches when they took away part of the congregation.

The enormous self-sacrifice and effort involved in raising money for new churches was a glorious introductory chapter in the annals of the Free Church. By their faith they were indeed rewarded. But others saw the results of the Disruption as a disaster. Norman MacLeod, then a minister in Dalkeith, near Edinburgh, and one of those who stayed with the Church of Scotland (the Assembly), recorded his horror in his journal:

While the "persecuted martyrs of the covenant" met amid the huzzas and applauses [sic] of the multitude, with thousands of pounds daily pouring in upon them, and nothing to do but what was in the highest degree popular; nothing but self-denial and a desire to sacrifice name and fame, and all but honour, to my country could have kept me in the Assembly. There was one feature of the Assembly which I shall never forget, and that was the *fever* of secession, the restless nervous desire to fly to the Free Church. No new truth had come to light, no new event had been developed, but there was a species of frenzy which seized men, and away they went.[29]

The most obvious concrete result was the growth of the Free Church, typified by the appearance of squat chapels built with no unnecessary adornment internally or externally. But at least as important was the reaction that set in amongst the established Churches both sides of the Border. In England a similar secession movement was taking place in the Anglican church where nepotism and wide divergences in clerical income were becoming apparent. Methodism and Congregationalism stem from this period. The establishment saw a new crusade was needed to unite their faithful, to prevent them from being swept away into the arms of the Secessionists, or in the case of the Church of England, into the scented embrace of Rome. Within two years a conference of sympathetic church ministers (MacLeod amongst them) was held in Liverpool. The following year (1846) saw the birth of the Evangelical Alliance.

'Evangelical' is open to more than one interpretation. Its literal meaning of acting in accordance with the true doctrine and spirit of the gospels soon became overshadowed by the quest to make these doctrines relevant to the increasingly secular world which the Church uneasily inhabited. Evangelicalism appealed particularly strongly to the young and vigorous; later the term 'Muscular Christians' came to be used to describe its adherents. For many young men in the turbulent 1840s its rallying cry was attractive. In Scotland serious-mindedness was the fertile soil where religious feeling sprouted, so it caught on with especial fervour. Sandie also must have been infected for a time, but probably not as deeply or for as long as his biographer Brisbane makes out in *The Early Years of Alexander Smith*. Despite his sometimes dour exterior, Sandie was never a killjoy. The increasing Puritanism of his evangelical friends probably began to grate and he found other companions who were more stimulating company. Some of these were not averse to passing the time in conviviality aided by tobacco and alcohol of the sort provided by the 'howffs' or taverns off the Saltmarket near Glasgow Cross. Here, in a piece anonymously written for the short-lived Glasgow Miscellany, Sandie purportedly records the proceedings of the respectable-sounding Sanct Mungo Club. It is in effect a drinking club, where the members meet in decaying splendour. He recalls the building was once

the deserted mansion of a merchant prince transformed into a comfortable modern tavern, rejoicing in crooked passages, inside stairs and cosie little rooms and snuggeries where the lover of good ale and other beverages of greater potency may nestle undisturbed over their tipple and their crack, or at least that portion of them who are not sworn foes of the social cup. The hostel to which we allude is situated somewhere in the bowels of the city, not quite a hundred miles from the locale of King William.[30] For certain reasons which need not be stated, we shall refrain from indicating more explicitly the whereabouts of this favourite haunt of creature comfort, good fellowship and genial mirth. We may mention, however, that the house, after being for several generations the residence of civic dignity, was in the process of time deserted by its former inmates, when fashion placed the locality under her ban, and that it was then fitted up for its present purpose by the grandfather of "mine host" who for many years, as he himself remarked, "drave a rattlin' gude business, and got weel on in the world by aye keepin' the genuine article in his cellar and a gude ceevil Scotch tongue in his head." The superior quality of the 'article' is still a distinguishing feature of the house, a circumstance to which is doubtless to be ascribed the fact that it has long been the howff of the Sanct Mungo Club, the members of which we shall by and by have the pleasure of presenting to our admiring readers.

This was entertaining stuff, a kind of urban *Noctes Ambrosianae* revisited, and one longs for more. However, with his career about to take a dramatic turn, Sandie had to postpone the pleasure of writing a sequel.

Chapter 3
1847-49

I seek the look of Fame! Poor fool – so tries
Some lonely wanderer 'mong the desert sands
By shouts to gain the notice of the Sphynx,
Staring right on with calm eternal eyes.
('A Life-Drama' Sc.1)

THE PEOPLE OF GLASGOW, that is to say the Goldocracy, have a peculiarly pleasant and amiable code of their own. They charitably presume every man to be a blackguard till he proves himself to be a gentleman. If a man has adorned his captivating person with peculiar care they believe him to be a swell – if he happens to be in the rough they pronounce him a snob – if he wears moustaches they think him a swindler or a foreigner; generally, indeed, they consider the terms synonymous. If you talk too much you are a bore – if you talk too little you are a simpleton – if two young people innocently chat and walk together there is an improper flirtation – if you play one of the beautiful ancient sacred tunes, or on Sunday, in meditative mood, stray into the quiet country lanes, as Isaac was wont to do at eventide, you are that worst of sinners, a Sabbath-breaking sinner.... In considering if you shall admit a man to your friendship, or to be the suitor of your daughter, such trifling little items as birth, connections, principles, amiability, habits, knowledge, are never taken into consideration. They may receive a passing notice; but the grand question, the question that swallows up all other questions, is How much is he worth?[31]

Mid-century Victorian Glasgow starkly epitomised rapid urban growth. The city's 400,000 population, already of some ethnic richness, represented a doubling every fifteen to twenty years since the beginning of the century. Although there was still a thriving folk culture, mainly among the immigrant Highlanders, the Irish and those whose rural homes were swallowed up by the city's ink-blot spread, only a minority had much interest in high or bourgeois culture. No one disputed that the Glasgow bourgeoisie knew how to make and spend. They were generous hosts and would turn out for visiting celebrities like Dickens, Thackeray and the singer Jenny Lind. Such were the high spots in what many regarded as a cultural vacuum. Municipal provision, far-sighted when it came to things like gas, water, transport and policing, was more cautious in the refinements of life. This was illustrated by the near-fiasco of the McLellan Bequest. A considerable collection of Italian masters and a purpose-built gallery in Sauchiehall Street had been left to the city by a well-known coachbuilder called Archibald McLellan the year before he died. Unfortunately he had considerably over-extended himself in making this generous gift. As a result the Town Council found itself picking up the tab for some

£40,000 of unpaid bills for work on the galleries. Debate raged back and forth amongst enraged rate-payers over whether the Raphaels should be auctioned to complete the work on the galleries, or whether the incomplete building should be sold off to the highest bidder. Eventually the Council bit the bullet and stumped up the money. McLellan's collection now forms the nucleus of one of the finest city art collections in the UK.

The ubiquitous Sabbath hush (no newspapers, no public transport, no licensed premises) was another symptom of the strong Presbyterian mistrust of frivolity. As evidenced in the above extract from *Alfred Leslie*, the first novel to use the city as a background, Sabbath-breaking was an infringement that only the most daring would risk. There were by the 1850s two or three theatres at most, devoted mainly to staging melodramas. The main artistic achievements of this era could be claimed to have occurred in architecture, as new-found prosperity was celebrated in stone and mortar. New developments of terraced housing were springing up well away from the trading and manufacturing heart of the city closer to the river. Three pleasantly rounded hills (Blythswood, Woodlands and Garnethill, formerly country estates) were situated strategically close to the west end of the new artery Sauchiehall Street which also took traffic eastwards to the two railway stations on Buchanan Street and also to George Square. In the main the "Goldocracy" favoured houses of neo-Georgian design, reflecting a more gracious lifestyle of bygone days. The main area where this new residential development took place became known as Charing Cross, an oblique reference to the second city's pretensions. It also demonstrates that the mid-century was the heyday of North Britishness. London was no more than ten hours away by train and a Glasgow merchant could be at his London club in time for supper.

As for Scottish education, it undoubtedly provided young men and women with many practical qualities, including the basic skills which would prove useful in business or in running a household. Unfortunately it was less good at encouraging artistic and cultural accomplishments. Scotland generally was at this time stony ground for artists, composers and writers unless they had gone south and made a reputation there first. This was hardly a cheering prospect for 18-year-old Sandie as he began to consider what life might hold beyond pattern-designing. He would have become one of the main breadwinners for the household once his apprenticeship was served. This would have left him with little enough for discretionary spending on clothes and evenings with friends. Going to the theatre or the concert hall must have been regarded as unimaginable self-indulgence. In status he would have been above the rank of "hands" working in factories or shop assistants, but he was still a long way below those of his friends who attended the College and had their sights on a profession. That option, as we have seen, had been denied him, but he was still determined to make the best of himself. The improbable-sounding Glasgow Addisonian Literary Society was the chosen means for doing this.

Between 1847 and 1852 Sandie was a moving force in the Addisonians. A record of the GALS meetings and soirées was dutifully kept and miraculously it survives to this day. A large notebook (measuring approx 190x120mm) bound in pigskin, showing all the wear and tear of being carried about in Secretaries' pockets for almost six years, can be found in the Dick Institute, Kilmarnock. [32] On the title page is the copperplate legend "G.A.L.S. (Instituted 22 May 1847)". Following this are accounts, varying greatly in length and style according to the current Secretary's inclinations, of nearly every meeting the Addisonians held. In total there are more than a hundred and fifty. For a biographer this is an essential document for charting the development of a writer's mind at a formative stage. It is akin to discovering a first-hand account of the Apostles meetings when Tennyson was a member during his undergraduate days at Cambridge, or reports on Burns' contributions to the Tarbolton Bachelors evenings in the 1780s. However, the keynote of the GALS soirées was earnestness. They met on Saturday evenings, firstly at Anderson's Temperance Coffee House in Candleriggs, a street mainly occupied by the city's fruit market and the newly-opened City Halls. It was here that the seven founding members resolved what were to be the general purposes of the Society:

It was agreed that we meet fortnightly, every alternate Saturday at 8 o'clock evg., and that an essay be read each evening by one of the members, to be followed (as far as time will allow) by remarks and criticisms...

Amongst the first office-bearers Tom Brisbane was elected Chairman and Sandie the Honorary Secretary, so the first ten meetings are minuted in his hand. Notable at these first meetings are three sets of brothers: the Brisbanes, the Niels [sic] and the Wardrops. John Connal and Jamey Bennie (who joined later) were also stalwarts. The complete list of names is there in the minute book, mainly in Sandie's spidery hand. Meeting places varied until October 1849 when they settled on the classrooms of Prof. Ange Simeon, a French teacher at 280 George Street, on the north side of George Square. Little is known of the other Addisonians. It is reasonable to assume that several might have been undergraduates and others young men in trade who would have ceased work by the Saturday afternoon. Several are characterised, but not named, in Brisbane's biography.

From the start the GALS' aims were avowedly evangelical, although the full rules were not written into the book until 6 January 1849. A stipulation was made that all members had to be "young men of strictly moral character and evangelical principles." The maximum number was limited to twenty, an unnecessary requirement as hardly more than a dozen ever attended. Amongst the rules were the imposition of a quarterly subscription of one shilling (nearer £8 equivalent value) to pay for the use of the room with any surplus going to a book fund. Also one hour per session was to be spent on *Parker's Progressive Exercises in Composition*. Finally theological or sectarian topics were expressly banned from all the Society's discussions. Sandie's part in setting up the Glasgow Addisonians was major; in fact, the choice of title was probably his. One of the papers he delivered was on Joseph Addison, mainstay of The Spectator whose well-bred humour and sense of nicety in matters social and literary were clearly a model for these self-improving young men giving several hours of their scarce leisure time every other Saturday to deliberations of this nature. From the minutes we can read of other papers given by Sandie: 'The Power of Intellect', 'Reason' (followed by a "somewhat spirited discussion"), 'The Claims of History Upon Man', 'Religious Poetry', 'Progress'. 'Music' ("in language chaste and truly classic"), 'Earnestness', 'Thoughts Anent Life' ("remarkable for its unique and eccentric style both as regards the composition and the ideas expressed in this production... but with the gloomy and despairing view the Essayist took of our present state of civilisation the Society almost wholly disagreed"), 'Thoughts on Napoleon', 'Thoughts on a Friend', 'John Keats', Ebenezer Elliott' and finally 'Burns as a National Poet'.

In this last talk, considered the finest delivered by any member, there is a considerable degree of self-identification. Burns' power over readers of very different tastes and cultures, Sandie suggests, stemmed from his "intense nationality... a condensed Scotland." For a poet who wrote so little in Scots this identification with Burns might appear strange. A few paragraphs later, though, all becomes clear:

Many well-meaning men have lamented the deficiency of Burns' education and amused themselves with speculations as to what he might have become had he been thoroughly trained in the schools and sent into the world fully equipped and armed as an intellectual workman. What he might have been I do not pretend to say, but this I know, that he would not have been Robert Burns, the maker of his country's songs... Difficulties are necessary to a man's thorough development. A pent stream has the greatest force. Much of our finest poetry has been written in circumstances which the majority of mankind would have considered unfavourable.

This paper was given in November 1852, just as his *Poems* was going to press. It shows how keenly Sandie remained aware of his lack of any formal education after the age of eleven. He suspected that, in a literary career, it might be held against him. This was prescient. Several critics reacted with utter disbelief that his early work could have been written by someone with his background. The full range of topics chosen for the Glasgow Addisonians' fortnightly debates is fascinating. A list was regularly drawn up in advance for the succeeding ten meetings. In April 1848 the following topics were entered in the minute book:

1st Ought the conduct of a man to be influenced by public opinion?
2nd Should there be a national system of education unconnected with Religion?
3rd Whether is an extension of the suffrage or a more extended system of education more requisite in the present state of Britain?
4th Whether was Pitt or Fox the greater statesman?
5th Is bad legislation the chief cause of the present depressed state of Ireland?
6th Was Britain justified in the war it waged against the American colonies for not complying with its demands?
7th Whether has the poet or the legislator the greater influence on the community?
8th Was the conduct of the British Government towards Napoleon Bonaparte, after the Battle of Waterloo, just?
9th Would a reduction in the British armament be injurious to the welfare of this country?
10th Is there a strong presumptive evidence that Mary Queen of Scots was accessory to the death of Darnley?

Such were the kinds of topics that occupied the minds of those earnest young men. If the discussions turned out to be not quite as intellectual as anticipated, at least the participants gained the opportunity to cultivate some self-assurance and become used to thinking on their feet. The outcomes of most of the debates were not recorded. One can imagine that they would have been conducted with all the serious-mindedness and national fervour for which Scots are famed. And, to spur on the more ambitious of the Addisonians, on their way across George Square to Prof Simeon's schoolroom, they would pass the new column erected to the memory of Sir Walter Scott only ten years ago. If literature and fame needed a joint icon for impressionable minds this was surely it.

A number of Addisonians, like Brisbane, would undoubtedly have gone on to become ministers or professionals. However, at the annual New Year soirées there was a much lighter side in evidence. These were usually held at McNair's Coffee House in Union Street, beginning with a high tea at 7pm to which each member was expected to bring a partner. Then the tables were pulled back, not for dancing but for around three hours of recitations, light-hearted speeches, songs and catches, all for the ladies' entertainment.

According to Brisbane in his rather partial biography, Sandie was not at ease in mixed company. Yet the accounts of the New Year events in the minute book suggest his contributions were often the highlight of the evening. In January 1851 his address on 'The Characteristics of Woman' "produced a considerable sensation" whilst his mock-epic account of the first five years of the Addisonian Society showed "a fluency of speech...pursued with astonishing success." This paints a surprising picture of a character who, according to contemporaries, was averse to standing out in any company, mixed or otherwise.

The first soirée (in 1848) was a joint effort with the Glasgow Coleridge Club. This was supposed to be a warm-up session for a possible amalgamation, but it seems to have gone badly awry despite the "four fleeting hours pleasantly occupied" by the recitations from members of both. The following Saturday a joint meeting was held "for the purpose of agreeing upon the designation of the Society and forming rules etc, when a spirited discussion ensued, which terminated unfortunately in a draw" [possibly *brawl*: the word is scored through]. Was the choice of name for the amalgamated society the cause of bad feeling? No minute book of the Glasgow Coleridge Club has yet come to light.

During 1851 and 1852 Sandie's attendance became noticeably less regular. The original *esprit* seems to have dwindled away. In May 1851 Brisbane proposed a three-month adjournment because no essayist came forward. In October a meeting "separated tumultuously shortly after 9 o'clock" (the normal time was 10.30) and the next month Sandie had to step in and give an impromptu reading from the work of Ebenezer Elliot, the "Corn-Law Rhymer". Although elected Secretary again the following January, Sandie must have realised he had by now outgrown any positive influence the Addisonians could provide. Some pages are in fact missing from the minute book before the account (13 November 1852) of his address on Burns. The last recorded minute was four weeks later. His commitment to the GALS would have been eating into precious writing time by the beginning of 1852. His feelings about its demise would therefore have been fairly mixed. Brisbane recalls the final meetings in his biography:

The fame which Smith at length suddenly acquired as a poet, by the pages of the Eclectic and Critic in 1851 and 1852 proved indirectly the chief cause of the death of the Addisonian Society. Although it had now served, for him and his most intimate friends, the purpose for which they had joined it, he still loved it as a place of pleasant intercourse and desired to remain connected with it; but several of the members now treated him and spoke to him with such unwonted [sic] tokens of deference, on account of his rising fame, and made such allusions to his poetry as galled his manly spirit. They often brought also young students and silly literary aspirants to the club, who sat and so stared at the poet that the place became unendurable, and he consequently failed to be present. With a few others he endeavoured to save the society by reconstituting it from a limited selection of the oldest members, and changing the place of the meeting; but, after all, a few hilarious students from the country got in, and so changed the character of the club that Smith and his chief friends withdrew altogether, and it soon became defunct from lack of earnestness of purpose and sobriety of spirit.[33]

The Early Years of Alexander Smith, Poet and Essayist. A Study for Young Men gives a very detailed account of the years 1847 to 1853 when Tom Brisbane and Sandie were in each other's company frequently. It was during this time that Brisbane was studying for his degree in Humanities at Glasgow, the very same course that he had hoped Sandie would take, in order to qualify for the ministry. Brisbane was six years older, also hailing from Paisley, and the relationship seems to have provided him with an elder brother role initially. To give him his due, he must have been one of the first to learn of Sandie's poetical ambitions and therefore to have offered some encouragement even though he had originally hoped to groom him for the ministry. It is difficult to imagine what other benefits Sandie would have derived. From the tone of his biography Brisbane was a rather controlling, overly literal-minded and fairly humourless character. Add to this his self-appointed role of preserving the sanctified memory of his former friend, and we end up with a portrait (as well as the original entry on Smith in the *Dictionary of National Biography*) that shows signs of crude retouching. One of the most obvious is the need he felt to omit fairly innocuous passages from letters by Sandie to him, and even an occasional rephrasing. A paragraph from the Preface to *Early Years* shows that Brisbane, even while being unable to avert them, was aware of the dangers of this closeness to his subject and the risk of partiality:

> The only requisite I possess for the task I have undertaken is a fuller knowledge of Mr Smith's early years than others may have. This advantage is, however, counterbalanced by a fear lest my unpractised pen may, after all, fail justly to present the well-known features of so fair a life before the reader's view. Still I cling to the hope that, with a hand moved by affection and steadied and restrained by truth, the work may be so done that the limner and his art may be forgotten, and the face growing before him on these pages alone command the attention of the reader, - or at least so to command it that he and the critic shall find it easy to exercise charity sufficient to cover any multitude of literary sins which a tyro in book-making may commit.[34]

In his rather distinctive prose Brisbane admits that Sandie by the early 1850s "had indeed outgrown all his Glasgow associates. The period had then arrived when the necessities of his genius and whole mental nature required that he should be severed from these and mix with men of larger growth as his friends and equals." Yet, despite this noble resignation expressed as biographer, Brisbane seems in reality to have clung onto the friendship well beyond the point at which it was giving mutual benefit. The description of their first real exchange of confidences is probably more revealing about Brisbane's personal obsessions than was intended. Before one of the early meetings of the Addisonians in October 1846 he bumped into Sandie:

> While passing along Argyle Street, purposing to get out of the city in quest of solitude, he suddenly accosted me and proposed a walk previous to the assembling of our club. And, as he had heard of my intention to enter College on the following Monday, we were speedily engaged in conversation on our respective hopes and aims in life. Mine were so far fixed, and interested him; but his were dim and uncertain. As he then informed me, however, he had till very recently ardently entertained a similar prospect to that which I was about to prosecute. Our conversation thus became close and confidential as, walking on, we left the city behind us and journeyed several miles along the Cathcart Road, aided by the light of the Hutchiesontown furnaces. At length we returned to our club, no longer acquaintances but friends, and under a mutual promise to meet again on the afternoon of that day week. That was to me, and I hope in some measure to him, a fortunate though accidental meeting. I had then no idea of the character and calibre of the youth I had ignorantly endeavoured to shun. The treasure of friendship…cannot be told nor estimated.[35]

It seems to have been a relationship of extraordinary intensity, for the biographer maybe his first such relationship. The way Brisbane describes the next six years is indeed just as if he had discovered a soulmate. The rest of the winter they "spent every Saturday afternoon together, and very rarely was there a third person present."

Then, as summer drew on, and the College had closed for the session, we met almost every night as he came out of the warehouse. This practice we continued for more than six years. Talking much on many themes, we frequently conversed of personal matters; rehearsed each other's history, forecast our hopes and told the secrets of the soul as far as one may to his fellow-mortal, and as one can only do to the closest and sincerest friend in the spring of unsophisticated youth. Each summer evening when the sky was clear, we walked from eight till ten o'clock. Our favourite and most frequent path being "beside the river that we used to love."[36]

This is extraordinarily revealing and it is followed by several pages of rapt description of sylvan and riverbank walks and of reading Keats,

Byron and Shakespeare whilst reclining in banks of flowers. The biographer also recounts that he has, for purely biographical purposes, revisited the village of Carmyle which by the 1860s had been linked to Glasgow by rail. Here Brisbane notes the changes that progress has wrought upon his nostalgic vision, but he is able to go back to an inn where the two of them were "wont to partake of bread and cheese and porter" before walking back into the city. Then, as if drawn irresistibly, he goes on to visit nearby Kenmuir where, as he enters the wood, "there came upon my spirit one of the strangest and most powerful experiences of my life."

All was so startlingly familiar that I felt as if I had renewed my youth; the past was restored; the [fifteen] intervening years became a vanished dream. At one moment I could not resist obeying an impulse to turn round and make sure that Smith was not behind me. Had I then seen his form I do not think it would have surprised me much; nor had I heard him pronounce my name would it have startled me. My imagination was in that state of heat and tension in which apparitions may be begotten.[37]

There is something clearly being suppressed here. Suffice to say Brisbane eventually married a sixteen-year-old farmer's daughter and led an outwardly uneventful life as a Unitarian minister, the major part of it at Cambuslang, only a few miles from the places he described in the above passage. He would surely never have dared to publish such rose-tinted reminiscence while Smith was still alive. Be that as it may, from 1848 he was Sandie's regular companion on five annual walking holidays in the West Highlands and the north of Scotland. This was Sandie's one week of holiday, taken during the local trades "fair" in mid-July. Each of the holidays, except for one, is described in detail by Brisbane (and much of the detail of the itineraries is corroborated in the early chapters of *A Summer in Skye*), so it is unnecessary to duplicate this in detail. A brief synopsis will show the ground they covered; in some cases it was considerable.

In 1848 the pair went to the isle of Arran, a journey of three or four hours by Clyde paddle-steamer. They had failed to book a hotel room in advance but they were able to take a room in a private house for the week. It was agreed on this first trip that the following year they would do something more adventurous, "Smith insisting, as a special part of the agreement, that no third person should be of the party." The next year saw Sandie and his "genial friend" travelling by train to Stirling to visit the historic town and the field of Bannockburn. Then they did a 16-mile walk to Callander, arriving at sunset. Resting on the Sabbath, the following Monday saw them embarking on a 30-mile trek round the head of Loch Katrine and on to Inversnaid. From here they were rowed across Loch Lomond to spend the night at Tarbet. The next day they walked to Inveraray via Arrochar, a mere 24 miles this time but the route took the Rest and Be Thankful pass (around 500m at its highest point). From Inveraray they took the steamer back to Glasgow where they arrived "with scarcely a shilling between us; but in truth we had not one pound sterling each when we started."

The other trips can be quickly summarised. In 1850 (with rather more money in their pockets) they went to Strone and Kilmun on the Holy Loch. Then taking another steamer the next day they crossed the Clyde to Greenock and then on to the Kyles of Bute, through the Crinan Canal and up to Oban, a full day's sail. The next day another steamer took them to Ballachulish. Spurning the waiting coach, they walked the road through Glencoe and across Rannoch Moor intending to reach the inn at Tyndrum. They only got as far as Bridge of Orchy where they were put up "in a very humble and smoky Highland hut." Another extraordinary hike of at least 25 miles took them across to Tarbet where they caught the steamer to Balloch and then the train home. The 1851 trip took them once more to Inveraray via a Saturday afternoon steamer to Lochgilphead where they spent the Sunday. A 5am start got them to Cladish in time for breakfast. At the head of the Pass of Brander they joined the mail coach and rode with the driver who entertained them with local lore and history. On reaching Loch Etive they left the coach at Bonawe and decided on a dip. This proved too much exertion for Sandie who started vomiting uncontrollably. Somehow they walked another ten miles into Oban where a doctor advised a day's rest. They then took the steamer to Rothesay on the isle of Bute and "spent the remainder of our vacation time in boating, and making short rambles". In 1851 they must have gone somewhere but Brisbane omits the journey details. The final pedestrian tour was in 1852, at a time when Sandie was working furiously on 'A Life-Drama'. This began with a train journey to Dundee and Perth, then the walkers took in Crieff, Comrie and Loch Earn and back to Stirling.

Sometime in the early 1850s Sandie's photograph was taken, a head and shoulders view, the only full-face portrait in existence. The most striking features are a determinedly set mouth, a large broad forehead and a right eye with a wicked squint to it. The shoulders slope slightly and there is a sense of unease in the figure confronting us. Tradition has it that the *carte de visite* photo was taken as part of a pact with Hugh Macdonald, who had his photo taken at the same time. Whichever of them survived longer would write the obituary of the other. Macdonald, thirteen years Sandie's senior, died first. Another indefatigable pedestrian, he was totally different from Brisbane, energetically playing a kind of Falstaff to Sandie's Prince Hal as he became famous. He had earlier been active in the Chartist movement.

They seem to have taken regular walks from Glasgow Green, similar in route to the ones taken with Brisbane, but there was never any intermingling and gradually the non-Evangelicals took over. Amongst them was Patrick Proctor Alexander, the precocious son of the Professor of Greek at St Andrews. He was living in Glasgow with the avowed purpose of following a career in commerce, but secretly writing what he called "fugitive pieces" for the Evening Citizen, founded and edited by James Hedderwick. Macdonald was the assistant editor, brought on board because of his prodigious local knowledge of Glasgow and its environs, particularly in the area of natural history.

In his Memoir in *Last Leaves* Pat Alexander gives a colourful portrait of Hugh Macdonald. Born in Glasgow, Macdonald spent part of his childhood on Mull and he seems to have cultivated a Highland wildness. For a number of years he was a printing block-maker and then weaver in Bridgeton, where he tried setting up a shop. But he was spending too much of his time getting out of the industrial city to ramble the nearby country lanes and villages which he then wrote about for whatever publication would take them. He also committed his sensations to verse. Sometimes Macdonald's poems attain a freedom and naturalness that makes them memorable, but too often they are pale imitations of Burns. This would probably have pleased him as in his estimation there was no greater poet. According to Pat Alexander he gloried in the name of 'Scotchman' and spoke in broad Doric whenever possible. In the country he usually sported a Glengarry bonnet with a sprig of heather, cutting a figure quite at odds with his conventionally dressed walking companion:

He [Macdonald] had much of the Celtic vividness, vivacity, enthusiasm; the "flash and outbreak of the fiery mind" was perpetually expressed in his speech and his various odd modes of procedure. Smith, on the other hand, fronted the world, as I said, as quiet an embodiment as may be of the right Saxon sense, shrewdness and solidity. The contrast was fundamental; and at almost every point of detail it was so marked as to make the friendly amalgam of the two amusing not to say absurd.[38]

On their riverbank walks Macdonald was always accompanied by a bulky tubular tin case used for collecting specimens. For Pat Alexander, nearer in age to Macdonald, this would be the subject of frequent (and probably increasingly tiresome) speculation about its alternative uses. A large bottle of whisky and several rounds of ham sandwiches seem to have been the favoured contents. Their route took them from the Green, where there is now a drinking fountain erected to Macdonald's memory, along the north bank of the Clyde which winds in the form of a distorted S and at that time contained within its loops the filter-beds of the city's two main water companies, taking water directly from the upstream river. There were also printing and cotton dye-works nearby, but within a couple of miles they would be in open country, dotted with farms and an occasional estate. At Carmyle there were a number of inns and hostelries that thrived off bona fide travellers and here there was a favourite of Hugh Macdonald's (the same one immortalised by Brisbane?) where the landlady "made you feel as if, in entering her hut, you had walked into a Waverley novel."

Too long a stay at the "modest hostelrie" was not without its perils as there was the return journey to be made by moonlight. And nearby was Kenmuir bank (soon to be removed by quarrying) giving through the branches a view across the surrounding country and westwards to the glowing city skyline. Smith later recaptured the mesmerising effect it had upon him:

In a quarter of an hour we reach Kenmuir bank, which rises some seventy feet or so, filled with trees, their trunks rising bare for a space and then spreading out with branch and foliage into a matted shade, permitting the passage of only a few flakes of sunlight at noon, resembling, in the green twilight, a flock of visionary butterflies alighted and asleep. Within the wood is jungle; you wade to the knees in brushwood and bracken. The trunks are clothed with ivy, and snakes of ivy creep from tree to tree, some green with life, some tarnished with decay. At the end of the bank there is a clear well in which, you and your face meeting its shadow, you may quench your thirst. Seated here you have the full feeling of solitude.[39]

Such were the few moments of escape that young Sandie enjoyed in an increasingly tedious life of drudgery lasting ten or more hours per day. He must have been aware of the deadening effect it was having upon him as he entered his twenties. In 1853 The Illustrated London News published a full-spread bird's eye view of Glasgow probably taken from a hot-air balloon. From the forest of masts and funnels at the quaysides up to the slender smokestacks at Port Dundas the face of mid-Victorian Glasgow was scarred with diagonal parallel trails of dense smoke. This was evidence of what enormous wealth was being created by and for the Goldocracy and the Cotton Bags. For hundreds of thousands of others life was lived at bare survival level. Many were Highlanders who had fled the ravages of the potato famines. Few remained to take the hand-outs of the Highland Relief Fund; they preferred to take their chance in the close-packed wynds around Glasgow Cross. Here typhus and TB preyed as effectively as starvation on new arrivals with no immunity to the latest strain of contagion.

Irish immigration began early in 1848 and it has been calculated that 43,000 came within the space of four months. As a result, basic foodstuffs like bread began to rise in price and even became unobtainable. The unemployed were offered meat and soup in return for spells of stone-breaking. Then in early March 1848 the Bread Riots broke out, creating four days of aimless looting around the Trongate where the better shops were situated. Troops were called in and blood was shed in restoring order; those arrested received sentences varying from two years imprisonment to eighteen years transportation to the colonies. Smith witnessed the 1848 riots (and recorded them in the Glasgow chapter of *A Summer in Skye*) as he travelled every day to work along the Gallowgate and Trongate to Queen Street. Some have claimed[40] that he was there as a participant, but (apart from Hugh Macdonald whom he probably didn't know until afterwards) there is no conclusive proof. He would certainly have witnessed countless other scenes of horror on a daily basis caused by poverty, disease and alcohol. Whether by typhus or gibbet, life for most citizens was unnaturally abbreviated. Twenty-five years was the average for those who survived childhood and lived at the bottom of the heap. Sandie was living only a few hundred metres away from some of the worst of the city's slums and he must have rubbed shoulders with the residents. To harden the sensibilities until awareness fades is not an ideal way of life for a budding poet.

Some idea of the formative effect all this had upon him can be discovered from probably his best-known poem 'Glasgow'. Although it first appeared in complete form in *City Poems* (1857) a much earlier version (entitled 'To a City') exists which must have been written in 1853 or earlier. (See Appendix 1.) In both versions the sardonic opening verse is the same:

> Sing, poet, 'tis a merry world,
> That cottage smoke is rolled and curled
> In sport; that ev'ry moss
> Is happy, ev'ry inch of soil –
> Before *me* runs a road of toil
> With my grave cut across.
> Sing, trailing showers and breezy downs,
> *I* know the tragic heart of towns.[41]

The italicised 'I' and 'me' were not in Smith's original version, but nonetheless it is a poem that goes to the very core of the individual's fight for self-preservation in an environment that is a mixture of creation and destruction. By the time the new decade approached he must have sensed that time was running out. He had to do something to get away from such a deadening existence. But was poetry really the route to a new life? Brisbane recalls how, in late October 1849 he went round to the drab tenement in Charlotte Street. Up in the attic Sandie was seated in his "snug little room before the fire". A spell of subdued conversation ensued until, just as Brisbane rose to leave,

> He also rose to his feet, saying "Sit down a little. I have something I wish to show you." He then went to a drawer and took out a mass of MS and, sitting down again, began to read from it with a rather tremulous voice. When he was done reading, we sat for some moments in silence; for I was as one bewildered with surprise.[42]

Brisbane was probably the first to know of the poetry. They met again the following day (Sunday) when Brisbane tried to express his appreciation of the work he had heard him read. Afterwards he sent Sandie a letter intended to convey his ideas more clearly. Eventually he received a reply. This was much more than a letter, or even an "epistle". Brisbane surely must have realised it was a manifesto addressed principally to a wider audience.

> Dear Tom,
> As we talked this night last week, few stars were visible in my spirit sky; those visible looked dreary and cold. One has gone out since. [A reference to a love affair ending?] Let it go. A star, 'my life's star', burneth and *will* burn: when it sets, I set.
> Your letter, I need not say, was read with interest. You have my sincere thanks. You have been very frank with me of late; I will return you like for like. I will unclasp my soul to you and you may read what I had hoped one day to have avowed proudly; or, that hope failing, to have buried it for ever – a dead hope in a dead heart.
> You may recollect, on the evening which has given rise to this epistle, you made a guess as to what mine aspirations tended – you guessed poetry. I made some evasive answer. I could not then say "Aye". I can *now* say you guessed aright. It has been the seventh heaven of my aspirations for years; a passion running as deep as the aboriginal waters of my being. At the present moment the 'passion poesy' standeth on the necks of all others like a king, and it will ultimately swallow them as the serpent of Moses swallowed the serpents of the Egyptian magicians. It is with a feeling of humiliation I make this confession.
> I know not how you will receive it. I trust, however, you will do me justice in your thoughts; that you will not place me in the category with the D---s, K---s, J---s.[43] I believe my spirit is something different from theirs – deeper and sincerer. I am unconscious of that pitiful vanity (the Alpha and Omega of their hopes) to see one's name in print; the immortality of five minutes in the Poet's Corner. Above all, don't laugh or sneer, however much you may pity. I could bear sneers on this point from no one, least of all from you. I might keep silent but I would suffer like a martyr in his shirt of fire. Believe me it's no laughing matter.
> Underneath those wide doming heavens, that ancient sun, those pitying stars, of all the miseries this is the chiefest – when one has the soul, blood, heart, pulses of an angel – all but the wings! This is egotism with a vengeance,

but we are all egotists; and all we are, feel or see – this universe of souls, stars and suns, is but a sublime egotism of Deity.

You tell me you wish I should yet fill a pulpit; this may never be. I speak in sober sadness when I say I am unfit for public life. That fire once burnt brightly on the hearthstone of my heart – the flame flickered, waned and died; a mighty wind scattered the red embers like autumn leaves: the hearthstone is now cold; I do not wish to fill a pulpit.

You may be inclined to ask, "What do you intend to do?" I might say "Nothing." To attempt to become a preacher is useless: incapacity within – *without* difficulties no capacity could overcome – prevents it. What I would like is just some way of living which would feed and cover this carcass, and allow much time to roam through book-world, and the world of my own spirit like the new-born Adam in the new-born Eden. You may say this life I desire to lead will not be a useful one for my fellows. Granted! I do not intend to gird on an apron and become waiter to the world.

If you judge me by the length of my letter you may think me rather ungrateful. I am at the confessional and, certes, the confession is no pleasant task. I do not know, however, that anything more need be said. I have unbosomed myself as well as I could. I fear this night's work will lessen your esteem for me, as I have fallen somewhat in my own in the course of it. If it be so, I will be the only loser.

Jog along, Tom; the road of life is rough, but the eternities are ahead. We will reach them soon.

Yours truly,
A.Smith[44]

Chapter 4:
1850-52

I'd grow an atheist in these towns of trade,
Were't not for stars. The smoke puts heaven out;
I meet sin-bloated faces in the streets,
And shrink as from a blow.
('A Life-Drama' sc.9)

TURNING HIS ATTENTION to his father's occupation of a pattern-designer, his good taste and natural quickness soon made him a master in this artistic department of trade, while he still continued to cling to his poetical studies; and on removing to Glasgow it was with the double object of finding employment among its manufacturers and intellectual improvement among its literary society. In the latter and more important aim he was especially successful...[45]

This laundered account of Sandie's early development as a pattern-designer is taken from *Chambers' Eminent Scotsmen*. It was published sufficiently soon after his death to have been written by someone who must have known him in life. By 1850, as his apprenticeship drew to a close, he was equipped to launch himself on a fully-fledged career in the textile industry. However much his employers may have admired his "good taste and natural quickness", this admiration was certainly not mutual. The designing of patterns may have sounded artistic, but it was very much market-driven and originality would seldom have been the main requirement for commercial success. The Robertson brothers were a Dickensian pair if 'A Boy's Poem' is anywhere close to reality. In this passage two seamstresses meet on the stair to exchange gossip and grouches about their working conditions:

> "I hate that wretch
> Stealing upstairs in India-rubber shoes,
> Creeping from room to room, till, ere you know,
> He is beside you; in each corner poking
> With his white weasel face. He cooks his meals
> Within his empty house; his sole companion
> A wretched cat that on his lonely bounty starves –
> A shadow like himself."
> "His brother too,
> The upper and nether millstones they,
> And we are ground between..."[46]

Making allowances for his employers' eccentricities, working life was probably pleasant enough, even if it lacked stimulation. Sandie would have been earning enough to make a major contribution to the household at 12 Charlotte Street now numbering seven. Although the 1850s would see a recovery in trade, anyone employed in manufacturing was always at the mercy of slumps accompanied by staff lay-offs, nowhere more so than in the textile mills. Here, apart from the subsistence level of wages, legislation had still not made many inroads into dangerous practices in the workplace, often involving children. While Sandie was designing his tasteful patterns for dresses, bonnets and shawls the actual work of weaving them would be undertaken with frequent industrial injury and even loss of life. Another Glasgow novel *The Factory Girl* made the point without laying on the sentimentality:

The iron shuttles flew to and fro, carrying the fine threads along, and weaving them into the woof, while the web of the beautiful fabric grew behind it so close and even. Behind every loom was a girl, watching it with quick careful eye, ready to unite any broken thread, and to supply it with proper food. There were girls of all sorts in that room, some of them pretty, others more commonplace, but all neatly dressed in clean short-gowns and skirts which left foot and ankle free. They looked quite brisk and happy, though day after day they had to keep watch by their looms in the midst of the deafening roar of machinery while the sun shone without, and the flowers blossomed in the woods – and fields without the city glistened fresh and green under the summer sky.[47]

A city centre warehouse was no place for a poet, one might have thought. But by this time he was writing feverishly, continuing his "poetical studies" and now also planning ways to get into print and find recognition. Meanwhile the Addisonians were debating who should succeed Wordsworth as poet laureate. Would it be a fairly safe choice such as Henry Taylor, W.S.Landor, Samuel Rogers or possibly Tennyson, in his early forties still considered by many as too young? In the event Samuel Rogers declined the honour because he considered he was far too old. The Athenaeum had canvassed support for Elizabeth Barret Browning, a daring choice but one that would have heralded the opening of a brave new decade. Others overlooked included her husband Robert Browning, Ruskin and Arthur Hugh Clough.

Meanwhile in Queen Street Sandie was paying less and less attention to the designing, employing pen and paper for other unauthorised purposes. Pat Alexander tells how years afterwards he and a traveling companion fell in with one of Smith's former employers at a Highland inn. Plied with local beverage, this 'muslin bag' (maybe it was one of the Robertson brothers) became more communicative. The two young men pumped him for more information about the fledgling bard as designer. He replied that for years he had been paying the wages of a man who had clearly been giving the job only half his attention: "he asserted that the poetry had been written 'at my expense sir, every --------- line of it!'" according to Pat Alexander.[48] Of course, Smith was told about it at the first opportunity and it raised merely the ghost of a smile.

It was in 1850 that he took the first serious step towards becoming published. Through Hugh Macdonald he had a line to the Citizen, whose editor was James Hedderwick, the London-educated son of a wealthy printer. In 1842, after a spell as assistant editor of The Scotsman in Edinburgh he came to Glasgow to start the weekly Citizen. In 1864 he was to take the bold step of turning it into a daily evening paper selling at a halfpenny, following the lead of the Greenock Telegraph. Hedderwick was exceptional for a newspaper proprietor-editor in enjoying poetry. He seems to have personally been frustrated both as poet and actor, so he did the next best thing by encouraging local talent. As well as taking on Macdonald and serialising his *Rambles Round Glasgow* and *Days at the Coast*, he instituted a poets' corner in the paper. At the top-left of the front page there was a regular space for 'Original Poetry' and it was here that Sandie's first published work appeared. In the issue of 6 July 1850 there was a seven-verse poem entitled 'Lines to a friend', written in Spenserian stanzas and signed 'Smith Murray'. The pseudonym was based on his mother's maiden name; it was coincidentally the name of a law firm situated close to Queen Street that he must have passed almost every day. Why not use his own name? Maybe it was from natural modesty or just a safeguard in case the Robertsons were growing suspicious.

The poem owes several literary debts. Most obviously imbued with a Keatsian "melancholy fit", the poet shares this mood of world-weariness, and he seeks in natural beauty oblivion from an oppressive workaday world. Although "lull'd, atmosphered in beauty" he feels "fated To sicken amid beauty", since what the world calls beauty is to him a sham. There are debts to Byron's Childe Harold, including the wandering, disillusioned protagonist and the choice of Spenserian stanzas. There is much here too from other Romantics, but the writer makes the well-worn coinage gleam just a little. Conventional as it is, one can see why 'Lines to a Friend' impressed his contemporaries.

> Dear Friend! Thou lovest well this summer weather;
> Up and away to the unconquer'd land
> Of storm and grandeur, mist and purple heather
> And gleaming lakes! We will tread hand in hand
> Song-hallowed paths; we will exulting stand

On barren summits, where the sun-gazing bird
Mates with the tempest, where our souls expand
With mountain joy, - such rapture as ne'er stirred
Your stagnant hearts, ye cold and money-grasping herd!

A kisser swooning on a luscious lip;
A blessed soul asleep in fields benign,
Lull'd, atmosphered in beauty; a dream trip
To streamed Elysium, laid in lap divine;
Rained kisses warming all your heart like wine;
A father's first sight of his first-born child;
A twilight-bowered love-whisper, "I am thine",
Joys deep as these are in the mountain'd wild
Rambling 'mong summer woods, and lakes all greenly isled.

Then steals a sense of pleasure still and quiet
O'er the lull'd brain stretch'd, by green-margined streams –
How drowsily it calms the warm blood's riot
And steeps us in a blissful sea of dreams!
Oh, are there beating hearts wherein there beams
No passion for green fields and forests old?
The purple clouds rich rimm'd with ragged gold?
When these I cease to love, may mine be hushed and cold!

Heart-weary of the world, its fret, its noise,
Oh, could I fade to some enchanted wood,
With one I love, tasting all sylvan joys,
And by her eyes of radiant darkness wooed,
On kisses fed – young Love's ambrosial food;
Pied earth our couch, our roof noon's bluest sky –
Or roam the dim paths with faint violets hued,
Drinking the soul of pleasure like a bee,
Calming this heart, unquiet as the unresting sea.

It may be a weak wish, but I am fain
To die in autumn, ere the leafless bowers.
Methinks that dying would lose half its pain
To die with sunshine, leaves, sweet-smelling flowers
And linnets' songs which charm the summer hours –
Dying with beauty; nor 'mid churchyard tombs
I pray to sleep, but where the ringdove cowers
Far in the dimmest of the forest glooms,
Where the wild song-bird builds, where the faint primrose blooms.

> Ah! there is that within me which is fated
> To sicken amid beauty, a lone guest
> Caged in the body, which will not be mated
> With earth or earthly things. As to its nest
> The worn bird turns, that weary and unblest
> Would fain seek shelter, but oh, where is its home?
> Like a spent arrow will it sink to rest
> In the sateless grave? No, no, 'twill upward roam
> And furl its wearied wing in the Eternal's dome!
>
> Beauty and Fame, twin cheats, twin idols, grow;
> Alas that both, starlike and beautiful,
> Should prove but garlands on an anguished brow,
> A golden halo round a grinning skull!
> Alas! Alas! that Life should be a school
> Teaching us unbelief in love and truth!
> Alas! Alas! that Time has power to cool
> The warm aspirings of our fervent Youth
> To loving money-bags – most worthless aim, in sooth!

It would be fascinating to know what else Hedderwick was offered (some of those "masses of MSS" observed by Brisbane). It would give an idea of when Sandie started writing the original poems that were to be later incorporated into his first major work. Already, just nine months after his manifesto letter, 'Lines to a Friend' is solid proof that Sandie had already learnt how to absorb, digest and reformulate all his systematic reading. The choice of the Spenserian stanza (used by Keats in 'The Eve of St Agnes' and by Shelley in 'Adonais') is particularly curious. Imitated from Italian verse, it has a strict, repetitive rhyme scheme more easily achieved in Italian than in English. To avoid the scheme becoming intrusive the poet needs to work sense against rhyme by reducing end-stopped lines and varying the stresses within the line. As Shelley intended in his tribute to Keats' memory, the straitjacket of the rhyme should add a solemn and suppressed quality to the emotion behind the lines. Maybe it allows the final stanza here to emerge with more pent-up emotion as the young poet dismisses the twin Sirens of Beauty and Fame that were obviously very much in his thoughts.

The 1851 Census showed how much the social tone of 12 Charlotte Street had dropped. There were around thirty adults living in the tenement and few were what we would now call white-collar workers. However one name stands out. This was Samuel Edwards, a 23-year-old teacher of English, who was lodging with the Lecks on the floor below Sandie. Maybe he was a source of fresh reading matter and possibly more, but he remains just a name. The other residents included dressmakers, seamstresses, a warper and cloth-lapper, a bookbinder, a shoemaker and a cabinetmaker. Meanwhile on the top floor there were now four younger children: David (13), Marion (11), Christina (5) all at school, and little William who was three. This made for a not excessive Victorian family, but still the four-room apartment must have become intolerably overcrowded. The urge for Sandie to move out and find accommodation must have been discussed, but that would effectively have meant the loss of his wage which would have had to go on his own rent.

His resolve to break free of Glasgow altogether may well have been strengthened by an occurrence which dates from early 1851. According to Brisbane the account of a young woman's accidental drowning, mentioned in 'A Boy's Poem', actually happened at this time. The girl, Barbara, possessed "a singularly gentle disposition combined with a thoughtfulness of mind" and there was a growing relationship between them. They had agreed to meet in the city centre early one foggy evening, but she failed to show up. He assumed that Barbara had thought better of it and stayed at home.

But early on the following morning the mournful intelligence was brought to him that she had been found that morning lying dead in the Glasgow and Paisley canal. On the afternoon of the previous day, having made a call at the southern extremity of the city, she had endeavoured to reach home the nearest way by going, as she was accustomed to do often, for a short distance by the canal bank – although her friends had advised her not to do so on this occasion; and in groping her way by the oft-frequented path she must have fallen into the water.[49]

"For several days" (Brisbane recounts) "he shunned all society." On the day of her burial the two of them took a long afternoon walk long the Clyde. After a few miles in silence, Sandie began to speak aloud the lines of what was to become one of his best-known poems. Later incorporated into 'Horton' in *City Poems*, it had first appeared in The Leader on 27 November 1852. It was also included in the revised *Palgrave's Golden Treasury* where it was given the title 'Barbara'. The poem's throbbing, overwrought quality recommended it to the late Victorians and Edwardians; its constant refrain made it into a popular drawing room recitation piece. A writer in the Pall Mall Gazette (12 January 1898) refers to it as "Alexander Smith's one famous poem" and continues: "This is that 'Barbara' which no reader ever quite forgets, whether you have come upon it early or late, or heard it read by chance, or lighted upon it in some collection of popular verses, whether it keep long hold of the fancy and the ear or newly capture them, 'Barbara' is better remembered than many a better poem." This anonymous critic refers to some lines having the "remoteness of a real emotion... they may not have the solitariness of fine poetry, but they are at least aloof, aloof enough." A verse should suffice:

> In the years I've changed
> Wild and far my heart hath ranged,
> And many sins and errors now have been on me avenged;
> But to you I have been faithful, whatsoever good I lacked;
> I loved you, and above my life still hangs that love intact –
> Your love the trembling rainbow, I the reckless cataract –
> Still I love you, Barbara.[50]

Brisbane is insistent this was written soon after the event. Recalling that wintery riverside walk, he writes: "the effect produced on the mind by reading it cannot equal that produced by hearing it repeated by the poet's own lips, as it came fresh from his wounded heart."

The Reverend George Gilfillan is not a name that features largely, if indeed at all, in 21st century histories of literary criticism. As we have already seen (Chapter 2) from the mid 1840s his pronouncements on the literary scene, prolific and verbose as they appear now, were avidly read especially by the younger set. According to Carlyle his offerings, whether published in periodicals and books or delivered verbatim at public lectures (he was of course a practised preacher), represented "a kind of opium style". Although the literary establishment tried to ignore him, they were aware that through the growing periodicals press writers like Gilfillan could speak directly to readers and affect the way new work was received. One could argue that Tennyson, EBB and Arnold (to name the most celebrated) had also trimmed their sails to Gilfillan's gusty critical breeze for a time at least. More importantly for recently arrived poets and others still to come, all eventually to be tarred with the label 'Spasmodic school', Gilfillan was a trusted interpreter and mentor, a self-appointed herald whose trumpet summoned the mid-Victorian reading public into new awareness.

The articles he wrote for Thomas Aird's Dumfriesshire & Galloway Herald were gathered together by William Tait (who founded Tait's Magazine, a more radical rival to Blackwoods). They appeared as *A Gallery of Literary Portraits* in three volumes between 1845 and 1854. Gilfillan's enthusiasm for championing the "rugged and wrathful" spirit (expressed in his article on 'Genius' for Hogg's Instructor), as opposed to a recognisable literary tradition, set some people's teeth on edge, particularly in the academic world. With his tough upbringing, somehow coming through in the face of poverty and rejection, he was a natural nonconformist both in his religious and social thinking. As well as Hogg's he was invited to add some literary dash to the British Quarterly Review (an upstart rival to the august Quarterly), the Eclectic Review and The Critic (where he wrote under the pseudonym Apollodorus). As a talent-spotter he sensed that there was a public out there hungry for overnight sensations, perhaps a new Shelley, Burns or Byron for a newly literate generation.

Gilfillan was a warm-hearted and often impulsive man, generous with his time when it came to reading and advising new writers. He was clearly imbued with an abundant energy that enabled him also to undertake his pastoral duties, dying in harness much loved at the age of sixty-five. He had a streak of vanity in his make-up, probably an advantage when mounting the pulpit, but potentially volatile when writing about his protégés. He would sometimes mix his métiers, rifling through the divine's style toolbox for his published periodical work. In this way he opened himself up to attack from more forensic critics. This sample of his technique comes from his portrait of J. Stanyan Bigg, a new poet living in the Lake District :

The poets who are at present acting with most power on the young mind of the age, are intensely subjective, and some of them to the brink of morbidity. The influence wielded over the lovers of poetry by Homer, Scott or Burns is slender compared to that which Wordsworth, Keats, Shelley, Coleridge, and the rest of the bardic brotherhood – the sons of Mist by Thunder – are exerting. The writings of the former are devoured like new novels and then thrown aside. The writings of the latter are tasted slowly, and in drops – are studied – are carried into solitude – are read by the sides of lonely rivers, or on silent mountain tops, and ultimately surround the young aspirants with an atmosphere which goes with them where they go, rests with them where they rest, and hovers over their pens when they write. To the charm of these poets, it adds mightily that they are said to be, and are, more or less heterodox in their creeds. This gives a peculiar gusto to their works, the reading of which becomes a sweet and secret sin, smacking of the taste of the "stolen waters" and the "pleasant bread". Thus are two luxuries – that of the indulgence of daring thought, and something resembling contraband desire – united in the perusal of our later subjective poets.[51]

This iconoclastic approach would have appealed more to twenty-somethings. So it was to George Gilfillan in Dundee that Sandie sent samples of his work after discussing the matter with several of his Addisonian cronies. Gilfillan returned home (in August 1850) to a large pile of MSS sent in his absence. Sandie's "written in an unfamiliar, boyish, unformed and straggling hand" was hastily looked at and put aside. A second letter prompted him to scrutinise them more carefully.

No correspondence has survived, but Gilfillan's reply was encouraging enough to make Sandie redouble his efforts while still working at Robertsons'. Under Gilfillan's encouragement he burnt with a bluer flame. The following July Sandie and Brisbane were off again, this time on the ill-fated expedition to Loch Awe where Sandie suffered an attack. Back in Glasgow he worked unstintingly on a long semi-autobiographical poem (called 'A Life Fragment') but on Gilfillan's advice he appears to have abandoned this in favour of a poem in the form of a drama. This way he was able to weld together other shorter lyrics, fragments and songs, possibly some already written, onto a much more ambitious framework. It was this, now titled 'A Life-Drama', that in 1853 appeared between hard covers as the major part of *Poems*.

Critics later accused Gilfillan of deflecting the young poet from his true course, playing Svengali to Sandie's Trilby. In October 1851 the two of them met for the first time, at an event held in Glasgow called Preaching Monday. Here Gilfillan was able to tell his protégé that he had just completed a long review for The Eclectic under the title 'Recent Poetry'. It covered eight published books of poetry (including *The Angel World* by P.J.Bailey, one of Sandie's models) as well as "A Life Fragment by Alexander Smith (MS)". He preceded his comments with a warning:

Mr Smith's language is, in a great measure, derived from his readings of such peculiar poets as Keats, Bailey, and Tennyson, but his thought and imagery are always his own. He is yet, but need not remain an hour longer, in that imitative stage as to occasion, language and rhythm, in which many great poets have commenced their careers.[52]

This warning (not strictly necessary about a work still in progress) shows that Gilfillan was sensitive to possible critical dangers ahead. Of more immediate interest are the extracts quoted in this article and then the ones used two months later when portions were previewed in The Critic. By comparing these with the final version that appeared in *Poems* eighteen months later Gilfillan's editorial interference (if such it was) may become clearer. Among the pieces that came under his scrutiny was the long ballad-like elegy known as 'The Garden and the Child'. It was printed under this title in the 15 December issue of The Critic and it also comprises the first half of Scene VI of 'A Life-Drama'. A textual comparison shows only minor changes, usually grammatical but one or two made with the intention of creating more sensation, e.g.

~~Cool~~/Blue lakes and slumb'rous palaces
and

Stars ~~glimm'ring~~/shuddering through the ~~ghastly~~/ghostly room

These lines refer to a solar eclipse witnessed by Sandie and Brisbane at loch Lubnaig in 1849, and used as the centrepiece of the poem told by an old man in flashback. Remembering seeing a golden-haired child, he returns from a long trip to India to visit a small graveyard beside a loch and the solar eclipse takes place, a potent omen of bad news. The mother confirms that her child is buried here after suffering a lingering death. She sings a song that seems to be the dying child's attempt to comfort her mother by declaring that she is happy now. It is in this song that the most noticeable changes have been made. In The Critic version there are only three tightly-knit verses, somewhat reminiscent of Wordsworth's Lucy poems, with a short final line:

Cold the death dews on my brow
Blight and cold as polar morn,
Cold is death, O colder now,
On my heart thy scorn
Lieth like snow.

Round thy words and looks and smiles
Memory lingereth, as heaves
The ocean with most loving wiles,
On calm mooned eves,
Round incense isles.

When the sun is in the west,
The golden-hearted marigold
Shuts its eyes. – Upon my breast
My white hands I fold,
And go to rest.[53]

In their place (in 'A Life-Drama') are six free-verse triplets that seem limp and sentimental by comparison. Here are two:

The callow young were huddling in the nests,
The marigold was burning in the marsh,
Like a thing dipt in sunset, when He came.

My blood went up to meet Him on my face,
Glad as a child that hears its father's step,
And runs to meet him at the open porch....[54]

Was this the influence of the evangelical minister? Gilfillan's advice (according to Brisbane in *Early Years*) was that "the select literary world would be best satisfied with some longer poem than any he had yet written, in which the sustained concentration of his powers might be shown." It was to provide a linking background for pieces like this that the pseudo-dramatic format was dreamed up, and one suspects this was also responsible for the inordinate length and bewildering plot of 'A Life-Drama'. But whose idea was this really? According to Gilfillan he recommended starting afresh on a new work. However Sandie was in a hurry and could see that there was a way of recycling much of what he had written already. With hindsight Brisbane admits that it "bore traces of being a patchwork".

Whatever Gilfillan's actual impact on the final version (as distinguished from the advice freely offered to the young poet), his Eclectic piece attracted widespread interest. George Meredith immediately set to and produced a sonnet on a sonnet: 'To Alexander Smith, the Glasgow Poet, on his Sonnet to Fame proclaiming "The mighty warning of a Poet's birth". This was published in December in The Leader. Gilfillan also received a letter of inquiry from Sydney Dobell, another of his protégés. He was clearly impressed by the extracts, indeed almost star-struck:

> Alexander is sensuous beyond even Keatsian intensity. Indeed the sensuous approaches to the sensual sometimes with a luscious power of passing the boundary which makes me anxious for him.[55]

This was prophetic indeed. On that mellow October Monday Sandie and his herald walked arm in arm along the Trongate in friendly conversation. Again they must have made a noteworthy pair, the facial contrast between Gilfillan's short-sighted beam and Sandie's farouche squint being especially marked. Around this time he was introduced to John Pringle Nichol, Professor of Astronomy at the College who had risen from origins almost as humble as Sandie's own. The son of "a respectable trader" in Brechin (according to Chambers' *Eminent Scotsmen*) Nichol was able to study at King's College in Aberdeen by doing school-teaching on the side. He then became Rector (headteacher) at Montrose Academy and began a series of public lectures there to "popularise the abstruse sciences and make them intelligible to the general mind which had hitherto been excluded from their mysterious circle by subtle distinctions and an unintelligible nomenclature." At thirty-two Nichol came to Glasgow and continued his pioneering efforts in further education. In 1841 a new observatory replaced the eighteenth-century one on the College Green, right in the heart of the old High Street. This was several miles to the north-west at Dowanhill, then very much a green-belt area beyond the city boundary.

Here, due to the value of the equipment, the Professor was required to occupy an adjoining house. This seems to have suited Pringle Nichol because, as well as being a voracious polymath, he enjoyed nothing more than playing host. The house (now part of Notre Dame school) was obviously large enough to accommodate guests comfortably. De Quincey, fleeing his Edinburgh creditors, came in 1845 and stayed for six months. Journalist Charles Mackay recalls a dinner party at the house with himself and the English Opium-Eater as guests. Nichol appears to have had a strictly empirical mind with little time for the unscientific, openly questioning the doctrine of the immortal soul with a bluntness that was unusual for the time. It is interesting that Gilfillan, a church minister, had an easy acquaintance with Professor Nichol through their shared passion for astronomy.

Gilfillan's December piece in The Critic ('A New Poet in Glasgow') claimed Smith's poetry to be the best since Thomas Campbell. *The Critic, or London Literary Journal* was started in 1844 as a rival to The Literary Gazette. In 1851 it was enlarged to twenty-four pages, consisting mainly of reviews and extracts from new books, but also with an occasional column entitled 'Gossip of the Literary World'. This new formula pushed circulation up to around seven thousand, allowing the editor to claim it was "the largest literary review in Europe." Although it only survived until the 1860s The Critic was now at the height of its influence, thriving on a mixture of hot-off-the-press reviewing and insider news about authors and publishers. In March 1852 its decision to serialise in bi-monthly sections almost the whole of 'A Life-Drama' was a welcome boost to Sandie's morale. Gilfillan undoubtedly had argued the case for this unusual step with his usual forcefulness.

All this must have felt a little like Byron's sensations post-*Childe Harold* ("I awoke one morning and found myself famous."). Perhaps it was more of a drip-feed process that effectively built up public anticipation in time for the release of *Poems* the following spring. And in Glasgow itself the grapevine was starting to hum. First mention of this New Poet would probably be heard in the College where Pringle Nichol and his son John, a final-year student, could be relied upon to spread the word; from there it would spread to church congregations, dinner tables and cultural soirées down to coffee houses, howffs and dram shops, even perhaps to the one in the basement of the building in Charlotte Street where Sandie lived. He was, of course, still putting in his ten hours a day at Robertsons. As the early spring sunshine of 1853 began filtering through the smoky air around Queen Street local attention would have become quite noticeable. Brisbane says it often took the shape of a would-be poet with manuscript in hand waiting to catch the New Poet's eye as he emerged through the pend into the main street for his lunch break.

The publicity machine was helped by one Daniel Lawson who ordered multiple copies of The Critic and circulated them widely among his friends. According to Brisbane he "sought out Smith, formed a personal acquaintance with him and invited him to his house which became for him, during his future residence in Glasgow, almost a second home." In the PO Directory there is a Henry Lawson & Son, coach proprietors and livery-stable keepers at 128 Queen Street. After publication of Poems he found himself invited to gatherings in places he would never have dreamed of entering previously. John Nichol recollects Sandie being present at a dinner given for Ruskin at the College during an unsuccessful bid for the Rectorship. But throughout 1852 the pressure was on to have the next extract of 'A Life-Drama' written and ready, despite the claims of sprigged muslin on his time. Not surprisingly the strains were starting to become apparent to his immediate circle of friends. They now comprised two separate groups – the earnest Addisonians and the more flamboyant later associates such as Hugh Macdonald, Pat Alexander and John Nichol with his college connections. Inevitably as literary fame beckoned the Addisonian connection weakened and Sandie became a less frequent GALS attender.

Brisbane noted that at this time "his Sabbaths were most frequently passed altogether apart from the church." He explains this as a "defection in practice, not in principle."[56] The main side-effect was that he increasingly avoided the company of friends who would sooner or later bring religious issues into the conversation. He had less and less time for the Church Militant. The work of creating poetry took over his waking hours; this, rather than any religious backsliding, got in the way of their formerly intense relationship. In addition his emotions might still have been raw after the death of Barbara. As we have seen Brisbane was given fair warning in the manifesto letter (quoted in chapter 3). But he found it difficult to accept that alongside the writing of 'A Life-Drama' there was also taking place in Sandie's mind a radical re-examination of the world around him. Issues like the nature of sin and the redeeming power of love would have been at the core of this re-evaluation. As can be seen from the resulting poem, conventional Christianity had little contribution to make. Brisbane can only flail around for a convincing explanation for the change in his friend:

The mind of Smith, in fact, was never in such an abnormal state as went [sic] he wrote that work. Hence is it that it is so unlike his other works, unlike the man himself... In this state of mind then the poem was too hastily conceived, then, by far too hurriedly written during the nights of 1852, and next, too quickly sent to the press. This is the real cause of its imperfections. Before it was quite finished, its author had himself begun to see its unnatural feverishness, and other faults; but the public had been promised, and was waiting for the book; and so it required to go before the world, ere he had time to perfect it by calm reflective thought. And it is almost certain that had it lain for a few months in manuscript in Mr Smith's desk, for reconsideration, it would never have been presented to the public as it is; much of it would have been recast, and much of it pruned. But written as it was, the chief wonder connected with it is, that it is what it is.[57]

Naturally the relationship with Brisbane cooled. Summer evenings were spent with freer spirits or more often alone as Sandie composed. The demands of monthly serialisation must have forced him into some tough prioritisation. The Trades Holiday once again approached and they had already agreed to visit the Trossachs for a week. Brisbane is rather tight-lipped about this tour, mentioning only that they visited Gilfillan in Dundee "for an hour's consultation" and then went by train to Perth, returning at the end of the week via Stirling. In hindsight it seems clear that the six-year friendship was effectively over. Circumstances would dictate they must go their separate ways, so it may have been with relief that Sandie later heard that Brisbane had taken up a parish in Aberdeenshire. Letters were still exchanged and visits made, but with lessening frequency.

In October an intriguing notice appeared in The Leader (and strangely was repeated in The Critic whilst it was still serialising 'A Life-Drama'). It sounds like Gilfillan but is just as likely to have been the editor G.H.Lewes. As a gossip piece it was strangely ill-timed, given the drowning of Barbara only eighteen months previously:

Alexander Smith's Poems ... Our readers have seen enough of this young poet to feel an eager curiosity about him; and we are frequently asked a variety of questions on the supposition that we have the pleasure of his personal acquaintance, whereas we must assure our correspondents that all we know of him is limited to the facts of his youth and residence in Glasgow, and his unquestionable genius – which is that of a born singer. Berlioz, in one of his playful tributes to Alboni's incomparable voice, expressed a wish that he were young and handsome: "I would make Alboni love me. I would maltreat her, and after six months of wretchedness she would be the greatest singer in the world."

Is there no cruel fair in Glasgow that can do this for Alexander Smith...? This, then, is what some woman may do for him, if he be misfortunately fortunate enough. How to look at nature and see new meanings in her evanescent forms he can already teach us; how to look at Life and see deep symbols in its vanishing perplexities and inevitable heartaches, can only be taught by one who, like Ulysses, has gained experience through suffering.

The gambit was successful. The Leader was sent 'Barbara' to make it plain that here was a poet who had already experienced his share of suffering. But far more substantial developments awaited Sandie as 1852 drew to a close. Maybe even as he gave his final Saturday evening address to the Addisonians ('Burns as a National Poet') he would have already received the news that his first book of poems would appear the following spring under the imprint of David Bogue of Fleet Street. One hundred pounds was offered for full copyrights, a sum that would enable him to hand in his notice at Robertsons almost immediately.

Fame at least greeted him, and her embrace was to be a warm one. For the time being, however, Beauty looked on impassively from the wings.[58]

Chapter 5:
1853

It [the harvest moon] came circling large and queenly o'er yon roof of smoky tiles,
And I saw it with such feeling, joy in blood, in heart, in brain,
I would give to call the affluence of that moment back again
Europe, with her cities, rivers, hills of prey, sheep-sprinkled downs –
('A Life-Drama' sc.2)

COMPARED TO TRANSITIONS from one century to another, mid-centuries in Britain lack the same spirit of innovation and ferment of ideas. The 1850s were no exception, perhaps as a reaction to the 1848 Year of Revolutions in Europe. In the literary world established names were industrious in becoming yet more established. Tennyson's *In Memoriam* and *Idylls of the King*, Arnold's *Collected Poems* ('Sohrab & Rustum', 'The Scholar Gypsy'), Browning's *Men and Women* and EBB's *Aurora Leigh* all belong to this decade. Only in the closing years did new names emerge like Fitzgerald (*Rubaiyat of Omar Khayyam* published in 1859) and Swinburne (his first work appearing under the umbrella of the iconoclastic Old Mortality Society, formed by a group of undergraduates at Oxford). Despite such a crowded field Smith's *Poems* (also known as 'A Life-Drama and other poems') attracted considerable attention on publication in the Spring of 1853 and critical interest remained intense for the remainder of the year.

Running in Smith's favour was a gradual change in the style of reviewing. Gone were the confrontational, partisan times when John Gibson Lockhart and J.W. Croker ruled the roost at the Quarterly Review with a personal vindictiveness. Keats' *Endymion* was dismissed as exhibiting "the most incongruous ideas in the most uncouth language". Now Lockhart (Walter Scott's son-in-law) had resigned after a spell of twenty-eight years. The Westminster Review, a Radical mouthpiece, was acquired by the entrepreneur John Chapman who took on as his assistant one Mary Evans, later better known as George Eliot. Blackwood's Magazine had been founded in 1817 with Lockhart and James Hogg (author of *The Private Memoirs and Confessions of a Justified Sinner*) on the editorial team, with the business under the control of the Edinburgh bookseller William Blackwood. It was from the outset a Tory counterweight to the Edinburgh Review with its reformist agenda. For the past thirty-seven years its editor had been Professor John Wilson. On his death in 1854, his son-in-law William Edmonstoune Aytoun, also a Professor at the Edinburgh College, would take over. So the 'Maga' (Blackwoods

*Maga*zine) tradition of greeting anything faintly radical with extreme scepticism was in safe hands.

William Hepworth Dixon, a noted travel writer and agitator for political reform, took the editorial reigns at The Athenaeum in the same year. This was the review of choice for all who fancied themselves as intellectuals: week after week it reviewed all serious-minded books and publications in literature, science, the arts and politics. Snapping at the heels of The Athenaeum were less venerable publications, such as: The Examiner (a Liberal organ famous for promoting Shelley and Keats now edited by John Forster), The Leader (edited by George Henry Lewes to promote the humanist cause), The Critic (which, as we have seen, resolutely championed the new and upcoming) and The Saturday Review (launched in 1855 as a Conservative mouthpiece with its review columns still using anonymity to settle some personal scores). Along with the daily press and other weeklies these titles were the cultural communicators of the age. Professional full-time editors became the norm and they saw it as their mission to guide the new reading public towards solid and wholesome fare, only occasionally taking a risk in their recommendations.

So it might have been a surprise to Smith that *Poems* was so widely noticed when it appeared in mid-March (a week or so after Charlotte Bronte's *Villette*). The last thirty-six pages of the volume included eight sonnets (mainly on themes of love and fame) and two longer poems best regarded as apprentice work, awkward homages to Browning and Tennyson. The remorseful lyric 'To –' is more interesting with its reference to an intense love affair that was marred by a "fearful moment". Despite the many blissful hours spent with his "lovely cheat" the poet has rejected her, to his current regret:

> Too late, thy fatal beauty and thy tears
> > Thy vows, thy passionate breath;
> I'll meet thee not in Life, nor in the spheres
> > Made visible by Death.

The first edition sold out within a few weeks and there were two more printings in 1853 with another two years later, representing British sales of around 10,000. In North America sales were even better, with six reprints ordered during the year, and throughout the 1850s it was kept in print with total American sales of nearly 15,000. Given that large sections had already appeared in The Critic, these were impressive sales figures.[59]

Smith's publisher David Bogue remains an enigmatic figure, especially since poetry was not a major feature of his list. With his partner Tilt he built up a major backlist of popular education titles and reprints of the classics. He took full advantage of the 1851 Great Exhibition with illustrated popular science books and his catalogue also includes Webster's Dictionary. At the more outré end of the spectrum he had recently published *The Women of the Bible* and *The Gallery of Byron Beauties* ("highly coloured, £3"). Hardy annuals included *The Comic Almanack* which contained illustrations by George Cruikshank, the political caricaturist who illustrated both Dickens and Thackeray.

In such company *Poems* was published, a small (octavo) 238-page volume bound in green cloth selling at three shillings. Bogue had purchased the copyright for £100, then he later added £50 when sales exceeded expectation. Although this was probably equivalent to several years wages as a pattern-designer, Smith was hardly wealthy. As to proceeds from America, there are no surviving records, but attitudes to copyright were fairly cavalier across the Atlantic so he would have been quite lucky to see anything. By comparison Tennyson was earning around £1,500 p.a. after the publication of *In Memoriam* (5,000 annual sales in 1850) and could invest heavily in railway shares.

If Smith was not rich he was certainly famous. Soon there was a small coterie hanging around the Robertsons archway in Queen Street, waiting to catch sight of the poet in the warehouse. In *Early Years* Brisbane paints a typical teatime break:

It was at once amusing and pitiable to see, day after day, some lackadaisical-looking youths standing at the warehouse door… to get a glimpse of the poet as he came out and to hear the whisperings – "There he's, there he's!" – whisperings which he sometimes heard and was wont to hitch his shoulders, muttering an "Uh!" as, after hurried steps behind him, he was immediately the object of a not very polite stare.[60]

A nearby bookshop displayed a window placard mentioning "the Glasgow Poet" by name, so Smith eventually went in and asked the manager to remove it. According to Brisbane, who of course reveled in the more saintly side of Smith's personality, "His fame turned other heads; his own it never turned." Far more copies of *Poems* were selling outside Glasgow, mainly to the readers of the reviews in the Home Counties. There are several references in literary letters of the time. In May Matthew Arnold wrote to Arthur Hugh Clough, professing knowledge of only extracts of 'A Life-Drama''s contents, but insisting that they were quite enough. ("I shrink from what is so intensely immature… This kind does not go far: it dies like Keats or loses itself like Browning."[61]) From Bagni di Lucca Elizabeth Barret Browning writes to Miss Mitford: "I have read him only in extracts, such as the reviews give, and such as a friend helped me to by good-natured MS. It is extraordinary to me that with his amount of development… he has met with such rapid recognition." The following year, after a space of a few months, she wrote again in a tone that was close to waspish, expressing surprise that *Poems* should already be in a third edition.

Another letter (now in the National Library of Scotland) written to John Hill Burton indirectly evidences how widespread his fame had become. Writing from Kinloch Rannoch this party, also an Alexander Smith, complains that his life is made a misery by acquaintances congratulating him on turning poet:

I see some clever extracts in The Athenaeum of a vol of poetry by my namesake (who the devil is this Sanny Smith?) which show far greater marks of genius than ever my poor and now almost mangy hide ever sported for the admiration of the ignobile or nobile vulgus... Let him look to poor Byron whose cruel breaking on the wheel by Professor (of Bosh) Aytoun has appalled the souls of all those [whose] memory can carry them back to 1826.[62]

The reference here is to six public lectures on poetry given on alternate evenings at the Queen Street Hall in April. The Scotsman gave an almost verbatim report of the final one, entitled "Modern British Poetry in its Most Remarkable Forms". The packed house was treated to a number of memorable thumbnail assessments by the Professor. Scott was "unquestionably beyond compare the grand poet of his age". But Byron's stock was on the wane ("So much of his sentiment was false and feigned… and thus would ever be the case with authors who wrote, as Byron did, for startling momentary effects and who were rather desirous to astonish rather than to please."[63]) If Smith had read this, it would have forewarned him of the frosty reception awaiting him in the world of literary academe, personified by the impressive figure of William Edmonstoun Aytoun, the new Professor of Rhetoric and Belles-Lettres.

By this time the Robertson brothers would have known that they needed to find a new pattern-designer for their sprigged muslin. Bogue's £100 provided a measure of security. As a guest at some of Glasgow's best dinner tables Smith might have been quizzed about his future plans. Perhaps some vague promises made him optimistic. Surely if the reviews of *Poems* were to be trusted his future as a writer was to be a secure and glorious one.

'A Life-Drama', the main component of *Poems*, is hardly remembered and never read these days except by specialists.[64] A long work of more than three thousand lines, it is divided into thirteen scenes (hence the *Drama* of the title) prefaced by atmospheric stage directions. In reality they are a device to break up the series of long and short lyrics and monologues which make up a kind of sequence but contain no vestige of drama whatsoever. Tennyson later adopted something similar in his "monodrama" *Maud*. The keynote of 'A Life-

Drama' is major rather than minor. Instead of the Tennysonian passionate lethargy the new poet uses an almost Jacobean intensity of imagery and expression whose richness and exotic qualities struck all reviewers, whether they approved or not.

"Passionate" was the epithet most frequently used to describe the character and tone of Smith's writing. This was seldom intended as a recommendation. Brisbane describes the style as "turbid", glossing over the fact that certain elements of the plot (insofar as they can be made out) were certainly risqué. It certainly created a stir throughout the land. This, as with Charlotte Yonge's *The Heir of Redclyffe* which came out later that year, would have increased sales. It would also have made the book one of those that should not be left lying around where a servant might pick it up. But the expectant reader of 1853 would surely have felt short changed on telling detail. Compared to the programme for Berlioz's *Symphonie Fantastique* (first performed some twenty years previously) with its drug-intensified eroticism, Smith's story of a gentleman poet's soul-searching, angst and occasional *amour* is pretty tame stuff. A brief synopsis of its very episodic narrative follows:

Sc.1 ("An Antique Room: Midnight") After tearing up a newly penned invocation to Poetry, Walter muses on the fame that he could earn by becoming a great poet.

Sc.2 ("A Forest. Walter sleeping beneath a tree. Enter Lady with a fawn.") The Lady finds slip of paper in Walter's book. It is a poem in praise of love ("a terror and a glory!"). He awakes and confesses that his experience of life is mainly from books. However he believes that he may be destined to be the poet who will speak for his age, as predicted by a dead poet (unnamed) whom he greatly admires. Walter then recites his own long poem in hexameters that foresees a day of judgement when all mercenary values will be discarded: "God! Our souls are aproned waiters. God! Our souls are hired slaves."

Sc.3 Back in his Antique Room, Walter recites a poem about "A lovely youth in manhood's very edge" living in pastoral seclusion. This youth awakens from sleep in the forest to hear a maiden singing: immediately knowing her to be his soul-mate he leads her off towards the setting sun. Walter wonders whether he might similarly win his Lady's love with poetry.

Sc.4 ("The Banks of a River") Walter and the Lady meet as arranged. He describes a glorious sunset over a city, but the Lady wants to hear the poem he has promised. It is about a languishing lady and her Indian page boy whose advances are mercilessly rebuffed. Walter then declares his love to the Lady. To his dismay she says she is to be married against her will to an older man. She believes it will hasten her death. She advises Walter against seeking a poet's crown.

Sc.5 Walter walks a country lane at sunset. Unconsoled by Nature's beauty he sees signs of unrequited passion everywhere he looks. He ends up confessing his broken heart to a peasant who has just expressed his contentment with his lowly lot.

Sc.6 ("A Room in London") Some time later Walter reads aloud the manuscript of The Garden and the Child (see chapter 4). He realises that many of his friends are dead and wonders about the Lady. To Edward, a friend, he confesses his current feelings of purposelessness in a "troubled age". But for the future he still has a grand poetic design:

> To set this Age to music – the great work
> Before the Poet now. – I do believe
> When it is fully sung, its great complaint,
> Its hope, its yearning, told to earth and heaven,
> Our troubled age shall pass, as doth a day
> That leaves the west all crimson with the promise
> Of the diviner morrow, which even then
> Is hurrying up the world's great side with light.[65]

Edward argues that the material advances of the age chime with some kind of divine providence, but that to ensure its continuity "We must go down and work our souls like mines, make books our lamps." Walter rejects this evangelical justification for progress.

Sc.7 ("A Balcony overlooking the Sea") Walter celebrates the beauty of an early Spring day. Still in Church Militant vein, Edward complains that it is not enough to stand and admire. We must work hand in hand with God. He then invites Walter down to Bedfordshire where he promises congenial company in the shape of a merry old squire and his daughter Violet.

Sc.8 ("Evening – A Room in a Manor") Walter is seated apart from his friends. When Violet enters he is smitten and says so in poetry. To lighten the mood the Squire asks for "a roaring song" and several of these follow. When it comes to Walter's turn he tells a story of a boy growing up in a large town, depending on books for company. On Sundays he takes long country walks "to efface the scars of scorn, the rents of hate." He develops a brain fever and rushes to climb a mountain to accuse God of ignoring his gifts. He dies soon after. Edward scoffs at this gloomy tale, but it strikes a chord with Violet. Walter admits it is based on his own experience and that he has just visited the Lady's grave. Violet then sings a mournful song.

Sc.9 ("A Lawn – Sunset") Walter tells Violet about his first meeting with the Lady. Then they confess their love for each other.

Sc.10 ("A Bridge in the City – Midnight") Walter indulges in a long monologue on his recent decline into debauchery. A prostitute approaches and he confesses to her how he has mistreated Violet. She says she pities him more than Violet and he runs off.

Sc.11 (Night – Walter standing alone in his garden") He broods on his childhood, but then shakes off his nostalgia to issue a poetic challenge to the waiting world.

Sc.12 Some time later Walter has written the poem that has made him famous but his mental equilibrium is worse than ever. Two friends worry that his dissolute lifestyle will bring him to an early grave. Edward believes, nonetheless, that he will return to a life of conventional evangelicalism.

Sc.13 It is three years later. Walter returns to Violet and they visit the garden of his childhood. Violet reads a passage from his poem about sin destroying healthy pleasure. In the summerhouse Walter confesses it was truly inspired by love for her rather than desire for fame. In tears, Violet wonders whether all their turbulent past can be redeemed by love. Walter says he needs her to keep inspiring him:

> Lift, lift me up
> By thy sweet inspiration, as the tide
> Lifts up a stranded boat upon the beach.
> I will go forth 'mong men, not mailed in scorn
> But in the armour of a pure intent.
> Great duties are before me and great songs
> And whether crowned or crownless, when I fall
> It matters not, so that God's work is done.
> I've learned to prize the quiet lightning-deed,
> Not the applauding thunder at his heels
> Which men call Fame.[66]

As the stars come up in the evening sky they go into the house together. *Finis.*

As can be seen from the quotations 'A Life-Drama' rejoices in imagery that is startling, sometimes discordant, invariably profuse. Today's reader might well echo Ben Jonson on Shakespeare's lesser known plays ("Would he had blotted..."), whilst acknowledging that several lines or phrases do have the power to resonate in the memory. The language may be over-ripe in places, but at least the poem avoids the fascination with sentimentality that besets so much Victorian verse. Smith had an innate sense that warned him off second-hand sentiment and that is something to be grateful for.

Later accounts of Smith's life make it appear that the critical response to *Poems* was a string of eulogy. This is far from the case.

Although the tradition of anonymous reviewing was disappearing, personal animosity or literary partisanship still made their way into the reviews. And this can be detected in the case of 'A Life-Drama'. The trouble was that he had been remorselessly championed by Gilfillan and The Critic before *Poems* appeared. This factor ran the danger of making Smith *persona non grata* with those in the opposite camp or at the very least appear as secondhand goods. Add to this that he was still considered a freak, since he had apparently enjoyed no formal education, belonged to no Oxbridge faction and most significantly was working a ten-hour day as well as writing copiously. Ergo the work he produced must be "second-rate" (a contemporary assumption that was woven into much of metropolitan criticism). To many Victorians poetry was the outpouring of mind and soul, so the pattern-designer's well-publicised artisan background sent out warning signals to any reviewer, especially one who considered himself to be in the morality business. (Keats had suffered from this form of critical snobbery a generation earlier.)

Smith had friends in the literary world, but not many in London or college circles where literary verdicts counted. In Glasgow, thanks to Addisonian friends and University figures like John Pringle Nichol, he understandably received a more sympathetic reception. Probably the only reviewer he knew personally was James Hedderwick, editor of the Citizen and himself a frustrated poet. Naturally this piece was one of the first reviews of *Poems* to appear (on 19 March). Although Hedderwick criticised the poem's lack of intelligible plot and characterisation, he makes a point about the language and imagery employed by Smith:

The whole current of [Walter's] thoughts and actions appears to us to be somewhat distempered; but the truth is that it is only natures greatly wrung that take successful refuge in poetry. Your good, easy, well-to-do man of the world is apt to be of the earth, earthy. Hence poets seek their most beautiful and glowing images in regions of woe, real or fictitious, and hence, too, all grandest thoughts seem to be born of sorest travail.[67]

Chambers' Edinburgh Journal ran an assessment where the first of many comparisons was made with Tennyson. Smith was seen as running a poor second when it came to mental rigour and the subject matter of his poems was dismissed as "decidedly crude and meagre notwithstanding their grandeur and gorgeousness of form." The anonymous writer implored Smith to "hallow" his gifts and seek "divine ordination". The Athenaeum also made the comparison and accused Smith of meretricious phrase-making.[68] This was from its chief literary reviewer Henry Fothergill Chorley who had been in post for almost twenty years. Warmer receptions came from other weeklies such as The Spectator and The Leader, but bizarrely The Examiner's reviewer makes it clear that Smith was (to his way of thinking) a very dangerous character:

Expression indeed, which is one of the subtlest tests, is also among the most erring of all the indications of poetry. Vices are the worst for being *dulcia vitia*. And where fancy brings together images which have no purpose and no connection; where character, knowledge, passion, imagination, the sustained and continuous flow of feeling are absent altogether, and in their place is found but the glare and glitter of broken and aimless imagery, we will give the writer every possible praise of ingenuity and merit, but dispute to the last his greater claim [to be a true poet]."[69]

In other words the allure of Smith's imagery and choice of subject matter implied a moral taint at the heart of his work. This was a charge that was answered by the first of the reviews in the quarterlies. The April issue of the Westminster contained a long campaigning piece by G.H.Lewes who claimed:

The language of passion, when sincere and reverent, is the language the poet is bound to use... With a strong sense of enjoyment he mingles the most refined perceptions of what is beautiful and tender. There are, indeed, many who object to any expression whatever of these imperishable and holy instincts; but the objection springs from a perverted and unhealthy conception of literature. It belongs to that mistaken view of Art which has idealised disease; which has created the type of sickly heroines and impossible refinements. We have deserted Nature for the Hospital, and our most poetic flowers are *immortelles.*[70]

Tait's Edinburgh Magazine also hailed the new poet as a freethinker and compared him to the *vates* of classical times held to have prophetic powers. Almost certainly by John Stuart Blackie, the newly appointed Professor of Greek at Edinburgh, the review verges on the contentious: "Thus the old heathen poems of Greece caught more nobility, and grandeur, and loveliness from Zeus and Aphrodite than ours have done from the loving God himself." It was Blackie who first employed the word later used as a dismissive epithet for Smith and other New Poets: "Too much there is of the spasmodic and hysterical, struggling uneasily where the ripe poet would be calm." In early June a sweet and sour piece appeared in the New York Daily Times. Once again the comparison with Tennyson proved irresistible:

He gives evidence of the possession of powers which were nowhere apparent in Tennyson's earlier works. Read by isolated passages he may challenge comparison with any poet of the last century [meaning 100 years].[71]

The piece later makes less favourable comparisons and goes on to suggest plagiarism is at work. The imagery is dismissed as "this diarrhoea of fancy" and the poet's "violations of good taste are frequent and enormous." There was a gap in the reviews until July, by which time Smith was in London. Arthur Hugh Clough in the North American Review was one of the first to claim that Smith was staking out new territory for poetry:

Under the guise of a different story, a story unskilful enough in its construction, we have seemed continually to recognise the ingenuous yet passionate youthful spirit, struggling after something like right and purity amidst the unnumbered difficulties, contradictions and corruptions of the heated and crowded, busy, vicious and inhuman town.[72]

Clough's review, entitled 'Recent English Poetry', included Matthew Arnold's *Empedocles on Etna and Other Poems*. The comparison was unfavourable to the classically educated Arnold and from his correspondence it is clear that he was alarmed at the evidence that some kind of sea-change was taking place in the taste of the new mid-Victorian readership. When reprinted the following year his *Poems* contained a trenchant Preface which replaced the vilified 'Empedocles'. This contained the notorious passage on Keats' background:

We have the tone, or rather the entire want of tone, the abandonment of all reticence and all dignity, of the merely sensuous man, of the man who 'is passion's slave.' Nay, we have them in such wise that one is tempted to speak even as Blackwood or the Quarterly were in the old days wont to speak; one is tempted to say that Keats's love-letter is the love-letter of a surgeon's apprentice. It has in its relaxed self-abandonment something underbred and ignoble, as of a youth ill brought up, without the training which teaches us that we must put some constraint upon our feelings and upon the expression of them. It is the sort of love-letter of a surgeon's apprentice which one might hear read out in a breach of promise case, or in the Divorce Court. The sensuous man speaks in it, and the sensuous man of a badly bred and badly trained sort[73]

Naturally enough this stirred the aesthetic debate still further, as noted by modern American critic Anthony Harrison who has charted its progress, categorising it as underpinned by class politics:

The ideological conflicts imbricated in the two markedly opposed systems of aesthetic value evident in Smith's and Arnold's poems are apparent in reviewers' responses to their work. Smith's poetry is founded in sensation (to employ the term Arthur Henry Hallam had used, twenty years earlier, to characterize Tennyson's poetry), while Arnold's is, of course, saturated with what we today, like Arnold's anonymous reviewer of 1852, would describe as "high culture." .... Clough acknowledges that he is puzzled by the "discrepancy" that "certainly does exist between the two books [of poetry].... We close the one and open the other, and feel ourselves moving to and fro between two totally different, repugnant, and hostile theories of life". Not "art," but "life." Clough understands, in the most comprehensive manner possible, the opposed fields of value delineated in the works of these "totally different ... and hostile" writers. The stakes of the battle, it would seem, were extraordinarily high: its outcome entailed not just matters of "taste," but, far more importantly to Clough, matters of morality, philosophy, spirituality, and social order.[74]

Arnoldian influence was evident at the Dublin University Magazine where the question of diction and purity took centre stage with their reviewer. The advice to Smith is to "use the universally received language of good sense and good taste."

Support for Smith came in August from the North British Review, published originally as a Free Church sounding board. David Masson, later to become Professor of English Literature at Edinburgh, tried to put the record straight on Smith's lack of education: "Mr Smith is perfectly on a level with the larger proportion of those who, in England, write novels, paint pictures and edit newspapers." He also put his finger on a distinctive feature of the way imagery works in Smith's writing: "His peculiarity is that he cogitates in a language of concrete circumstance – that, whatever meaning lies in his mind that meaning takes the form not of abstract proposition but of some imagined scene, object, or incident, or some *imagined tissue* of scenes, objects and incidents". In this, by far the most comprehensive and intensive review (covering almost fifteen pages)[75] Masson was able to parry some of the more unjust criticisms made in earlier pieces. He took the Examiner to task over its complaint that the imagery of 'A Life-Drama' was repetitive by carrying out some textual analysis, an unusual approach for a Victorian reviewer. He ended by suggesting the main fault of the pseudo-drama is its lack of planning and poetic stagecraft. And then, after conceding that parts of the poem are "rough, crude, unpolished and unmelodious" (as well as poorly punctuated), he outlined the more significant positive and ground-breaking features:

> Mr Smith, it will have been observed, is no calm unperturbed poet, with imagination lax, cold and leisurely, weaving together sensuous phantasies for the mere pleasure of the exercise. Nor is he a contemplative poet like Wordsworth. He is a poet highly impassioned, touched with fire and feeling, and allegorising a state of mind natural to strong and manly, and yet unsatisfied youth. A discontent, a sorrow not untinged with sarcasm, breathes through his verse. Yet he is never ungenial, never entirely Byronic. Nor, in any true sense, is Mr Smith's poetry morally unhealthy…

As we shall see, assessments such as this and the one by Clough, caused Arnold to have severe misgivings about the direction of his own work. Novelist, divine and social commentator Charles Kingsley, also appalled by the New Poets, still felt impelled to write about them in two essays for Fraser's Magazine. In 'Alexander Smith and Alexander Pope' (October 1853) Smith is depicted as one hopelessly blighted in sensibility by "the dreary Glasgow prison-house of brick and mortar" where he was raised and worked. A fervent adherent of Christian Socialism, Kingsley had little time for the "poetry of doubt". The following month ('Shelley and Byron') he lays the blame for the new literary disease of "morbidity and doubt" at the feet of Shelley resulting in a preference for "a spasmodic, vague, extravagant, effeminate school of poetry." The final adjective seemed to once again raise the issue of moral taint at the very heart of the writing.

Later reviews added little extra in the way of substantive criticism. Since there was no more credit to be had for hailing a new poetic genius, it was safer to sneer and dismiss with a hint of world-weariness. Blackwood's brought in their military writer E.B.Hambley. Dismissing any meaningful role for poetry in changing society, he sought to restore some backbone into this querulous young fellow with a dose of John Bull:

> We will tell Alexander how it will not be done. Not by uttering unmeaning complaints against fate and heaven, and other names of similar purport which will not be set down here, like a dog baying at the moon. Not by uttering profane rant, which… is horribly nonsensical in the mouth of a young gentleman who ought to have taken a blue pill because his liver was out of order.[76]

A more thought-provoking line of criticism is provided by contemporary critics who see the combination of Smith's humble background and immersion in classic literary works as a recipe for wish-fulfilment. Most compelling of these is Richard Cronin's essay 'Alexander Smith and the Poetry of Displacement' where all the energy put into the writing of 'A Life-Drama' is solely to enable Smith (as Walter) to imagine himself as part of this charmed circle.

> But this dream is countered by a sullen suspicion that the English poets and the class from which they come form a closed circle from which he will always be excluded. Then, his poems become futile: "shouts to gain the notice of the Sphynx / Staring right on with calm eternal eyes".... He can feel himself a grubby interloper in the refined regions that he aspires to enter, staining them "as a lewd dream stains the holy sleep."

Smith certainly could not complain that *Poems* had been overlooked. Somehow he had to capitalise on this widespread recognition and ride the crest of the wave. Fame beckoned, but in which direction should he go? It must have seemed like an obvious step to go to London, for the first and only time in his life crossing the English border. Since he knew little of metropolitan ways, a traveling companion was needed and the figure of John Nichol strode confidently forward. The son of Professor Pringle Nichol and three years younger than Smith, Nichol had already completed one degree and had privately issued a precocious collection of his own verse. He was about to spend a further five-years at Oxford where he would become a close friend and mentor to Swinburne.

At around this time Smith's parents, John and Christina, decided to return to the house in Gauze Street, Paisley. Suddenly he was a free agent, without home or employment but with Bogue's money in the bank. And July was a good month to be in London. The second printing of *Poems* would be ready and Bogue had promised another £50. It was something close to an act of impetuosity by this most level-headed of young men. The reviews were still appearing; in today's parlance he was bankable. Possibly, if he played his cards right, he might have dared to think that London would become his home? Whatever the ultimate purpose of the journey for Smith, the two must have made strange travelling companions. Nichol, barely twenty but already self-assured, had been brought up in the academic world and was not easily intimidated by even the sharpest intellects. His intention was undoubtedly to shine in London's literary circles and with Smith in his wake he must surely have thought his entrée was assured. Smith, by contrast, would have remained reticent about the whole business, sullen even. He would undoubtedly have cut a poor figure.

They went first by coach to the Lakes where an appointment had been arranged with the ailing Harriet Martineau at Ambleside. As celebrity introductions go, this one lacked fizz. Having largely kept the Westminster afloat, she presumably had the right to hold audience with any new literary lions. She makes no mention of Smith's visit in her memoirs; it clearly wasn't memorable for her. Since she was stone deaf it wasn't to be an easy opportunity for Smith to shine. By his own account his remarks seem to have been restricted mainly to the weather. With one elderly literary celebrity already encountered, Smith steered well clear of Dorothy Wordsworth. In letters to Brisbane he appears increasingly disenchanted: "she has been crazy for twenty years, is now very old and frail and when I saw her she was drawn about in a wheeled chair."[77]

The Glasgow pair also visited another New Poet, J.Stanyan Bigg who worked on the local paper at Ulverston. Again no record of the meeting remains. They left for Halifax, probably to meet up with a friend of Nichol's. Once again there is an air of disenchantment in the letters home. In his estimation Yorkshire has "the finest scenery and the stupidest people it has been my lot to witness". No invitations to

Haworth, then. A brief stopover in Manchester and then the pair continued their travels to Nottingham. Here he met P.J.Bailey, famous for writing (and continually re-writing) *Festus*, a sprawling verse saga which was a source of inspiration whilst he was still at work on 'A Life-Drama'. Grudging respect is as much as he is prepared to offer in his next letter: "Although I have modified my opinion of him vastly, I could not but look on him with eager interest." After a visit to nearby Newstead Abbey for its Byron connection they headed for the metropolis with no further diversions. There is nothing in the letters about the first impression made on Smith by mid-Victorian London. Images were probably already established in his mind's eye by the recently issued *Bleak House* and other contemporary fiction like Sala's bohemian stories often set in and around artists' studios. Nichol, as anticipated, had no difficulty in getting them invited to soirées. Soon Smith's letters to Brisbane started again, this time with himself cast in a leading role:

Last Saturday I was at a literary party and was much amused by a girl who fastened upon me there. She is a Miss [Brisbane's deletion]. She professed vast admiration for my bridge scene [A Life-Drama Sc.10]. Later in the evening she laid me completely on my back after this fashion: "I am going to ask you a question, Mr Smith, and you need not answer it unless you choose, you know. Would it not have been as well to have married Violet and Walter at once, and not to have sent him through such a career of sin and misery?" I did not think the time and place was suitable for an explanation, so I parried the question as dexterously as I could.[78]

If only the gossip columnists could have got hold of this! The intoxication of it all, and the additional pleasure of being able to write about it in a Byronically world-weary manner to cronies back home! It would have been good to have had Nichol's letters as well. We know from *Early Years* that the pair of them received many invitations, from both London and the Home Counties, but few names are mentioned. There was a visit to Martin Tupper, the doggerel poet. Smith was lionised by G.H.Lewes who had reviewed him twice, followed by Herbert Spencer the Social Darwinist and contributor to the Economist. The following week, between trips to Windsor and Buckinghamshire, he managed a stay of a few days in Cheltenham with Sydney Dobell, the most established of the New Poets and author of *The Roman*, a florid verse epic published in 1850, another strong influence on Smith whilst writing 'A Life-Drama'.

But who else would they have met during those two weeks? EBB might have entertained them, but she was in Florence. Harriet Beecher Stowe was in town, busy promoting *Uncle Tom's Cabin*. That would have been an interesting but unlikely encounter. In a letter to Thomas

Woolmer, Dante Gabriel Rossetti states that he is due to meet "This genius in a fragmentary state... It seems he is some Glasgow nobody of about 23 or 24 who has been in the habit of existing by drawing patterns for linen drapers, so I suppose he is an artist of some sort."[79] At least DGR had done his homework, but no record exists of this encounter either.

We know that they did meet David Bogue, his publisher. But Smith leaves no pen portrait or any indication of what sort of a man he was. As well as the extra £50 Bogue gave him some valuable books (maybe the *Gallery of Byron Beauties*?). The two Glasgow bachelors must have visited editorial offices as well as drawing rooms, attended the theatre or a concert or two, been seen in restaurants or coffee houses. But no salacious gossip appears to have accompanied them. An interesting account of the contemporary literary salon scene was published in The Critic which suggests a quite daring informality was encouraged:

At these gatherings the amusements are conversation and music only, and the entertainment is unostentatious and inexpensive, consisting of tea and coffee, wine or negus handed about in the course of the evening and sandwiches, cake and wine at eleven o'clock. Suppers are prohibited by common consent, for costliness would speedily put an end to society too agreeable to be sacrificed to fashion... Authors, artists, editors, musicians, scientific men, actors and singers, male and female, are grouped together indiscriminately, and peers, baronets, knights, lawyers, doctors, booksellers, printers – provided they possess the qualification of being authors, artists or musicians or be renowned as patrons of literature, art or music – here meet together in temporary social equality, but regulated by so much good sense that it does not lead to familiarity elsewhere.[80]

The London trip was over too soon. The febrile round of recognition and approbation had to end, possibly to Smith's relief. One of the last events on the calendar was dinner at a Cambridge college "with the professors and dons, very good fellows all of them." This was during the long vacation around the middle of July. A few days later they embarked on the return journey north; if Smith had entertained expectations of being offered a full-time literary post they had not materialised.

He had last stayed in the Gauze Street terrace cottage when he was eight years old. With all his younger siblings still under the same roof, it is most unlikely that he would have been tempted to return. The next few weeks must have been spent with Glasgow friends. In August he and Brisbane took a short walking tour to Aberfoyle and the Trossachs. Brisbane glosses over it and it must have proved something of an anticlimax for Smith. Soon afterwards he was invited to stay a few days at Inveraray Castle by George Douglas, the eighth Duke of Argyll, making his mark as a Liberal member of the House of Lords. He had just been appointed Lord Privy Seal and was later to become Secretary of State for India. Douglas and his wife were keen to be seen as cultured (they persuaded Tennyson to come all the way from the Isle of Wight in 1857) and Smith was put up in their 18th-century castle. He seems to have adapted to the unfamiliar ambience of the castle, possibly escaping to the village of Inveraray (which he would have known well from previous visits with Brisbane) or walks in the surrounding hills.

A fellow guest was Frederick Temple Blackwood, a career diplomat with a literary wife. Later he took the title Earl of Dufferin, after the area in Ireland where his family had ancestral estates. According to Pat Alexander an invitation to accompany them back was offered and accepted and Smith had a further week in novel surroundings. Maybe somewhat reluctantly he was back in Glasgow by the end of autumn to regale cronies with accounts of this gentrified existence. His old drinking companion Hugh Macdonald tried to cap it with a re-telling of how he went to visit Christopher North (Professor John Wilson) in his New Town Edinburgh home just to get him to admit that certain lines of Tannahill, the Paisley weaver poet, were indeed superior to a stanza from Wordsworth's Lucy poems. The Blackwoods veteran probably conceded the point just to be quit of this garrulous character in his dubious Tam O'Shanter. In fact, although Macdonald was delighted at his younger friend's success with 'A Life-Drama', he thought little of the poem, dismissing it (according to Pat Alexander) as "a bit coloured wab [web], the like o' whilk amainst any speeder [spider] might spin if ye gi'ed it vermeelion i' the guts o'it."[81] But in the Citizen's regular column 'An Hour with the Poets', a three-cornered dialogue between the Editor, Tom Croon – a naïve poet specialising in hand-me-down Scots versifying – and Caleb (Macdonald himself), there is a reference to the Inveraray visit and the reception given to Smith in London. Through the mouthpiece of Tom Croon the pretensions of various reviewers are mocked:

According to some he's a perfect miracle o'genius; ithers wad mak him out to be little better than a sumph [simpleton]; while there are not awanting wiseacres who throw out hints o'something akin to demoniacal possession. On ae point they a' seem to be agreed, however, and that is that the young poet maun be sadly in want o'advice, and advice accordingly o'every shade he has had in dauds [loads].[82]

Smith was now a local celebrity, but he was also in the unenviable position of waiting for something to turn up. Just about anything, he must have thought, as long as he didn't have to return to muslin. James

Hedderwick, editor of the Citizen, was amongst those looking around on his behalf. He wrote to the Chambers brothers in Edinburgh. Robert replied with the news that the College Secretary's post had recently become vacant. From his time on the Scotsman Hedderwick was also friendly with Duncan McLaren, by now Lord Provost and later MP for the city. He was an essential contact since it was the Town Council that would be responsible for making the appointment.

By the closing date in December Smith had gathered testimonials from Robert Chambers, Professor Blackie and John Hill Burton (more Hedderwick contacts) as well as Pringle Nichol from Glasgow University and, at the last moment, from the Duke of Argyll. These names were enough to persuade McLaren that he could safely back Smith's candidature in the Town Council. On 17 December The Scotsman reported: "Mr Alexander Smith, the Glasgow poet, is a candidate to the office of Secretary to the Edinburgh university, vacant by the resignation of Mr Blair Wilson." This was advantageous to Smith, since other candidates remained unmentioned in the media. McLaren's advice to Hedderwick was that the Secretary's duties "would be prosaic, and he had heard the fact of his being a poet referred to, not as a point in his favour but as a positive disqualification." Indeed The Scotsman's reviewer had only a few months previously hailed Smith as a new voice reminiscent of Byron producing work "fervent, bold and vigorous."[83]

To be in with a shout, though, was encouraging. The timing was a relief for another reason. Shortly after returning from Ireland Smith had been recruited by a local wholesaling bookseller and stationer called William Love to edit the first issues of "The Glasgow Miscellany (A Scottish Weekly Journal of Literature, Science and Art, price 1½ pence)". There was hardly any supporting advertising so the first issue (14 January 1854) was heavy with editorial pages, and these all had to be commissioned or written by the new editor. From the start Smith must have realised that producing a weekly with this level of content was going to be hard work. However, it was money in his pocket (and a rather unglamorous office near Glasgow Cross) so he shouldered his burden. Luckily the Addisonians were to hand and he fell upon them with requests for articles and reviews, also calling on Pat Alexander, Hugh Macdonald and probably John Nichol. His stated editorial stance was one of non-interference. But this soon led to several near-crises. For example the first issue of the Miscellany reviewed a new edition of Gilfillan's *The British Poets*. The reviewer took an unexpectedly aggressive line with Smith's mentor: "little of strictly critical writing has Gilfillan given to the world... In Gilfillan's mind the poetical rises and drowns the critical. Had he been less a poet he had been a better critic." This was bad enough, but in the second issue a review of

Sydney Dobell's *Balder* states that large passages "stand up before the reader in an impenetrable wall of darkness". This was the same Dobell that had offered Smith and Nichol his hospitality at Cheltenham only a few weeks previously.

In lighter vein there was a purported extract from *Young Glasgow, or the Gentrism of the Western Metropolis* by 'Ben Brick' (John Nichol?). The chapter quoted (on University Snobs) has some nice comic touches. Issue number 3 contains the first part of Smith's Addisonian address on Burns. Maybe this was a measure of his desperate thirst for material to feed Love's presses. And maybe he was so busy writing he didn't even have time to read the reviews carefully before publication. An anonymous one on Aird's *Poems* refers to "pilfering and borrowing" which Aird sometimes does.

And so does Smith. We do not stigmatise this as a wilful crime for we are convinced it is unconscious. Embued [sic] with Keats, Shelley, Tennyson, 'Festus', Longfellow, their thoughts, style, images and passions have been wed to his, and the offspring of the union naturally bears their impress.[84]

With friends like these... The urge to cut this contribution must have been strong. In the same issue Smith's own 'Sederunts of the Sanct Mungo Club' (quoted in Chapter 3) also appears, showing him to be comfortable adopting the couthy vein of *Noctes Ambrosianae*. On 4 February the last Miscellany appeared, containing a long review of De Quincey's *Selections Grave and Gay* ("the greatest master of style and expression now left amongst us.") This, as well as most other contributions to this number, was by Smith. By now he would have known there was to be no fifth issue. It is difficult to know whether editor or publisher would have been the more relieved. For Smith, at least, it was a useful introduction to the world of the literary journalist and essayist. Interestingly he seems to have been unwilling later to admit to the episode.

On 31 January the Edinburgh Town Council voted Smith to the Secretaryship by a three vote margin. According to Pat Alexander his only reaction was "an air of impassivity as if the matter were of no personal concern to him."[85] He sent a letter of acceptance two days later, appointing James Clelland, an accountant, and James Campbell of Tillichewan as 'cautioners' (guarantors) for a total sum of £500. By mid-February he would be packing his bags for the short journey east. The prospects in Edinburgh were undoubtedly brighter. Glasgow was still relatively stony ground for contemporary arts. Although local pride was strong, only the wealthy few invested in life's refinements. For the many their wealth, such as it was, got spent in other ways. Statistics of Drunkenness for every major town were published by the government on an annual basis. In 1853, as for many years before and after,

Glasgow topped the table for truly staggering amounts of alcohol consumption. The Scotsman claimed that one in thirteen of the population had been arrested for drunkenness. But this was almost a case of pots and kettles since in Edinburgh the figure was one in eighteen. The Reformer's Gazette, under its new editor Peter Mackenzie, reported: "Glasgow is one of the most drunken and disorderly cities on the face of the civilised globe. This is a fact which, laying aside all sham and equivocation, we hold to be perfectly incontrovertible. Anyone with eyes in his head who chooses to go abroad on a tour of observation ... will see it demonstrated daily by reeling and staggering arguments."[86] Such things may have reminded Smith of his early evangelism and the intuitive awareness of the city's power to pollute and destroy. Early 1854 was also marked by the beginning of a cholera epidemic in the wynds of the old city centre. In Bridgeton the cotton spinners were threatening a long and ultimately bloody strike. There was a scent of unease in the air, and it must have seemed like a good time to leave.

His former traveling companion John Nichol was at this time editing the annual *Glasgow University Album* and he received two contributions from Smith just as he was leaving. One was a heavily revised version of 'Burns as a National Poet' ("Much of our finest poetry has been composed in circumstances which the majority of mankind would have considered unfavourable."). There were also two poems, one an early draft of 'Glasgow' which would not emerge in final form until more than two years later. The spur for this early version was his imminent departure from the city that had shaped him and brought him to manhood, a poetic reassessment of what had developed into a love-hate relationship.

> Of me thou hast become a part –
> Some kindred with my human heart
>   Lives in thy streets of stone;
> For we have been familiar more
> Than galley-slave and weary oar.[87]

Chapter 6:
1854-56

Bare, bald and tawdry as a fingered moth
Is my poor life, but with one smile thou canst
Clothe me with kingdoms. Wilt thou smile on me?
('A Life-Drama' Sc.1)

IN AN AGE OF WIDELY AVAILABLE higher education it is not easy to picture the enclosed world of the early Victorian universities in Scotland. Any similarities with today's academia are few and often exist only in shared terminology. Dr Johnson's observation on Scottish students, made eighty years before, was still not too wide of the mark: "for the most part [they] go thither boys, and depart before they are men; they carry with them little fundamental knowledge, and therefore the superstructure cannot be lofty."

The Edinburgh Town College (its official title until 1859), less socially exclusive than Oxford or Cambridge, was nevertheless for the sons of the professional and commercial elite and a few other young men on philanthropic bursaries. The student body was extremely young (often matriculating at the age of thirteen or fourteen), entirely male, and mostly concerned with obtaining useful connections that would stand them in good stead in professional life. Few bothered to gain a degree: Professor Blackie categorised them as "soft milky boys and unkempt lumbering clowns". Each academic year comprised two long sessions. Professors lectured once or twice a week, marked essays and exams, and tried to take a personal interest in their scholars. They saw themselves more as teachers of the basics rather than true academic specialists. The college atmosphere resembled one of the more academically inclined English public schools (a model still relatively rare north of the Border) with deference towards teachers expected. Educationally little had changed at Edinburgh since the opening of the new college building in the 1790s. Principals, all ordained ministers, enjoyed long tenure. It was a cosy, self-assured world strangely at odds with an outside world under rapid transformation. Its teaching syllabus seemed uninfluenced by new discoveries in science and medicine and a whole range of technological advances , for example the transatlantic cable.

As he took up the Secretaryship late in February 1854 Smith must have been aware of coming changes; his background was, after all, dominated by technology in manufacturing and what went with it, the phenomenon of rapid urban growth which formed the catalyst for the poem 'Glasgow'. As well as suffering culture shock in his first weeks at Edinburgh, he was probably trying to get straight the exact position of the Secretary in the college administration.

In 1824 the opening shots had been fired in what became a thirty years war between the Town Council – the College's founder with administrative powers vested in a 16th-century Charter – and the intellectual authority of the Senatus Academicus representing the professors. It all started when Dr James Hamilton had petitioned the Council to include midwifery as a compulsory subject for medical graduates. In their wisdom the Town Council bailies decided against it. The Senate then claimed the sole right to regulate graduation and the awarding of degrees. The Town Council demurred on this too. They then asked to see complete Matriculation Fund accounts, revealing just how much each professor earned including trivial items such as the "small fees" charged to students for providing coal to heat lecture halls. Eventually the professors, now in high dudgeon, took legal advice. They were told that the councillors "had not been disinclined at times to the extension and masterful exercise of their powers." Encouraged by this, the Senate twice took the Council to court. Both times they lost.

Despite posturing on both sides, plus the expensive litigation, the points at issue were important ones. A clash of interests was to be expected between a publicly accountable body (the Town Council) and those who jealously guarded their intellectual freedoms. The issue still confronts those granting public money to cultural and community ventures today. In order to keep a closer watch on daily running the Town Council had appointed the first General Secretary to the College in 1833. His salary was paid by the Council and he was required to make annual reports of all expenditure. With an office in the New College building he was responsible for the supervision of student matriculation and matters of discipline. Residing in hostile territory, so to speak, the Secretary's task might well have become impossible. But by choosing non-partisan appointees the Council ensured that the system jogged along smoothly enough. Smith's predecessor was, in fact, the son of Professor John Wilson.

By 1854 the Senate had spent more than £900 of College funds (mainly from a bequest intended for a new medical school) in the courts. They were still awaiting a House of Lords decision to withhold medical degrees from students who did not complete studies within the College premises. In April they heard that they had lost once again. So when Smith took over as Secretary there was a growing movement towards reaching compromise with the Council through a set of administrative reforms, and it was the new Secretary's misfortune that devising the mechanics of introducing them would add greatly to his duties.

Smith's surroundings were undoubtedly impressive although somewhat forbidding. There was a startling contrast between all this neo-classical grandeur and the Scottish vernacular style of the Glasgow College in the High Street where Smith had occasionally visited friends like John Nichol or Brisbane. Edinburgh had, of course, rejoiced in this architectural gem for more than thirty years. The New College replaced buildings which partly dated back to the late 16th century. They had failed to impress. On one occasion a distinguished visitor had walked right past under the impression the buildings were an almshouse. So in the 1780s, flushed with a number of actual and promised bequests, the Senate and the Council commissioned Robert Adam to design a homogeneous building to cover a site bounded by North College Street (now Chambers Street), South College Street and the new South Bridge. A neo-classical design naturally bore no traces of Scottish vernacular; at the time it must have resembled a New Town garrison built to overlook the surrounding wynds and closes. Within its spacious arcaded quadrangle (recently grassed over) the College was a haven of academic tranquillity except when students, at the end of lectures, converged on the Great Court. Nowadays few of the original classrooms are used, the building (now known as Old College) being given over mainly to finance and admin departments. The Great Court now only witnesses sustained (and in the past violent) student activity during the Rectorial Elections held every three years.

An odd feature of Adam's design, understandable when one remembers it took over thirty years to build, is that the main porticoed entrance faces resolutely east when all subsequent University expansion has taken place westwards. The 18th-century student would have approached via the Cowgate, then an extremely busy thoroughfare. By the time the New Town was being developed increasingly the student body would come from there via the Mound. Then in the 19th century the new suburbs to the south were where the majority of students would have had comfortable homes, in addition to an underclass of bursaried students in digs, with homes further afield outside the city.

Some of the surrounding wynds, leading steeply down to the Cowgate, survived until the 1870s. The house where Scott was born in 1771, at the head of College Wynd whose cobbled and often slimy surface was the main route up from the Cowgate, still stood when Smith arrived. Many of these dark, foul-smelling fissures between rickety tenements were barely wide enough for a horse and cart. On the upper streets, immediately adjacent to the College, there were booksellers, printers, druggists, a tailor, grocery shops and a coach-hirer as well as a sprinkling of licensed premises. On the tricky descent down College Wynd, the social fabric changed dramatically. Every other main door entry seems to have been a spirit dealer. In Horse Wynd, where the tenements reached six storeys in places, there were a few honest sons of toil – a cabinet-maker, a smith, wrights (building workers) and a ropemaker – wildly outnumbered by howffs and shebeens. The young gentlemen from the College may well have enjoyed slumming it on occasions. According to the 1854 Post Office directory there were also a Mrs Kelt and a Mrs Temple, occupation unspecified.

This ugly underbelly of Edinburgh in the College backyard would have been familiar territory to Smith. There was unlikely to have been anything he had not already witnessed in the vicinity of the Saltmarket in Glasgow. But the social topography of Edinburgh allowed areas of ill-repute to flourish in a literal underworld. Ten years later, when Smith had moved away to the city's northern coastal suburbs, his recollection of the wynds was still detailed and intense, clearly the observations of a man who had been there and observed:

The Cowgate has fallen into the sere and yellow leaf of furniture-brokers, second-hand jewellers and vendors of deleterious alcohol. These second-hand jewellers' shops, the trinkets seen by bleared gaslight, are the most melancholy sights I know. Watches hang there that once ticked comfortably in the fobs of prosperous men, rings that were once placed by happy bridegrooms on the fingers of happy brides, jewels in which lives the sacredness of death-beds. What tragedies, what disruptions of households, what fell pressure of poverty brought them here! Looking in through the foul windows, the trinkets remind one of shipwrecked gold embedded in the ooze of ocean – gold that peaks of unknown, yet certain storm and disaster, of the yielding of planks of the cry of drowning men. Who has the heart to buy them, I wonder? The Cowgate is the Irish portion of the city. Edinburgh leaps over it with bridges; its inhabitants are morally and geographically the lower orders. They keep to their own quarters, and seldom come up to the light of day. Many an Edinburgh man has never set foot in the street; the condition of the inhabitants is as little known as are the habits of moles, earthworms and the mining population. The people of the Cowgate seldom visit the upper streets. You may walk about the New Town for a twelvemonth before one of these Cowgate pariahs comes between the wind and your gentility.[88]

Although Alex. Smyth [sic] is listed among the College's office-bearers in the PO Directory there is no address given until 1857. In Adam's plan for the New College building provision was made for six 'houses' or suites of rooms. One was for the College Principal, one for the Librarian and four more for senior professors. The professors' apartments were never built. Dr Lee, the octogenarian Principal, occupied his premises, but Mr Small the Librarian already had a house in Duncan Street (now Drummond Place). It is significant that Smith's

£150 salary did not include the £30 housing allowance granted to previous Secretaries. This may point to his residing, for his first year in Edinburgh at least, in a four-room apartment adjoining the Library and overlooking South Bridge and the narrow South College Street. Today these handsome rooms are approached by an imposing staircase adorned with portraits of the College's most celebrated professors. He makes no mention of this, but he would have had as near neighbour Thomas De Quincey who, after a spell in Glasgow, had returned to his rented rooms in Lothian Street overrun with books. He was to spend the last five years of his life laboriously revising work for Hogg's 15-volume collected edition of his work. As we have seen, Smith had already met the Opium-Eater in Glasgow at Pringle Nichol's house. De Quincey could, however, be exhausting company as he rarely slept and (fueled by laudanum) was prone to long monologues delivered in a breathy voice that was sometimes too soft to be audible.

On 25 February at noon the Town Council selection committee and some of the professors met in the Patrons' Room at the College to welcome the new Secretary and also "for the purpose of inducting Mr Smith into office." The formalities complete, he was left in the care of Mr Small to face the lacklustre realities behind his imposing title. The actual office, due perhaps to Blair Wilson's frequent absences, had fallen into disrepair – the minute book even makes a veiled reference to the unreliable state of the toilet. So in the interim Smith was offered a small space in the Library just by the entrance. The Playfair surroundings were certainly magnificent even if as Secretary he was working from something resembling a cupboard. In addition to other duties the Secretary was supposed to keep a daybook recording all purchases or presentations to the College Library. This was in a resolution passed just before he had arrived, the minute book explaining helpfully: "the effect of this arrangement will be to fill up the time of the Secretary"! Smith was eventually allowed back into his office near the gatehouse in November 1855. At that point it was minuted that the new Secretary had not undertaken this new duty. Mr Small had probably preferred to do it himself.

One of the first Professors to make himself known must surely have been William Edmonstoune Aytoun. He had held the Chair of Rhetoric and Belles-Lettres since 1845 and, with his legal training, was now a power in the Senatus. As the son of a successful Writer to the Signet, and Christopher North's son-in-law, he seems to have switched from writing and reviewing to legal affairs and back again with no great strain. His unruffled manner, tinged with a trace of *ennui*, did not always appeal to his students. One of them recalled "he was not a stimulating teacher, although an admirable literary man."[89] His weekly lecture began at 4pm, and at 4.45 without fail "he indulged in a most extraordinary and portentous yawn." For ten years Aytoun had been on the staff of Blackwoods, contributing pointed articles on the follies of the age, such as the advertising craze and railway mania. He also undertook translations from the German and wrote light verse. His most popular work was *The Ballad Book by 'Bon Gaultier'* (written for Tait's in collaboration with Theodor Martin) which contained parodies of national and personal verse styles. The speculation over Wordsworth's successor as Laureate gave the Bon Gaultiers a golden opportunity. The dying falls of Tennyson were adroitly captured:

> I'd lounge in the gateway all day long,
> With her Majesty's footmen in crimson and gold.
> I'd care not a pin for the waiting-lord;
> But I'd lie on my back on the smooth, green sward,
> With a straw in my mouth and an open vest
> And the cool wind blowing upon my breast,
> And I'd vacantly stare at the clear blue sky,
> And watch the clouds as listless as I,
>   Lazily, lazily![90]

The *Bon Gaultier Ballads* were revised and added to every now and then, so they remained in print for thirty-two years. Now Professor Aytoun was toying with an idea which would surely be even more of a popular hit. That it would burst like a thunderclap over the head of the new Secretary may have crossed his mind. But this latest spoof was very close to Aytoun's heart, so he did not breathe a word to anyone, except presumably to his Blackwoods cronies in their New Town salon.

Apart from Aytoun there were several others on the professorial staff with reputations outside the College boundaries. Pre-eminent was Sir William Hamilton, whose views on perception were later challenged by J.S.Mill in launching his theory of causation, but at this time Hamilton headed the revival of British philosophy and had held chairs at Edinburgh since 1821. By 1854 he was a stricken man and his lectures on metaphysics and logic were often completed by an appointed student whilst the old man watched silently. The figure most responsible for Edinburgh's later reputation as a centre for advanced surgery was James Syme. He had no small talk, was always in a rush and lectured sitting down but with mesmerising force. Dr Robert Christison had pioneered the study of toxicology and James Young Simpson, who was offered the chair of Medicine and Midwifery before he was thirty, later helped to develop chloroform for surgical use. The Church of Scotland's right to control the selection of professors through the Test Act was opposed eloquently but unsuccessfully by the minister of Greyfriars church, Dr Robert Lee, who was also Professor of Biblical Criticism and Antiquities. Finally, the burning issue of university reform was a particular interest of John Stuart Blackie who had taken up the Chair of Greek at Edinburgh in 1852. A benign if garrulous figure, he strode up the High Street unmistakably bedecked in long cloak and broad-brimmed hat.

One wonders how the 24-year-old Secretary would have reacted to this goulash of brilliance, eccentricity and self-importance as he first encountered it in the spring of 1854. Was he tempted to put on airs too? Sticking with his customary reserve would have been the safer course, listening and observing closely. He must have felt extremely isolated, feelings exacerbated by being entombed in the College building day and night. A letter written to Brisbane one Sunday morning conveys something of his underlying unease:

I feel Edinburgh very dreary occasionally, a sad want of old habits, places and companions, and worst of all
"There's nae toddy noo, Tammy,
There's nae toddy noo."
By my teetotalism there hangs a tale and a year hence this abstinence will either be the most heroic or the most insane proceeding I ever engaged in.[91]

In *Early Years* this letter is quoted without the jingle, presumably because Brisbane, its recipient, thought it better that impressionable readers should not know that the poet's lips had been profaned by alcohol. But clearly this was one of those "old habits". Perhaps there had been a pattern of social drinking with friends and work colleagues that had got a little out of hand. Certainly the pace of his creativity in 1852 might have required some stimulants, and all around him there must have been examples of his peers indulging in alcoholic excess. But 1854 was also the date of the new Scottish Sunday Closing Act, so temperance was in the air. Perhaps his evangelical principles reasserted themselves with the taking up of the new post. For whatever reason Smith decided to refrain for a year and he seems to have stuck with it.

His resolve must have been sorely tested in the succeeding weeks. In the May issue of Blackwoods a spoof review appeared, a peg on which to hang an attack on the then unnamed School of new poets. The writer asserted *ex cathedra* that "it is full time that the prurient and indecent tone which has liberally manifested itself in the writings of the young spasmodic poets should be checked." Although the indignation behind the piece was real there was a hidden joke. The subject of the supposed review (to be published two months later) was itself a devastating parody of the worst excesses of "spasm". It was entitled

Firmilian; or the Student of Badajoz: A Tragedy . It was purported to have been written by one 'T. Percy Jones'.

Tortured grammar, wilful obscurity and excessive egocentricity were all shown up by *Firmilian*'s gaudy verse. Whether or not it accurately parodied stylistic elements of 'A Life-Drama' has been debated by a number of critics up to the present day. Prof. Saintsbury said it guyed Marlowe, Byron's *Manfred, Sonnets from the Portuguese* and Tennyson's *The Princess*. 'T.Percy Jones' (as Victorian literature specialist Florence Boos has pointed out) made links to "the new poets' alleged Shelleyan extravagance ("Percy") as well as their homely origins ("Jones")". But to most people Smith and Jones are not really so far apart, and in addition the reviewer devotes a paragraph to Smith by name:

Alexander Smith possesses abilities which, if rightly directed, cannot fail to make him eminent as a poet. The real danger to which he is exposed arises from the superlative commendation lavished upon him by men, who in the present deluge of cheap literature, have been let loose upon the public as critics...[92]

This is a clear shot at the Rev. George Gilfillan, and there is more of the same ("in the eyes of a considerable body of modern critics extravagance is regarded as a proof of extraordinary genius") providing an immediate clue to the identity of the writer – not that he made any serious attempt at disguise. To some extent Smith, Dobell, Massey and Stanyan Biggs were all caught in the crossfire between Aytoun and Gilfillan, where there existed real personal animosity. Aytoun had never forgiven him for a dismissive review of his *Lays of the Scottish Cavaliers*. So when (as an unexpected sequel to the review) the complete poetic drama *Firmilian* was printed in Blackwoods two months later the effect on Gilfillan must have been difficult to bear. Sydney Dobell, particularly his interminable poetic-dramatic monologue *Balder*, was also accurately taken off. The hits on 'A Life-Drama' are less quantifiable.

The comic idea behind the parody is that the poet Firmilian is writing a drama about Cain and feels he has to emulate his fictional creation in the area of mass destruction of human life and buildings, principally churches, temples and mosques. Whether or not contemporary readers would have associated this with Walter in 'A Life-Drama' (here the parallels with Dobell's *Balder* and *The Roman* are much stronger), two characters in *Firmilian* are fairly clearly based on Gilfillan and Smith. Apollodorus, as we have seen, a *nom de plume* already used by Gilfillan, and his costermonger sidekick Sancho would have been readily identifiable to contemporary Blackwoods readers. Apollodorus is portrayed as a star-gazing talent scout (Gilfillan wrote also on astronomy) with a need to compensate for his own deficiency in literary recognition. "Why do men call me a presumptuous cur, A vapouring blockhead, and a turgid fool, A common nuisance and a charlatan?" he asks. There was some truth in this since Gilfillan, despite achieving considerable notice with his *Galleries of Literary Portraits* and his many collected editions of canonical poets, never made an impact as a poet himself. In *Firmilian* Apollodorus meets a grisly end when he is crushed to death by the falling body of another self-styled poet.

The Sancho episodes are fairly crude put-downs of the humbly born aspiring to areas of culture which should be beyond their reach. Sancho is depicted as having a sound knowledge of farmyard affairs but being on shakier ground when it comes to producing a well-turned out quatrain. This strain of class snobbery runs through *Firmilian* and, although parts are still humorous for today's reader, it might detract from fuller enjoyment. If Smith had felt excluded from the charmed circle a year earlier in Glasgow, it was clearly no delusion. Prof. Boos dismisses it more harshly: "I find it hard to see much more than class-antagonism, jejeune snobbery and a sort of displaced self-loathing in this oddly grotesque cartoon."[93]

One speech in *Firmilian* at least would have sounded familiar to readers of 'A Life-Drama' ("I have a strain of a departed bard; One who was born too late into this world" Sc. 2):

> I knew a poet once; and he was young
> And intermingled with such fierce desires
> As made pale Eros veil his face with grief,
> And caused his lustier brother to rejoice.
> He was as amorous as a crocodile
> In the spring season, when the Memphis bank,
> Receiving substance from the glaring sun,
> Resolves itself from mud into a shore.
> And – as the scaly creature wallowing there
> In its hot fits of passion, belches forth
> The steam from out its nostrils, half in love,
> And half in grim defiance of its kind;
> Trusting that either from its reedy fen
> Some reptile-virgin coyly may appear,
> Or that the hoary Sultan of the Nile
> May make tremendous challenge with his jaws
> And, like Mark Antony, assert his right
> To all the Cleopatras of the ooze –
> So fared it with the poet that I knew.[94]

The joke was not yet quite complete. The August issue of Blackwoods rounded things off with a Preface by 'T.Percy Jones' where he justifies Spasm as a creative doctrine and poetic method. This reveals Aytoun's sharp legal mind at its most forensic, allowing Gilfillan, the Spasmodics' mouthpiece, to hang himself as if under skilful cross-examination. In acknowledging himself as a Spasmodic poet T.P.Jones responds to the charges: "Remove that element from Lear—from Othello – from Macbeth – from any of the great works which refer to the conflict of the passions – and what would be the residue?" A great deal more would have been Aytoun's response, as well as certain things which innate good taste would have prompted better known writers to omit. Accusations of profanity and prurience underpinned much of the hostile criticism of the new poets championed by Gilfillan. If the boundaries in such matters were to be relaxed, who knows what else in society might have to yield to change? It is hard to over-emphasise the influential role that literature was playing in a fast-changing, more technocratic age where mid-Victorian institutions such as the church, the universities and the plebiscite were all in the firing line.

One could argue that the *Firmilian* episode scored its most effective hit on George Gilfillan, guying him mercilessly in the character of Apollodorus but also providing an accurate pastiche of Gilfillan's own reviewing style in the initial spoof review that appeared in the May edition of Blackwoods. Gilfillan's headlong approach to critical writing was easy meat for Aytoun's keen dissection. His listing of the four main failings of the Spasmodic School (where the fourth just repeats the first in more florid language) seems accurate when set beside Gilfillan's own work. In his review of J. Stanyan Bigg's *Night and the Soul* four failings are similarly listed, giving rise to "considerable monotony and tedium", yet after listing them Gilfillan still praises the work effusively. Aytoun killed him as a critical force. After *Firmilian* he found it impossible to find a market for more literary discoveries among the new generation of poets.

Smith's only published comment on it was in the essay written on Dobell some ten years later. He concedes that Aytoun's catchphrase had found public favour but refrains from making any comment on its personal impact. There was clearly something about 'Spasmodic School' that made it stick. 'Spasmodic' had already been applied on at least three previous occasions in reviews, most notably in a round-up review by Charles Kingsley in Fraser's ("a spasmodic, vague, extravagant, effeminate school of poetry") but also by Professor Blackie in Chambers' and in the original Blackwoods review. At the time the word had two meanings. As an adjective it suggested the convulsive and unpredictable quality of diction and metre, but as a noun (an anti- spasmodic) it referred to a medicine administered to relieve muscular spasm, like giving someone a shock to stop the hiccups. Maybe this would have made it an even more appropriate label to stick on the likes of Dobell who had been repeatedly hailed as Tennyson's rival since the appearance of *The Roman* in 1850. Spasmodic was to become a by-word for weird style and questionable opinions (a parallel with the Yellow Book group in the 1890s suggests itself). It was also probably very effective at imposing some self-censorship on future poets about to venture into print. Kingsley was so incensed by the new poets that he incorporated a caricature into his novel *Two Years Ago* where dreamy John Briggs cuts a poor figure beside his level-headed companion Tom Thurnall. He works as an apprentice pharmacist, is very aware of his defective education and so relies on Dr Bolus to lend him books and guide his early attempts at poetry. Although achieving some early recognition, Briggs lacks the right stuff and becomes an opium addict.

Recent writers on the *Firmilian* episode and Aytoun's Blackwoods group have suggested that the satirical ripples also spread over the toes of established writers such as the Brownings, Clough, Ruskin, Emily Bronte, George Meredith and even Matthew Arnold with his later disowned 'Empedocles on Etna'. The effect was to reintroduce a note of stylistic caution into the mid-Victorian literary scene. Even Tennyson was not immune to the trend. In August 1855 the publication of *Maud* reignited the whole issue, some seeing the poem (largely written by the time of *Firmilian's* appearance) as a Spasmodic kite to test public reaction. He received his worst reviews by far, even Coventry Patmore in the Edinburgh Review awarding it "the serious defect of leaving the mind of the reader in a painful state of confusion as to the limits of the sane and the insane". Although there was no lack of opportunity Smith was believed to have refrained from intervening in the *Maud* controversy. In fact an anonymous piece in the West of Scotland Magazine is almost certainly by him. This was a one shilling quarterly published by the enterprising Thomas Murray (who also published *Alfred Leslie,* the first novel set in Glasgow) which ran for five years from October 1854. 'Mr Tennyson and His Critics' appeared in the first issue of 1856, making a powerful defence of the Laureate as a poet dedicated both to his art and the national interest. On *Maud* specifically the writer is judiciously fair-minded:

Mr Tennyson has written 'Maud' to prove that he too can strike out a new vein, and show us unlooked-for images of ourselves on the polished marble of his verse. And if the author of a new pleasure is to be considered a benefactor of his species, surely it is not right to blame Mr Tennyson for trying to be so, even though he may have failed of success. The attempt was laudable, and he deserves our thanks.

'Spasmodic' influences made their way into other branches of literature, most notably the sensation fiction that became popular in the late 1850s and 60s. "Aytoun played successfully to a receptive claque," Professor Boos writes, "but subsequent generations have largely consigned his sensibilities to a literary and political backwater. Then as now, it was easier to be a clever critic than it was to write a memorable poem. More dispiriting were the enduring triumphs of the iron laws of class and education that Aytoun exploited. No acknowledged 'major' poet of Victorian Britain came from working- or lower-middle-class origins, and none of the Spasmodists is likely to gain more than token entry into any twenty-first century anthologies. Even here, however, Dobell, Smith and others might have found a measure of vindication in the vast palette of subsequent generations' preoccupations with despair, recovery, aberrance, marginality and self-examination – a palette they helped, in the face of withering critical abuse, to configure." [95]

Smith had already become close friends with Sydney Dobell (who palindromically wrote as Sydney Yendys) and he was one of the first to make him welcome in Edinburgh. Since meeting in Cheltenham after publication of 'A Life-Drama' they had kept up a correspondence, exchanging poems and ideas. Dobell had been in Edinburgh since the previous autumn to take medical advice. He and his wife stayed for three years, moving to a cottage in the Highlands each summer. Dobell's animation and quicksilver mind would have created a strange antithesis to Smith's more dogged manner. Obviously Firmilian would have brought them even closer. During that first year as Secretary Smith must have spent many evenings at the Corstorphine villa with its view of the Pentlands. From a letter by Dobell to his father (a wine merchant and member of a rationalist Christian sect who was initially opposed his literary inclinations) we know that one evening in April they staged a lavish entertainment with historical tableaux designed by James Drummond, a popular painter of historic scenes, and the portrait painter James Archer. Dobell and Smith provided the verbal accompaniment to scenes of Flora Macdonald and Bonnie Prince Charlie, Mary Queen of Scots and the bride of Lammermoor representing Scottish tragic heroines. Smith provided a prologue to the tableaux, drawing a parallel with the Crimean War which was coming to a head with the siege of Sebastopol.

> The curtain rises on our mimic scenes.
> Pale Flora, watching o'er the Prince, forlorn;
> Ruth, standing like a poppy 'mong the corn;

> And Mary, saddest, fairest of the queens,
> Bending, in tumbled and dishevelled grief,
> Above melodious Rizzio, stabbed and torn:
> Frail Lucy, shrinking neath her lover's scorn,
> With faith as worthless as a withered leaf
> That o'er the waste by every wind is whirled.
> > Another curtain, o'er a stage of gloom,
> > Is slowly rising: calm and pale with hate
> > Two foes are closing in the tug of doom.
> > Upon this stage shall rise our mimic state,
> > But on that other stands or falls the world.[96]

In August 1854 Dobell included a verbal portrait in a letter to Gerald Massey who was to arrive later in the year to work for Chambers Journal. This had been Massey's annus mirabilis. *Babe Christabel & Other Poems* had gone through five reprints, even being hailed by the Athenaeum. He was the son of a canal boatman, starting work in a silk mill at the age of eight, going later to London to support the Chartists and subsequently espousing Christian Socialism. He was supposed to have been the original for George Eliot's *Felix Holt*. Massey spent just over two years in Edinburgh writing articles and giving lectures at literary institutes. His background was similar to Smith's, so the curiosity must have been mutual. Dobell's description opens by warning that "anything more than such sheer statistics is (due to his Scottish reserve) impossible from anyone with whom he is not intimate." After describing facial features ("a somewhat brown complexion") Dobell tries to convey the impression made on a first meeting:

> ...a broad strongly-built figure approaching with a lounging, thoughtful step. The face that might not have attracted you on the street brightens, as we meet, into very sunshine. He sits down; and during our talk he beams first one and then the other of those blue, clear, living eyes upon me, each of which in turn seems to take up the conversation with a force all the greater for its interval of rest, and to shine while employed with the combined light of both.

The letter (missing a final page) ends with a passage about Smith's social graces:

> With me he speaks freely and at length, but in ordinary society he has little conversation. With friends or strangers, however, his manners are alike quiet and simple... The conclusions which certain critics have drawn from some overcoloured passages in his writings are strangely inconsistent with the purity of his conduct, the chastity of his speech, the firmness with which he has maintained his water-drinking in the face of the banter of Edinburgh drawer-tables *[sic]* and the large development of the religious element of his mind.[97]

Apart from this bond of friendship there was another reason for Dobell and Smith to associate frequently: they were planning a jointly written book of sonnets. That autumn the Russian evacuation of Sebastopol meant that the Crimean War was in its last stages. A poetic tribute was surely due to the valour of the Allied troops, of whom nearly five times as many died from epidemics as fell on the field of battle. Although the conduct of the generals had been questioned in the press, notably in The Times, the poets resolved to write largely of military exploits on the battlefield and the heroes' welcome the returning soldiers would receive. David Bogue offered to publish and before the Treaty of Paris was signed on 30 March 1855 *Sonnets on the War* had appeared in soft covers at a shilling. It was credited on the title page "by Alexander Smith and by the Author of Balder and The Roman." One reason for the collaboration is immediately clear: the collection had to be produced in haste and 39 sonnets (of which Smith wrote twenty) are produced more quickly if the job is shared. They seem to have made a list of titles and then taken turn about to write.

The choice of sonnet form is less easily explained. Perhaps it was a joint decision to show that these two arch-Spasmodics could actually write poetry in an immediately familiar form. It is still slightly strange to see Smith's name on the title page, given his aversion to anything political. He obviously saw the Crimean campaign, as did most of his compatriots, as a new version of the Crusades. In many ways he was typical of his age, and of course Tennyson was to join the ranks of bellicose poets later in the year with his 'Charge of the Light Brigade'. The *Sonnets on the War* that Smith wrote are easily identifiable. The best of them still have a slight Spasmodic echo, otherwise they are just well-crafted technical turns. This one is called 'Volunteers':

> Take us, O England! In thine hour of need.
> We hold our lives out in our eager hands!
> Take us, O England! Gather us in bands!
> We come to rot in winds or wildly bleed,
> We come in crowds from glen and milky mead,
> From homes, fir-saddened on the sunset-wold,
> From Fortune's pathways, littered thick with gold.
> From tarry towns that on the ocean feed,
> From lowing fields, from blithe cock-crowing farms.
> From proud brides nestling in our happy arms,
> At thy command we dare the chilly grave,
> And dying we have one wild thought above
> The pang. This guerdon, England, we would crave –
> Take us into the heaven of thy love.[98]

It's the kind of thing W.E.Henley was to turn his hand to twenty years later. Assuming you accept the prerequisite that involvement in a war can be just even if your own borders are not threatened, *Sonnets on the War* is written with style, flair and a willingness to bang the drum a bit. This time the Spasmodics received ecstatic reviews, with one exception. Blackwoods once again sent a copy to their man on the spot, Edward Bruce Hambley (who had previously written a dismissive review of 'A Life-Drama'). Hambley had been sending regular reports from the battle zone whilst serving as a Brevet-Major in an artillery regiment. At the battle of Inkerman he had his horse shot from under him and narrowly escaped capture. He was mentioned in dispatches four times and received the Crimean medal. At a loose end, one suspects, by the time Sebastopol had been relieved Hambley enjoyed getting stuck into *Sonnets* and produced his copy in short order. His review appeared in the May issue and seems to have questioned from the start the credentials of anyone who had not witnessed the battles to write about them. At one point he upbraids the two milksop poets for their over-gruesome descriptions, culled almost certainly from colourful reports in Blackwoods and elsewhere. Other reviewers were openly surprised at how orthodox the two arch Spasmodics had become. For neither was this collection a step forward, more a diversion. However it helped to reposition both writers and their opportunism was rewarded with healthy sales.

As the spring of 1855 turned to summer and the end of the academic year, the new Secretary's thoughts no doubt turned to his annual report to the Town Council due for completion before the summer vacation which ran from July to October. This apparently generous break was in fact curtailed at either end by the necessary Secretarial focus on the closing accounts for the previous academic year and the preparations for matriculation of new students for the following one. In the summer of either 1855 or 1856 (or possibly both) Smith went to Skye for the first time in the company of Horatio McCulloch the landscape painter. McCulloch, who hailed from the west coast but had lived in Edinburgh since 1830, was twenty-five years older than the poet but they seem to have struck up an immediate *rapport*. The link between them may have been Alexander Nicolson, a man nearer Smith's age who had been brought up in Skye and had then come to Edinburgh to take an Arts degree. Having got it, and been commended as an outstanding philosophy student in his year, he seems to have drifted into journalism and hackwork for the Encyclopaedia Britannica while thinking about studying for the bar. McCulloch and his wife were famous for entertaining a wide circle at late dinners in his home and studio in Danube Street. Now a stalwart of the Royal Scottish Academy (RSA) McCulloch was entering the peak period of his success, with public demand for his wild and luminous Highland landscapes seemingly insatiable.

Every summer he packed his paints and easel and headed north. We can tell that in both 1855 and 1856 he was on Skye by the canvases he exhibited the following spring at the RSA annual exhibition. His wife Marcella was a Macdonald from the Sleat peninsula, which forms the southernmost tip of the island, with the steamer pier at Armadale its main link (at that time) to the mainland. She had as cousins the eight children of Captain Charles Macdonald, the tacksman or tenant at Ord, a small community of cottars overlooking Loch Eishort. It was from the shore of Loch Slapin, just round the headland from Ord, that McCulloch painted his 'View of the Cuchullin (Cuillin) Mountains' which was exhibited in 1857. It is reasonable to assume that on one of these visits Smith met Charles Macdonald's eldest daughter Flora, just a few months younger than himself. It must have been a *coup de foudre* for both. By the time the poet had departed south there was an understanding between Alexander Smith and Flora Macdonald. In a letter to his erstwhile companion Brisbane (1 December 1856) he hints that a date for the wedding had been fixed. Brisbane had just been inducted as minister to the Congregationalist congregation at Duncanston, a rural parish near Inverurie in Aberdeenshire and had invited Smith to join him for Christmas. The poet has to decline for a good reason:

A certain lady from the Hebrides is to be in Glasgow at that time, so I cannot come. If Duncanston lies on the line of the railway from Inverness, I may perhaps drop in upon you in April. Take a wife, Tom. Now is your opportunity. You have a position, a house and everything now.[99]

By October it was back to the inflexible routine of the Secretaryship as the winter session got under way, arriving at the College by 10 am and leaving at 4pm. Around 1,200 students could badger him with questions at any moment in between. There were also occasional visitors from Glasgow, many of them wanting to be introduced to Dobell.

Fairly early after his arrival he joined the Edinburgh Raleigh Club, probably at Alexander Nicolson's invitation. Although it's tempting to find a parallel with the Glasgow Addisonians, the Raleigh seems to have attracted mainly ex-graduates and drop-outs from the College who enjoyed wide-ranging intellectual discussion rather than the more earnest debating format of the Addisonians. There were other important differences. A hint of its priorities is given by his Glasgow friend Pat Alexander:

Once or twice I went with him to the Raleigh Club (so called in honour of Sir Walter, the introducer of the fragrant weed), a weekly meeting of such of his intimates, with some pretext of an intellectual aim, in the reading of an occasional paper or so; but obviously convened in the main for good, honest, social purposes of the pipe and modest tumbler.[100]

It would seem that Smith's year of teetotalism was now at an end. The Raleigh was not the only conviviality group he belonged to. Amongst other friends and fellow-Raleighans was John Downes who had come from Galloway to study at Edinburgh, almost inevitably after graduation becoming involved in compiling the eighth edition of *Britannica*. He had recruited Nicolson, and Smith had already written the entry on the poet Cowper. It is a sympathetic piece, stressing the disabilities under which Cowper worked and trying to account for the popularity of some of his work:

His muse does not sit apart in sublime seclusion – she comes down into the ways of men, mingles in their everyday concerns, and is interested in crops and rural affairs. You see by the slight tan on her cheek that she has been much in the harvest fields. Cowper talks rather than sings. His blank verse makes no pretensions to majesty; it is colloquial sometimes in its bareness, yet in it artless flow is ever delightful as the conversation of a beloved and gifted companion.[101]

Downes would hold smoking evenings for fellow contributors and others at his house in Barony Street on the edge of the New Town. On Saturday afternoons the same group would undertake a long circular walk out to the shores of the Forth, remembered here by a regular attender:

We used to start from our favourite rendezvous, viz the Philosophical Institution Rooms in Queen Street, about mid-day; and we walked westward by the Granton shore. Then we dined and smoked, and sauntered out for a time; returned again to the modest inn, and in the later hours walked home to Edinburgh, often in wonderful moonlight.[102]

To Smith these bucolic jaunts must have been pleasantly reminiscent of the rambles with Hugh Macdonald and Pat Alexander beside the Clyde out to Carmyle. One of his fellow-walkers by the Firth of Forth was John Ferguson McLennan, an Inverness man of Smith's age who had been educated at King's College, Aberdeen, and then at Cambridge. Another aimless spirit, he was compiling a long and scholarly entry on 'Law' for Britannica. He had arrived in Edinburgh in

1856 to apply to the Scottish bar, and it seems that Smith shortly afterwards shared rooms with him at 25 India Street, at the west end of the New Town. McLennan was to create something of an anthropological furore in the 1860s with the publication of *An Inquiry into the Origin of the Form of Capture in Marriage Ceremonies*. Smith, contemplating just such a 'capture' himself, would have found his flatmate interesting company.

About this time (December 1856) the publisher David Bogue died. Although he was a shadowy figure we may assume he had an influence of some kind on the young poet when the 1853 *Poems* was being prepared for press. He had also done well with *Sonnets on the War* and would have been impatient to receive Smith's next collection. In fact, it is likely that he would have already received a large proportion of what was to become *City Poems*. There was a brief period of uncertainty. By mid-December Alexander and Daniel Macmillan were in touch, in the hunt for the most lucrative of Bogue's copyrights. On 23 December Smith writes to them on College notepaper:

I did not expect that you were in a position to make an offer for poems yet unfinished. Happy to let you have first offer when I get them finished.[103]

The offer, when it came, was handsome: £200 for the copyright plus the American rights. As an indicator of their confidence the Macmillans also agreed to instigate a fourth reprint of *Poems*, still with Bogue's imprint on the title page, making it into a publishing curiosity. It was a nice gesture to bring 'A Life-Drama' back into print, but were they a little apprehensive of becoming tarred with the 'Spasmodic School' brush and therefore left the colophon unchanged? The reissue gave an opportunity for reviewers to look back on the *Firmilian* affair, one of them (in Hogg's Titan) showing that 'Maud' had still not recovered from the association:

they have appeared to cup our young singers in a different fashion [since 'A Life-Drama' first appeared in 1853]; even hinting that an assured immortal like Tennyson, when he presented his latest poem, was wandering in his wits and passing into second childhood, and unfairly classing together a band of totally different writers, and calling down on them howls and execrations as the 'Spasmodic School'.[104]

This was almost certainly Gilfillan, sensing that now at last he could get in a late return of Aytoun's serve. It was a good moment to choose. The Professor had just published *Bothwell: A Poem in Six Parts* in which the captured laird recalls at considerable length those halcyon days when he was consort to the Queen of Scots. The ballad strains at times come perilously close to a desperate doggerel:

> My blazon has been long erased,
>> My name struck off the knightly roll.
> But what of that? The time has been
>> When I was highest of the high –
> Yea – was the husband of the Queen;
>> And so they shall not pass me by.[105]

The critics were in the main unimpressed. In October Smith could write to fellow Spasmodic J.Stanyan Bigg:

> Have you seen Aytoun's Bothwell? A clear case of literary suicide, the Professor has cut his throat from ear to ear, and no surgeon in the world will ever sew it up. He is a good fellow, Aytoun, and I wish he had made a better appearance.[106]

A few weeks later, on Boxing Day, the city was rocked by a real case of suicide. The pioneering geologist and radical writer Hugh Miller shot himself with a revolver and a few days later shops were closed on the route of his funeral cortege. Only two years earlier his *My Schools and Schoolmasters* had been published to acclaim and for more than fifteen years he had been a legendary editor of the Free Church Witness. Like Smith his origins had been relatively humble and he had worked as a stonemason on several buildings in the Highlands and Edinburgh before turning writer in his twenties. The parallels with Smith's early career are striking, but there is no record that the two ever met.

With his wedding arranged for the following spring and a contract for *City Poems* in his pocket, as 1856 drew to a close it looked as if 1857 would surely turn out a memorable year for Smith. And so it was to be, but in a fashion quite different from anything he could have reasonably expected. For during the closing weeks of the year another letter was being written, this one addressed to William Hepworth Dixon, editor of the Athenaeum. It was signed only 'Z' (in algebra, an unknown or variable), its author having several good reasons to keep his identity unknown.[107]

Chapter 7:
1857

The land is covered with a net of iron,
Upon whose spider-like, far stretching lines,
The trains are rushing, and the peevish sea
Frets 'gainst the bulging bosoms of the ships
Whose keels have waked it from its hour's repose.
  ('A Life-Drama' sc.6)

BY THE MID-VICTORIAN ERA Britain had taken an unassailable lead in most fields of science and technology, underpinning an advance in mass industrialisation that was only later matched in mainland Europe and America. The early 1850s had seen pioneering and partly successful attempts at steam locomotion that would grow rapidly into railway fever. Imbue an engineer such as I.K.Brunel with both imagination and access to wealthy backers and just about anything was possible. The *SS Great Eastern*, the largest ship the world had ever seen, was launched in 1857. Despite gloomy predictions she floated and she went on to cross the Atlantic in eleven days, powered by both screw propulsion and paddle wheels. She was also to play an invaluable role in the saga of laying the first transatlantic telegraph cable. Despite consuming huge amounts of coal, the *Great Eastern* soon became an icon, a floating demonstration that British technology had no foreseeable limits.

In the 1860s far-reaching advances in science made ripples that spread to today's world. The chemistry of the ovum had been observed under the microscope, Pasteur had developed his germ theory of infection, and both Darwin and Wallace were investigating variation of species. By 1863 more powerful optical lenses were revealing the secrets of cell formations. Mendel exploited this when he published the results of his heredity experiments in 1866. *Origin of Species* in 1859 had proposed a theory of evolution that influenced Galton and others who advanced into the equally contentious area of eugenics and improvement of the gene pool. Pasteur's discoveries were being developed by Lister into an antiseptic regime that would dramatically reduce surgical mortality rates. It was also the era of applied science when, particularly for the emerging middle class, daily life in an increasingly urbanised environment began to resemble our own. Prototypes of a carpet-sweeper, a dishwasher and a chain-driven bicycle went into the manufacturing stage. The first oil well was sunk, the first safety lift was installed, celluloid and a range of synthetic dyes were discovered, and the electric dynamo was invented. Technological progress would eventually lead to social improvement. Admittedly it also included iron warships, Gatling guns and Nobel's dynamite works, but for the majority progress (linked to the rapid spread of basic literacy) was bringing some comfort and even entertainment into their lives.

Others were not so happy with what The Quarterly called "overwrought materialism" taking over. Biblical Christians were being exposed to a succession of cold blasts from the laboratory. The faith of some, such as Arthur Hugh Clough, was shaken as the doctrine of free will seemed to be fatally compromised by the Darwinian mechanism of natural selection. As we have seen the Evangelical Movement spearheaded the church militant's diversion into areas of social concern. For a small number the stupendous discoveries of science were but greater evidence of an all-knowing Creator's hand, a starting point for other pseudo-sciences which would spawn an industry with the ability to prey on the suggestible and vulnerable: the growing influence of mesmerism, clairvoyance and the spiritualists.

In the midst of such bewildering novelty people looked increasingly to the printed word for guidance, in books if they could be understood, but more often in the many periodicals which jostled for public attention. Satisfying the thirst for knowledge became a major industry in itself, creating opportunities which generated many publishing dynasties of the twentieth century. With greater depth of literacy becoming the norm the quest was on for material that demanded extensive rather than intensive reading. First-generation readers may have used the King James Bible as their primer, but publishers now looked for material to satisfy reading skills produced by more systematic education. In mid-century Scotland, through the efforts of parish schools and later school boards, there was a higher rate of literacy than almost anywhere else in Europe. Even the eighteenth-century suspicion about women being literate was beginning to dissipate. Harriet Martineau (whom Smith had visited in 1853) recalls the situation in her youth when she was expected

to sit down in the parlour with her sewing, listen to a book read aloud, and hold herself ready for female callers. When the callers came, conversation often turned naturally on the book just laid down, which must therefore be very carefully chosen lest the shocked visitor should carry to the house where she paid her next call an account of the deplorable laxity shown by the family she had left.[108]

With the introduction of rotary presses in the 1830s larger print runs reduced unit costs. There was a wave of weekly periodicals at prices almost any family could afford. As we have seen, the most influential of these was The Athenaeum, a paper founded in 1828 as a weekly independent commentary on works of literature, philosophy and science. According to the original prospectus it was to be "like the Athenaeum of antiquity, the resort of the most distinguished philosophers, historians, orators and poets of our day." (To some it appeared dauntingly self-opinionated and trenchant. In *The Wrong Box* intellectual lightweight John Finsbury cheerily dismisses it as "all full of the most awful swipes about poetry and the use of the globes ... the kind of thing that nobody could read out of a lunatic asylum.") By the 1890s it may have fallen into something of a rut (it closed in 1923), but fifty years before its reputation was as impressive as its most famous editor Charles Wentworth Dilke who had just halved the price to fourpence. The fact that every review and article was anonymous somehow gave The Athenaeum's pronouncements greater authority. It had built up a fearsome reputation for championing progress and asserting the highest standards in all branches of the arts, politics and science. On the literary front Dilke had favoured women writers such as Charlotte Bronte, E.B.B., Mrs Gaskell and George Eliot as well as being a champion of Tennyson before public idolatry set in. His successors were to support a wide variety of causes, from penny banks and mechanics institutes to Arctic exploration and the Great Exhibition. Even the Public Record Office for England and Wales was established as the result of a campaign in The Athenaeum. Scotland had already set one up in 1785.

The letter – signed 'Z' – which appeared in The Athenaeum of 3 January 1857 under the heading of 'The Last New Poet'[109] occupied five full columns. By juxtaposing lines from *A Life-Drama* with similar short extracts taken from published work by Tennyson, Shelley, Keats, Leigh Hunt and even Spenser, Z demonstrated that since 1853 Alexander Smith had been perpetrating "a new poetic system of composition". More plainly, Z had established – to his own satisfaction at least – that Smith was a plagiarist. For the young poet trying to establish himself in the eyes of the Edinburgh professors, in particular, it must have been unnerving to discover that The Athenaeum had him firmly in its sights. The allegations aroused widespread and immediate interest. In the next issue the literary editor Henry Fothergill Chorley noted that: "Our table is covered with letters upon the subject of the wholesale poetical appropriations charged upon Mr Alexander Smith." Throughout the campaign Chorley outwardly maintained the stance of an independent observer, whereas in reality he seems to have played a much more active role in stoking the fires whenever they showed signs of abating.

This was probably the most public literary plagiarism *affaire* since De Quincey in Tait's Magazine in the 1830s alleged Coleridge had borrowed freely from contemporary German philosophical writers. Aware of the hornets' nest he was about to prod, De Quincey at least offered some extenuation. He was also insightful about the creative process:

Many of his plagiarisms were probably unintentional and arose from that confusion between things floating in the memory and things self-derived, which happens at times to most of us that deal much with books on the one hand, and composition on the other. An author can hardly have written much and rapidly who does not detect himself, *and perhaps therefore sometimes fails to detect himself,* in appropriating the thoughts, images or striking expressions of others.[110]

From their editorial offices in the Strand The Athenaeum men, writing for the nation's intelligentsia, took a much more cut and dried approach. Accusations of intellectual theft should not be made lightly, but once made they had to be made to stick. In publishing such a comprehensive letter (and in only using a relatively short one from John Nichol out of many that were sent in reply) editor William Hepworth Dixon was embarking on one of the celebrated crusades. Unfortunately, if there ever was an important issue at its heart it soon got lost in the mass of pedantic, almost laughable, detail that filled the correspondence columns. Each week piles of poetic small change were counted up and moved from one writer's pocket to another. Looking back on the affair four years later, David Masson, a future Professor of English Literature at Edinburgh, made light of it. But, even so, he hinted at an orchestrated campaign:

"Plagiarism!" was now the cry and "Borrowed feathers!" and straightway there were columns of parallel passages, to prove that there was not a sun, or a sea, or a star, or a tree, or any combination of thoughts or of images in Mr Smith's poems but it had been in somebody's pages before. Never was such a pecking. The feathers flew about, green, blue and crimson, as at the murder of a parrot. One recollects the affair yet with something like disgust. In the proportions perhaps of two percent of the alleged parallelisms there was distinct evidence of latent recollection or conscious reproduction – opening up what might have been an interesting inquiry as to how far every poet works in an element of transmitted diction, and makes permutations and combinations of ideas that have slipped into his memory from books.[111]

For Smith it was more difficult to take such a detached view of proceedings. For a start, it was problematic to know how to respond. Taking the view that any protestations on his part would probably make him appear yet more guilty, he kept quiet throughout the year or so it went on, and hardly seems to have referred to it publicly. Even today charges of plagiarism are dreaded by writers. Charges of libel can effectively be settled through the courts, but this seldom happens with plagiarism. It can in effect become a witch-hunt where old scores are settled. There was also the more worrying implication that as well as devaluing the worth of his writing, Smith was guilty of a kind of fraud ('debasing the poetic coinage') and therefore due some punishment. The word *plagiarism* relates to the Roman crime of stealing another man's slaves, an interesting analogy that also raises more troubling issues of original ownership. What must seem strange to a literary historian is the continuing need for identifying a crime of literary theft or borrowing. In the UK we have had effective copyright laws since the early 1800s to protect the writer against unscrupulous publishers and provide compensation for lost income. So what justification is there for labeling someone a plagiarist? How is it possible to prove that some borrowings are intentional and others are not? How to make a moral judgment if the borrowing has resulted in something palpably better? Significantly the charge is usually made by critics and academics rather than by other practising writers.

Before considering a few of the instances cited in the plagiarism campaign against Smith (both in the Z letter and the ensuing review of *City Poems*) it is instructive to examine the personalities behind it. Z was William Allingham, like Smith largely self-educated and needing to support himself. He worked as a customs and excise officer in County Donegal before coming to London to try and live on the proceeds of his writing. Unfortunately his *Poems* had appeared in 1850 and had not been very much noticed. In fact in a couple of instances it was lumped in with *A Life-Drama* for review three years later. For this Allingham was not grateful as the comparisons were unfavourable. Clough in the North American Review praises his "pure felicitous diction" in some of the poems but then adds ungraciously that the book "would have been better, certainly, for more perfect elaboration of several of the minor pieces and perhaps the entire omission of a considerable number..."[112] Allingham later turned to producing ballad and song lyrics with some success, but his early efforts to refresh former poetic genres and diction fail to impress. His *Day and Night Songs* (1854) seems to have done better with the critics. This time he made good use of the period before publication by ensuring that big names such as Carlyle and Tennyson were sent copies. Then, a touch ingenuously, he wrote to ask what they thought. When they replied he made sure that influential critics saw the letters. With Ruskin the stratagem presumably failed because the day after D.G.Rossetti gave him a copy Effie Ruskin ran off with the pre-Raphaelite painter Millais.[113]

In hindsight, viewing the Z letter charitably, one can see that Allingham was a young man in a desperate hurry to make his name (as well as bearing a considerable grudge) and saw a literary version of guerilla warfare as the best available means to this end. But he never seems to have admitted during his lifetime that he was Z, perhaps because he later achieved entry into the literary establishment by becoming editor of Fraser's Magazine and a regular houseguest of Tennyson and the Brownings. It was only in Arthur Waugh's biography of Tennyson that the truth came out in the 1890s (see Chapter 12). Later (after Allingham's death) his *Diary* was published, edited by his widow and a friend. Although often revealing about his contemporaries it is widely known that a number of the *Diary* items were omitted in the published version and later destroyed. Several others were in the know, including Rossetti who in April 1853 wrote with anticipatory relish to fellow-artist Thomas Woolmer:

> Allingham is heard of by nobody. I am sure he must be masticating his identity in a frightful way out at Ballyshannon about the news of Alex Smith. I should think that nothing were more likely than its bringing him up to London to do battle with tooth and nail...[114]

Allingham, seething with a self-imposed need for vendetta, had written to DGR on 15 March 1857:

> Don't waste sympathy on Alexander Smith. I hear he is coming out with Macmillan shortly; but if he ever produces a good book I undertake to eat it literally, as St John did, miraculously I suppose, that one in the Revelation.[115]

This was almost three months after the Z letter, but Allingham was not through just yet. The charge was redoubled in The Athenaeum of 22 August. This time Chorley was undoubtedly taking a more active role in drumming up support. A tireless reviewer of both literature and concerts every week for almost twenty-five years, Henry Chorley lived the life of a semi-recluse in a tiny house in Eaton Place. He also came from a humble background, working as a clerk in Liverpool until he was taken on by Dilke to persevere with the drudgery of copy-editing and proof-reading. He soon rose to become chief reviewer and the *confident* of figures such as Dickens, Thackeray and the Brownings. He was also a thwarted novelist. Although published, his long-winded historical fiction was seldom reviewed. Mortifyingly, it is possible that hostility created by his own stabbing reviews in The Athenaeum led to this situation. The trouble was that, since all the reviewing was done anonymously, occasionally an unsigned piece was attributed to him erroneously, creating further needless bad blood. Such was (and perhaps still is) the thankless lot of the literary editor, so maybe

Chorley is due some sympathy. To be deprived of the slightest recognition is gall to any writer. But, after years of ill-paid journalism, recognising the talent of others but gaining no reputation in return, he had taken to adopting a sneering tone towards new work that did not fit with his pre-conceived notions of literary correctness.

His piece on *City Poems* is a prime example. It starts off in mock-heroic style:

> He [Smith] announced himself a hero, and the busy world that takes so much on trust smiled on his burnished arms and dancing feathers. But time gave rise to doubts – whether the *preux chevalier* had forged the shining armour for himself or merely picked it up by the wayside… Everywhere we find the mutilated property of other bards, strewn about like wrecks of noble vessels thrown upon a wild Scotch coast.[116]

The "wild Scotch coast" jibe echoes some reviews of *A Life-Drama* where London critics could not manage to persuade themselves that this "uneducated" 23-year-old could have written that work unaided. Now the explanation fell into their laps: he had filched lines and couplets wholesale and stitched them together to make his first work such a success. On even a first reflection this should have struck someone as a particularly arduous way of composing poetry, as well as a risky one for a youngster without the education (nor presumably the reading) to make a decent fist of it. So what exactly were these "noble vessels" that Smith had lured onto the rocks and plundered of their cargoes? Allingham and Chorley worked hard to compile lists of parallel passages where there was an echo in Smith of some earlier work by another poet. Most of the New Poets seemed to admire the late Romantics and some of Tennyson's earlier work, so they started their search in Tennyson's *The Princess*, Keats' *Endymion* and the *Odes*, some lesser-known Shelley and even the arch-Spasmodic P.J.Bailey. In some of the juxtaposed passages the Smith lines do have more than an echo of the earlier work.

> From Tennyson there was:
> The full-juiced apple, waxing over-mellow,
> Drops in a silent autumn night.

> From Smith:
> Our beings mellow, then they fall
> Like o'er ripe peaches from the wall;
> We ripen, drop and all is o'er.

Conscious or unconscious? In some cases it seemed to The Athenaeum clique that Smith had taken particular words and phrases from a passage and conscientiously changed them around to throw the reader off the scent. In this way Keats' "Gold vase embossed With long-forgotten story" had become Smith's "Great cup of gold All rich and rough with stories of the gods". There was plenty more of this kind of thing as the case was assembled. So had he been caught out shamelessly fingering the small change of English poetry?

Pat Alexander was one of those who rushed to his defence by demonstrating the dangers of this kind of "evidence". But his letter to The Athenaeum was never published. In it he cited the couplet from *Maud*:

> The cruel madness of love,
> The honey of poison flowers.

This was published in 1855. From Smith's *City Poems* (published two years later) we have:

> Bring me love's honied nightshade, fill it high,
> I know its madness.

Ergo Smith is the plagiarist; but these lines from *A Life-Drama* could also be quoted:

> O God, I'd be the very floor that bears
> Such a majestic thing! Now feed, mine eyes,
> On beauteous poison, Nightshade, honey-sweet.

So who is the plagiarist now? In fact, Smith's last line also bears echoes of Keats' *Ode on Melancholy* (1819). And so on: the process of incrimination by juxtaposition could go on indefinitely but would it provide proof of either conscious or unconscious borrowing, De Quincey's "things floating in the memory and things self-derived"?

The Athenaeum's method was neatly parodied in Punch:

> Twinkle, twinkle, little star *(Original Poems for Infant Minds)*
> Each star that twinkling in the sky *(Alexander Smith)*

In hindsight much of the evidence painstakingly compiled by two thwarted writers, knowing their motives, seems unconvincing. But in 1857 the case for the defence still had to be argued and won; it was insufficient to claim that property rights to characters, plot-lines, imagery or poetic insight were effectively an abstraction. Pat Alexander's letter of refutation eventually appeared in *Last Leaves* (twelve years later) and perhaps it should have the last word on the matter:

> The truth is that no tolerably well read poet, and especially no young poet on his first wild plunge into poetry, reading fiercely and uncritically, is *or can be* in a position to discriminate between what comes to him as an occult suggestion from other minds and the original produce of his own.[117]

Just before The Athenaeum controversy erupted Smith had been busy on his contribution to the influential *Edinburgh Essays* which appeared in late January 1857. In a letter to Brisbane he mentions being "busy with an essay on the Scottish Ballads for a volume of Edinburgh essays on the same plan as those volumes issued by the Universities of Cambridge and Oxford." He was one of eight contributors gathered together by Alexander Nicolson, a Gael born in Skye but educated in Edinburgh. He had been a star pupil in Sir William Hamilton's metaphysics classes and was frequently called on to complete the ailing professor's lectures from his written notes. He enroled at the Free Church College but soon decided the ecclesiastical life was not to his taste. Thereafter Nicolson seems to have become an errant autodidact, making a kind of living by occasional writing and helping out in the law courts. As we have seen, he and Smith probably met through affable John Downes when he was recruiting writers for the eighth edition of *Britannica*.

Nicolson's collection of essayists is remarkable for having only two contributors with official connections to the Edinburgh College (later University). Apart from Smith, who of course was not on the academic staff, there was John Stuart Blackie who, as Professor of Greek and a pioneer of direct-method language teaching, wrote appropriately but at great length about Plato, and W.T.Gairdner (later to become Professor of Medicine at Glasgow and an early exponent of public health reform) who wrote more surprisingly on homoeopathy. There was a piece on early English drama by John Skelton who wrote essays under the pseudonym Shirley. The Buddhist Andrew Wilson, famous for his travels in India, Tibet and China, contributed 'Infanti Perduti'. This explored the proposition that men of genius are ordained to suffer and that they "appear in the world in order painfully to give their lives for the world's great gain". In many cases Nicolson seems to have gone for unorthodox linking of writer to topic. Apart from the venerable Blackie all the writers were in their early thirties or (in Smith's case) younger: some like James Sime and Thomas Baynes were on the verge of making their names. At least three holders of relevant chairs (Professors Aytoun, Playfair and Laycock) were overlooked, or maybe they were not over-interested when they heard who the other contributors were. However, *Edinburgh Essays* was widely reviewed and several mention the stylistic confidence of Smith's contribution:

The [essay] is everyway a remarkable production, the prose of a poet who can write prose and think prose with a felicity of expression and steadiness of conception which mere versifiers would find hopelessly impossible. We detect the poet in his love of concrete images and in the cadences of rhythm, but even when the style is most elevated it is always *prose*...[118]

Apart from his contributions to the short-lived Glasgow Miscellany in 1853-4 this was Smith's first published prose. The stylistic novelty, considered as a precursor to his later essays and *Dreamthorp*, is obviously significant but there is also a core of polemic here that made his topic much more relevant to his contemporary readers:

Poetry has a value in right of its truth and beauty; it also has a value of an historical and illustrative nature; the first may decrease, and be less regarded, from the changing habits and feelings of society; the second increases necessarily as the ages roll. Every bygone period of the world has reflected itself in its contemporary poetry. History storms on with siege and battle and political crisis, but Poetry runs alongside supplementing History, smoothing its austerities, filling up its chasms and interstices with music, catching up the life of the streets and the current talk and humours of men, chronicling the emotions, the desires that inflame, the fears and spectres that daunt the heart.[119]

The previous year his co-contributor Blackie had delivered a public lecture inviting poets to return anew to ballad form as a kind of national poetic principle "to enrich the blood and brace the nerve of the people". The balladists (including Aytoun who was preparing his *The Ballads of Scotland* for publication the following year) had found an indirect way of continuing the backlash against the New Poets. They cited *Marmion* and *The Lay of the Last Minstrel*, forgetting that Scott had already reinvented the narrative qualities of the ballad before accepting the greater freedom of fiction. Now Blackie, Allingham, Macaulay and others were claiming this as the poetry of the people, what Blackie called in a later (1889) essay "the harmonious dealing with the facts of life". Blackie's essay never quite manages to place the ballad tradition in a realistic contemporary social setting. Smith, on the other hand, continually stresses this dimension. If its words were simple and unremarkable, the reason was that the traditional sung ballad had to be readily understood by a live audience. It had to be about some extraordinary event of far-reaching consequence, rather than "the common raid and the skirmish of rival clans". He concedes the power of the best ballads but refuses to admit their relevance to his century. For the ballad-writer and singer conditions were quite different and the ballad was a product of that environment:

> They sang to rude and uncultured men; their task was to touch their spirits and evoke their sympathies; and from their peculiar environment and training they exhibit an artlessness and simplicity which becomes at times the very perfection of style, and which – whatever other merits modern singer may possess – cannot be expected to appear in anything like the same degree in an artificial and fastidious age. In pathos they are supreme. Nothing can be placed beside them. The feeling is so direct and simple, and goes so to the heart. There is an element of helplessness in it which is overpowering. It is piteous as the complaint of a little child.[120]

At the end of February his mind had to switch from The Athenaeum's mud-slinging back to official College duties. Among the Secretary's more mundane tasks was dealing with student indiscipline. Now he was confronted by a full-scale riot. Young hot-heads clashed with the local branch of the Temperance Society who were proposing an American-style prohibition regime in Edinburgh. This was unpopular with medical students who packed a TS meeting in the Queen Street Halls and caused a major disturbance (whisky bottles were provocatively flourished and drained in the gallery). The meeting had to be abandoned. Afterwards Dr Laycock went into print to say that in his opinion a moderate alcohol intake was not generally harmful. The TS reacted by putting up inflammatory posters ("Dr Laycock Dissected") suggesting the Professor of Practical Medicine was not worthy of his post. The student body was aroused once more and on 27 February several hundred formed an ugly mob outside the TS premises in Bristo Place. Smith, in his College office nearby, must have calculated that they would get bored and disperse, but by the evening they were still there. The constables had to be summoned.

From newspaper accounts it is clear that the College authorities decided to approve a firm approach by the police. The Caledonian Mercury reported: "Opposite the Baptist Chapel the Secretary formed them into a line across the street and gave them instruction to clear the passage. This they at once effected, and with such power that one man who was knocked down complained that his ribs were broken by the batons."[121] For Smith the role of custodian of public order would hardly have been congenial. True, he had witnessed with distaste the 1848 Bread Riots in Glasgow, but his preference would probably be to wish it all away. On the other hand, there is no record of the Secretary being vilified for his part. Student life then was a basic affair especially for those living on the sack of oatmeal. A few knocks were probably considered part of the average undergraduate experience.

Around this time he and his fiancée Flora were house-hunting, since the date of the wedding was approaching fast. McLennan's flat was unsuitable for raising a family, so somewhere had to be found and furnished by mid-April. From this time there is a jaunty letter to Brisbane outlining the profit-sharing arrangement for his next book of poems:

I know I have acted very badly in not writing earlier; but for my sin I must plead in extenuation a multitude of good intentions and, fortunately, some little business. I have been arranging matters for a certain great event which has, I confess, knocked all minor things out of my head and I start today. The wedding takes place on Monday first. To you and to all other friends of my bachelorhood I wave farewell, and trust that in that other life I may know you all again.

I have but little news. I am in the sun again. This time my publishers are Macmillans of Cambridge, who gave me £250 for the book, the copyright to remain with me. When they make the same amount of profit, the profits are to be equally divided so that if the thing is at all a success in a commercial point of view I will gain more by it. I expect £50 or £100 from America also. The people who printed the 'Life Drama' have been written to on the subject, and I expect an answer soon. I think Macmillan's offer extremely liberal; and taking the time I have been in Edinburgh, in which the greater part of the work has been done, and the little windfalls of money for other literary work (I got £20 for an Edinburgh Essay on the Scottish Ballads) in conjunction with my salary at the College, there is a tolerable prospect that, with thriftiness and economy, Flora and I will be comfortable enough.[122]

In central Glasgow the "dark ranks of masts" noted on the Broomielaw quay in 'A Boy's Poem' were soon to be outnumbered by the brightly painted funnels of the West Coast paddle-steamer fleets. To get to Skye one needed first to reach Oban; until the 1880s (when the rail link to Callander was eventually completed) it was easiest and quickest to undertake the whole journey by sea. The alternative was to take a combination of train, mail coach and the Loch Lomond steamer to reach Inveraray, a full day's journey from Glasgow. The next day involved starting at 9am and posting along a wretched road round the head of Loch Awe, in the coach that Smith and Brisbane had used five years previously when Sandie had taken ill. This was another full day's journey.

In 1855 William Hutcheson's *SS Iona* was launched. The sleekest and most spacious of the Clyde greyhounds and with a length of more than 225 feet (68 metres), it could achieve a speed of 17.5 knots. Now it was possible to leave Bridge Wharf in Glasgow at 7am and be in Oban ten hours later, weather permitting. The journey still had to be broken by changing to the Crinan canal boat at Ardrishaig and taking the remainder of the journey from Crinan in another steamer. Heavy luggage had to be sent on ahead. Such was her speed the *Iona* was sold in 1862 to American Confederate agents who needed vessels to beat the blockade at the mouth of the Mississipi. Painted camouflage grey and stripped of her luxurious furnishings, she sailed down the Clyde for the Atlantic but was run down by another steamer in fog just off Gourock. (The second *Iona* fared little better, springing a leak and sinking in the Bristol Channel two years later.)

During April there were two sailings a week to Oban and one can imagine the wedding party setting off down the Clyde on a balmy Monday morning in mid-April, leaving behind the roar of the foundries and cotton mills, passing the clanging shipyards on either bank, eventually gaining the open countryside:

> At length the stream
> Broadened 'tween banks of daisies, and afar
> The shadows flew upon the sunny hills;
> And down the river, 'gainst the pale blue sky
> A town sat in its smoke. Look backward now!
> Distance has stilled three hundred thousand hearts,
> Drowned the loud roar of commerce, changed the proud
> Metropolis which turns all things to gold,
> To a thick vapour o'er which stands a staff
> With smoky pennon streaming in the air.[123]

The party consisted of McLennan, the best man, and Alexander Nicolson who was to act as registrar, as well as the betrothed couple and possibly Flora's Glasgow aunt. After a protein-rich breakfast a stroll on the deck was probably called for before finding ways of occupying the interval until noon when luncheon would be served. On the closed-in hurricane deck reading and letter-writing could be carried on in tranquillity, while those gentlemen wishing to light their pipes retired to the saloon deck. For Nicolson the journey would have been already familiar, undertaken many times in the ten years or so since he had left his native Skye. But even so, it would have been strange if his pulse had not quickened as the steamer left Crinan and, across the Sound of Jura, Mull was clearly seen. Beyond, to the north, lay the craggy silhouette of the Cuillins and Skye.

But arrival was still another twenty-four hours away. After staying overnight in Oban the party proceeded at a more leisurely pace on board the *SS Stork*, not a "swift steamer" rather more of a plodding but reliable workhorse carrying much-needed supplies as well as passengers. Consequently she stopped frequently: Craignure, Lochaline and Salen (on Mull), Arisaig, Armadale, Glenelg, Balmacarra, Kyle (the last stop before Skye on Loch Alsh), then Broadford, Portree "and any other place that may be agreed upon". If there was no pier there you had to arrange for a boat to come out and meet you. Such would have been the arrangement for disembarking at Isle Oronsay on the Sleat peninsula at the southern end of Skye, a small fishing village with a harbour and an inn. From here it was a four-mile journey by horse and cart across the peninsula, precipitous in the final stage down to Ord, their destination.

On a small bay Ord House overlooks Loch Eishort and the Cuillin range. Here Flora's family lived in truly feudal style, surrounded by impoverished crofters living in the foetid 'black houses'. They helped out with animal tending, getting in the hay crop or even domestic work in exchange for the landlord's bounty. In fact Charles Macdonald was only the 'tacksman' or tenant of around 180 acres (70 hectares) of the Macdonald's estates which were managed from Armadale castle. Since resigning his commission in the Glengarry Fencibles in his late forties (on grounds of ill-health) he had come to Ord and married a local girl, Isa McLeod, still in her twenties. Over nine years she had borne him eight children, of which Flora was the eldest.

For Skye Ord House was spacious, but then it had to accommodate (according to the 1851 Census) more than twenty people. The "village" of Ord consisted of nineteen other dwellings housing around ninety people, nearly half of them registered paupers. Here, surrounded by this host of dependents, the Macdonalds grazed around two thousand sheep. The children were all educated by a tutor, so throughout the Sleat peninsula up to Broadford they would have been regarded as gentry. Charles Macdonald originally came from the mainland; on his army half pay he could set up in style amid destitution that, in the years when the potato crop failed, must have reached starvation level. In his book about the island *A Summer in Skye* Smith confronted the anachronism that Ord presented and tried to put the best face on it. By 1857 Flora's father was nearly eighty, a man of fiery temper and ingrained prejudice. When he started compiling the book in the 1860s Smith probably assumed that the old man would be dead by the time it appeared, but it was not to be. He changes his father-in-law's name to McIan and fails to name the area of Skye where he reigned supreme. Even so, the description of Ord House still rings true today:

The farm which Mr McIan rented was, in comparison with many others in the island, of but moderate extent; and yet it skirted the sea-shore for a considerable distance, and comprised within itself many a rough hill, and many a green valley. The house was old-fashioned, was harled all over with lime, and contained a roomy porch over which ivies clustered, a dining room, a drawing room, a lot of bedrooms, and behind, built out from the house, an immense kitchen with a flagged floor and a huge fireplace. A whole colony of turf huts, with films of blue smoke issuing from each, were scattered along the shore, lending a sort of homely beauty to the wild picturesqueness. Beside the house, with a ruined summer-seat at one end, was a large carelessly-kept garden, surrounded by a high stone wall. McIan kept the key himself; and on the garden door were nailed ravens and other feathered malefactors in different stages of decay. Within a stone's throw from the porch were one or two barns, a stable, a wool-house, and other out-houses in which several of the servants slept. McIan was careful of social degree, and did not admit everyone to his dining room. He held his interviews with common people in the open air in front of the house. When a drover came for cattle, he dined solitarily in the porch, and the dishes were sent to him from McIan's table. The drover was a servant, consequently he could not sit at meat with my friend; he was more than a servant for the nonce, inasmuch as he was his master's representative, and consequently he could not be sent to the kitchen. The porch was therefore a kind of convenient middle place; neither too high nor too humble; it was in fact a sort of social purgatory.[124]

The marriage ceremony took place at Ord House on 21 April, the following Monday, probably in the dining room which has one of only two windows in the house overlooking the bay. Since this was a 'mixed' marriage it was a ceremony with a priest attending "according to the forms of the Catholic Church", a simplified nuptial service without mass being said. Flora must have previously obtained a dispensation from the Bishop of Aberdeen to marry a non-Catholic. It might have been granted on two grounds. One was known as *angustia loci*, referring to lack of suitable Catholic males on the island. The other grounds for appeal was her age of twenty-seven, considered advanced for a spinster. Either reason might have been allowed on "grounds of compassion", but the bride and groom would have had to agree to all children receiving a Catholic education.

Naturally the groom and his two attendants slept elsewhere before the wedding day, perhaps at the Isle Oronsay inn, now a well-appointed hotel with its own whisky label. From the tone of his letter to Brisbane it is clear that Smith considered the marriage partnership to be all-important and likely to exclude other friendships. To outsiders it must have seemed a marriage made in heaven, an almost fairytale romance of a young poet and a descendant of Bonnie Prince Charlie's Flora, exchanging their vows in a remote place in the midst of loch and mountain.

An odd, almost chilling footnote to the nuptials is provided by Smith's poem 'The Night Before the Wedding' which was first printed in the National Magazine earlier that year. When it was included in *City Poems* it was split into two, so it presents a rare opportunity to study Smith's method of wholesale revision.

In *City Poems* the explanatory subtitle 'Ten years after' makes clear that the narrator looks back, perhaps as a widower, on the early raptures of the marriage which now remain a memory only. This might have seemed to friends a strange line of thought to be taking in the months leading up to his wedding day:

> The man who knew, while he was young,
> Some soft soul-subduing air
> Weeps when again he hears it sung,
> Although 'tis only half so fair.
> So love I thee, and love is sweet,
> (My Florence, 'tis the cruel truth),
> Because it can to age repeat
> That long-lost passion of my youth.[125]

Odder still was the prophetic accuracy in this and in other poems hinting at his own death. It was, in fact, almost exactly ten years from the writing of 'The Change' (the second part of the original poem) to the sudden end of their marriage. But for the two newly-weds on that spring day the future could have looked nothing but fair. They took the steamer back to Oban the next day, where they enjoyed a brief honeymoon before the new husband returned to his Secretarial duties in Edinburgh.

Soon after returning to Edinburgh they moved into a rented house just off Gilmore Place, near the Lochrin basin of the Union Canal. The location, although hardly desirable in a middle-class sense, had some attractions, not least of which was proximity to open countryside. Gilmore Place then ended as a cul-de-sac and there were fields stretching from the canal bank all the way round to Gillespie's Hospital for Pensioners. Further south, across more green fields, lay the village of Morningside, an area now covered by later Victorian tenements and a brewery. To reach the College buildings every morning the Secretary needed to walk across Bruntsfield Links and over the Meadows, already laid out with formal, tree-lined walkways. The row of six houses had been recently erected as a letting proposition by Miss Bow who also occupied one. On either side of the Smiths at no.4 Gillespie Place were a master plumber (employing six men and five boys) and a shoemaker employed by the NB Rubber Company. The houses were small, with two upstairs bedrooms and stone-flagged kitchen extensions. Because of the proximity of the Sisters of the Poor convent there was no space for gardens to the rear (occupied by the priest's house with a long garden). So the developer resorted to providing five garden plots across the lane opposite the front doors. As summer came it must have seemed a pleasantly bucolic setting to the newlyweds, although the Lochrin basin with its ropeworks and slaughterhouse not far away must have provided some unwelcome background noise. Furnishing would need to be purchased, and with a year's rent to be found in advance, not much of the Macmillan's £250 would have been left in the bank. One of the first items Flora would have hung on the wall of the drawing room was a portrait of her husband done in oils the previous year by James Archer, probably a wedding present from her. With a studio in York Place Archer was a fashionable portraitist who had a fondness for literary figures. In 1852 he had done a series of remarkable chalk drawings of De Quincey and his daughters, followed by a portrait of Professor Aytoun a few years later in the same medium.

The portrait (now in the Scottish National Portrait Gallery[126]) shows regular youthful features above a Ruskin-style beard. The left ¾ - profile conceals the squinty right eye but manages to emphasise the square forehead and the straight nose. By pointing the eye upwards Archer has tried to find an expression denoting inspiration. However, the overwhelming impression is of steadiness. The contrast with the farouche look of the full-face *carte de visite* photo taken ten years earlier (for Hugh Macdonald) could not have been greater. The new-look Alexander Smith had the well-scrubbed look of an eager young man with ambition and prospects.

By July the College was closed up until early October. The Secretary's duties were officially non-existent during those three months although there must have always been accounts, reports and matriculation minutiae for Smith to deal with. However, it was the couple's habit from 1858 onwards to spend the whole of August at Ord House, a place where there was absolutely no chance of any unfinished business finding its way to his door. In 1857 they went instead to the Trossachs, following the route up Loch Venachar, Loch Achray to Loch Katrine by pony and trap, as outlined in the second chapter of *A Summer in Skye*, then by the *P.S. Rob Roy* to Stronachlachar. From here a stiff walk might have taken them across to Inversnaid on Loch Lomond:

The aspect of the country now has changed. The hills around are bare and sterile, brown streams gurgle down their fissures, the long yellow ribbon of road runs away before you, disappearing out of sight sometimes, and reappearing afar. You pass a turf hut and your nostrils are invaded by a waft of peat reek which sets you coughing and brings the tears into your eyes; and the juvenile natives eye you askance, and wear the airiest form of the national attire.[127]

After returning from Callander they seem to have gone straight over to the west to stay at Strone or Kilmun on the Holy Loch near Dunoon. Being barely an hour away from Glasgow, by steamer and train, this was a favourite summer retreat for well-off families and the area was awash with substantial holiday villas, boat-houses and large gardens. From here the Cotton Bags could work a shorter than usual week in the city during the summer months, rejoining their waiting families on the pier head by 7pm on a Friday if the paddle steamers at Greenock made a quick getaway.

The need to keep expenses to a minimum after the cost of furnishing Gillespie Place may have been one reason why they did not go to Skye this year. *City Poems* was also due out in mid-August. As revealed in the letter to Brisbane, Smith's second book was published by Macmillan & Co. *A Life-Drama* had amongst its fervent admirers Alexander Macmillan, the younger of the two brothers behind the publishing firm set up by Daniel in 1843. The family came from Arran, but they moved to a farm in Ayrshire where the family increased to fourteen members. Despite their father's early death somehow the brothers got themselves educated and Daniel became a power in the bookselling trade in Cambridge. Alexander had a varied career prior to becoming a publisher, including a stint before the mast and working in a Glasgow chemist's shop. Then he joined his elder brother in his Cambridge digs and made up for gaps in his literary education. The story is that Daniel would read passages of Carlyle out loud every morning as they got dressed and had breakfast.

After the reception given to *A Life-Drama* in 1853 the poet must have thought it advisable to be in Edinburgh to ride the critical wave when it broke for *City Poems*. In fact, the response was more muted, perhaps proof that the plagiarism charges had made Smith too much of a hot potato for some reviewers. In fact, this collection contained what was to become Smith's best-known poem 'Glasgow' (see Appendix) and a long partly autobiographical narrative poem ('A Boy's Poem') that showed how far he had developed in poetic technique and mastery of material in the intervening period. But few seemed able to detect this. Even sympathetic reviewers expected more impact, more raw sensation perhaps. The Leader's reviewer put it down to lack of substance:

A sense of vagueness fatal to the effect of a story, and giving the whole volume an unfinished air, creates the disappointment we have alluded to. But on turning back to each of these poems we are impressed with the sense of exquisite power in the musical utterance of emotion, and of delicate felicity in the use of language.[128]

It was as if Smith had overnight turned miniaturist, perhaps an inevitable reaction after the stylistic histrionics of *A Life-Drama*. But a new control in several of the pieces could certainly be perceived even from a cursory reading, and 'Glasgow' proves that he could write a poem that has staying power. No critic, however, seems to have picked up on the underlying rationale of this very varied collection. Smith was consciously trying to pare down his diction and concentrate on everyday subject matter. It was a new direction already signalled in his article on Cowper for the *Encyclopaedia Britannica* ("His muse does not sit apart in sublime seclusion...His blank verse makes no pretensions to majesty; it is colloquial sometimes in its bareness, yet in its artless flow is ever delightful.") There are, however, dangers to this close-focus approach, the writing sometimes veering perilously close to prose chopped into lines to resemble verse. This example (from the opening to 'Horton') is rescued by the three-line image of the moonlight bathing the streets below:

> The other night I lay within my bed,
> Watching my dying fire: it mouldered out.
> I listened to the strange nocturnal cries:
> A ballad-singer 'neath my window stood,
> And sang hoarse songs; she went away, and then
> An oyster-man came crying through the streets;
> And straight, as if I stood on dusky shores,
> I saw the tremulous silver of the sea
> Set to some coast beneath the mighty moon.
> He passed into the silence. Wafts of song
> From arm-linked youths, as they meandered home,
> Came to my ears; the town grew still; and then
> Just when my soul was sinking into dream,
> Alarm of "Fire!" ran through the startled street,
> And windows were thrown up as it went past. [129]

In other poems, notably 'Squire Maurice', there are lines of uninspired dialogue that shift uneasily from self-conscious to banal. This is a monologue (or rather two monologues) with more than a nod to Browning's *Men and Women* which had appeared in 1855. Clearly the central character, writing in a letter to his brother for advice, is vacillating and cowardly so Smith wrote his lines in what he considered an appropriately evasive style. But the effect is to lower a thick veil over the reader's perception of him. Unlike Browning, who points his verse with irony that betrays the narrator's innermost thoughts, here we cannot begin to fathom what the intended effect might be.

City Poems contains three monologue poems and none of them, on the face of it, makes reference to the urban experience. Most had already appeared in periodicals, so reviewers were confused and maybe resentful. One of the more perceptive was W.C.Roscoe in the National Review:

> Every man who is capable of admiring [Nature] knows that there must arise some harmony between his own mind and the scene he gazes at before he can appreciate and thoroughly enjoy it... but Alexander Smith has no idea whatever of harmonising the different elements of his poetry. His is a fragmentary genius. His poems are a mass of little glimpses of scenery, and of similes heaped together like gravel that does not bind.[130]

He had previously been lambasted for sacrificing sense to sound, and for writing too much like Keats. Surely the title of the new collection should have given the reviewers some clue to what Smith was about. Just because he appreciated Nature (his childhood in semi-rural Renfrewshire, the excursions with Brisbane, evening walks with Hugh Macdonald, and now his first experience of the landscape of Skye) does not mean he saw himself as a nature poet. *City Poems* warns us as readers that the viewpoint will be that of a writer whose sensibilities are far from pristine and cloistered. Romantic angst was by then a little *passé*. Nature may contain great beauty, but it is not the only source for those deep-seated emotions that beauty evokes in humans: captivation of the senses, feelings of vulnerability, awe and not a little fear. Previously in poetry the natural and the man-made were placed in telling contrast, but now as more and more people grew up entirely in cities why should this continue to be so? A new generation, schooled in viewing Nature through the poet's eyes, was now turning its own on the urban environment being created. Not everything was ugly, oppressive and toxic.

It is instructive to contrast what Smith attempted in his first two books of poetry with some earlier and later poets. In Keats' sonnets there is occasional reference to the urban background that was so much part of his life as an apprentice surgeon. The city was something unhealthy and destructive (both to physical health and poetic sensibility) from which escape was essential:

> O Solitude, if I must with thee dwell
> Let it not be among the jumbled heap
> Of murky buildings; climb with me the steep, -
> Nature's observatory – hence the dell
> Its flowery slopes, its river's crystal swell,
> May seem a span;

Keats here is deep in a late Romantic convention that puts cities and countryside at opposite ends of the spectrum, the inhabitants of each doomed to extreme and often painful sensations every time they stray out of their allotted realm. For Wordsworth and Coleridge seeking healing in Nature was still a novelty. Even for Blake the appalling effects of rapid urbanisation must have been a shock and the "mind-forged manacles" a guarantee of blighted generations to come. But by the late 1870s, when G.M.Hopkins was posted to Jesuit missions in Lancashire, Liverpool and (briefly) Glasgow, poets were beginning to overcome the conventional revulsion and find fit subject matter in cities. Not so poor Hopkins who, whilst giving disapproving sermons on drunkenness ("they gabble and blur their words, they stagger and fall and deal themselves dishonourable wounds…"), did not attempt to create poetry out of crowded humanity. On a frosty morning in Liverpool, for instance, he noticed that the spit on the pavements was star-shaped, but such an arresting image failed to make it into his poems.[131]

Smith also has neo-Wordsworthian moments, most notably in the semi-autobiographical 'A Boy's Poem'. The bulk of the poem is a recollection of adolescent years in a city, retold for the benefit of a companion now living abroad. Here he recalls a group of friends leaving the city to spend a few days on an island:

> I and my cousins started in the morn
> To wander o'er the mountains and the moors
> How different from the hot and stony streets!
> The dark red springy turf was 'neath our feet,
> Our walls the blue horizon, and our roof
> The boundless sky; a perfect summer-day
> We walked 'mid unaccustomed sights and sounds;
> Firm apparitions of the elements
> That lived a moment on the air, then passed
> To the eternal world of memory. [132]

Although Smith luxuriates in these sensations of Nature, for a city poet he has added power to strike at the subconscious. Here, as in other passages, Smith juxtaposes light and shade to show how awareness of one adds piquancy to experiencing the other:

> The common sunshine in the common fields,
> The runnel by the road, the clouds that grow
> Out of the blue abysses of the air,
> Do not, as in my earlier days, oppress
> Me with their beauty: for the grief that dims
> The eye and cheek both touched them too and made
> Them dearer to me, being more akin.
> Death weaves the subtle mystery of joy:

> He gives a trembling preciousness to love,
> Makes stern eyes dim above a sleeping face
> Half-hidden in its cloud of golden curls.
> Death is a greater poet far than Love;
> The summer light is sweeter for his shade.[133]

For the city poet, says Smith, cities must always retain a fatal fascination, grimy surfaces suddenly transforming themselves into strident colour in extremes of light and shade. Unlike Nature, the urban scene is never still, never predictable; the chances of being caught unawares and unprepared for a revelation of beauty only make its perception the keener:

> Next morn the bells awoke me to my toil,
> And what a pageant of divinest sights
> Passed by me on my daily round of life !
> I bore a message, and upon my way
> The streets were swept by the impetuous rain,
> The lightning fluttered in my dazzled eyes,
> And thunder like a sea broke overhead.
> A fleece of thunder hung before the sun
> With a wild blazing fringe, while scattered shreds
> Burned on the marble sky. Black strings of ships
> Sat on the angry mirror of the stream
> Keen with the splendour, till the gusty rain
> Drowned the red sunset and the winds were loud.[134]

Perhaps Smith is sometimes content simply to catalogue brilliant effects, and there is not always a sufficient accumulation towards a final composite image. Maybe it was this shortcoming that was behind Coventry Patmore's extraordinary dismissal in the Saturday Review:

He shows himself to us in his poems as sensitive and melancholy – keenly alive to and almost absolutely dominated by the impressions of external circumstances and objects – given to pampering rather than to controlling his own sensations, with a mind wholly and constantly turned inward on itself, and therefore utterly destitute of creative and dramatic power."[135]

In The Athenaeum Chorley's review saw little merit in the poet's new concerns ("For charwomen – in England, far from attractive society – Mr Smith exhibits a strange preference."). He quoted the whole of 'Barbara', however, before returning to his well-worn theme: "the mutilated property of other bards". 'Barbara' was written several years earlier, according to Brisbane, and it is here incorporated into 'Horton', an attempt to provide a poetic narrative with a (semi-autobiographical) central character seen from different perspectives. Horton is someone of obvious natural gifts and sensibility who never manages to fulfil his potential. After the death of Barbara he plunges into a life of dissipation with the intention of escaping the burden of others' high expectations. This kind of character would be only too familiar to Victorian readers from the mould of the typical flawed Shakespearian tragic hero:

> The heavens seem
> To mar as wilfully their creature man,
> As one who limns a face, on which the world
> Could stand at gaze cheated of pain and time;
> Then lets, before the smiling hues are dry,
> His careless sleeve slur all as off he goes.
> Nature, who makes the perfect rose and bird,
> Has never made the full and perfect man.
> In every worthiness there is a Law,
> That, like a crack across a mirror's face,
> Impairs its value[136]

The year which had promised so much ended in disillusionment. *City Poems* was reprinted, but its sales hardly justified Macmillan's initial enthusiasm. For example, it was outshone by Massey's *Craigcrook Castle*, containing the popular ballad 'The Mother's Idol Broken'. Those charges of plagiarism, although ably rebutted, had been a severe irritation. Although he dismissed it all as "a ginger-beer bottle burst", Smith must have sensed the critical tide was now running strongly against him. Arnold was about to take the Chair of Poetry at Oxford. Balladists such as Aytoun and Blackie had published during the year to acclaim. The other Spasmodics were silent or (like Massey) diverted into more acceptable forms of literary production. Lacking actual Crimean experience Smith now faced the literary equivalent – establishment snipers on higher ground – more or less alone.

On the plus side he was a married man; this provided the steady emotional base he needed. But it also required a strong nerve to embark upon a new major poem that would occupy him for several years. There was no guarantee that he would even find a publisher. And even then, what kind of financial return would it provide? From whatever source, hard on the heels of skulduggery and disappointment, Smith now found the necessary vigour to write his longest and most ambitious work of poetry.

Chapter 8:
1858-61

Oh, thou art fairer than an Indian morn,
Seated in her sheen palace of the east.
Thy faintest smile out-prices the swelled wombs
Of fleets, rich glutted, toiling wearily
To vomit all their wealth on English strands.
('A Life-Drama' sc.4)

SIR WALTER SCOTT HAD DIED in 1832 after reinventing Scottish history. He had by his single-mindedness won for Edinburgh a position of significance in contemporary European literature, and for the next fifty years or so the city (and by implication Scotland) was bathed in exhausted after-glow. Endless editions of the Waverley novels poured from the presses, but any attempt to rival the Wizard of the North was regarded as a kind of impudence. Scotland had become to all literary intents Scottland. Historical fiction was a burnt-out case until Stevenson found a new angle on the genre, and at his heels came the Kailyard School, principally S.R.Crockett and Ian McLaren. But in the meantime those who might have earlier tried historical fiction looked for an easier living by contributing to magazines and periodicals in which Edinburgh, and to a lesser extent Glasgow, was abundant. At ten shillings a page a ready pen could raise a low basic wage to something closer to comfort as well as raising self-esteem. But periodical writing rarely made for ambitious literature. Smith wrote of it "What blazes a sun at Edinburgh would, if transported to London, not infrequently become a farthing candle."[137]

Scott's spectre was hard to exorcise from a city still bristling with familiar backdrops to scenes from his novels. Atmospheric photographs taken in the 1850s by Thomas Keith and William Donaldson Clark show the old wynds snaking away at either side of a steeply descending High Street. Brown Square stood, somewhat decayed since it featured in *Redgauntlet*, but still the recognisable milieu for a close-knit politico-legal fraternity. Other prints show the spacious streets of the ambitious New Town, begun during the Enlightenment period, still under construction during Scott's lifetime and only just completed by the mid-century. Hither the Victorian aristocracy and the burgeoning professional classes had migrated from the Old Town, some still displaying some eighteenth-century characteristics: a strong Scots accent with some French lexis, the habit of taking dinner late into the evening, a preference for snuff rather than pipe smoking, and a taste for claret over whisky. Sedan chairs were still a common sight into the 1840s as well as knee breeches and powdered wigs. It was into the heart of this self-conscious world of "douce" Edinburgh society that Alexander and Flora Smith moved in 1858, setting up in a three-room basement owned by their friend John Ferguson McLennan at 6 Northumberland Place. McLennan had qualified as an advocate (Scottish term for barrister) in January 1857 but he seems to have found little court work.

He and Smith had shared a flat in India Street before the marriage. With the year's lease on Gillespie Street coming up, the couple accepted McLennan's invitation to occupy the lower basement area. This had a separate entrance via a flight of steep steps down directly from the pavement. Economy can be the only possible explanation for the move, since they were now living in far less space with no garden, being overshadowed by a wall bounding the back gardens of Abercrombie Place. In addition, being in the basement of an early nineteenth-century building, the flat was probably damp. It was here that their first child Flora was born in March 1858. They stayed for the best part of three years with increasing unwillingness, but at a peppercorn rent. To Flora Macdonald particularly after Ord an inner city basement must have been most uncongenial.

The Smiths lived at the much less fashionable end of Northumberland Street. Further west were the residences of men like the painter John Faed, sculptor Alexander Brodie and physician George Keith, brother to the pioneer photographer Thomas. In nearby Fettes Row lived Professor Aytoun who entertained regularly with his wife Emily. After a long illness she died early in 1859 and Aytoun was left alone in the 3-storey house. One evening shortly afterwards he called at 6 Northumberland Place with a brown paper parcel under his arm, containing a complete silverplate dinner service which he thought might prove useful to the Smiths.[138] By Smith's account the "silky-voiced man" could be magnanimous; he apparently had a soft spot for Flora, often addressing her as Chieftainess.

The tenements at the east end of Northumberland Place, six floors high and situated on a peculiar Z-shaped junction of streets, would have been only too reminiscent of those early years in Charlotte Street. However fine it seemed on paper, the location was far from being sought after. A few yards to the east stood an inn, with a public weighing machine for measuring the loads of horse-drawn carts. Next to it was a tenement whose overcrowding would not have been out of place in Bridgeton. The 1861 Census records that 105 people lived at number 2 in eighteen flats, occupations including coachman, ostler, foundry labourer, dairyman and street porter. On Saturday nights especially it must have been a slice of Old Town life inserted behind a late Georgian façade. Meanwhile at number 6, as the Smiths strove to protect their baby daughter from the all too often fatal diseases of childhood, up above them the inquisitive mind of McLennan was probing the mating rituals of aboriginal tribes. It was he who devised the bride-catching theory, based on the common practice of female infanticide which led to the need to take wives from other tribes. He is probably referred to in the mysterious postscript to a letter from D.G.Rossetti to Allingham of January 31 1857. This was just as the plagiarism charges were being made (and rebutted on Smith's behalf) in the Athenaeum:

Some people say here you wrote A.S. Of course I have undeceived some, <u>and did not spread the report.</u> I believe *(entre nous)* Maclennan did, being a great friend of Smith.[139]

McLennan was one of that coterie of literary lawyers who formed the mainstay of the Raleigh Club. As we have seen, Smith joined as soon as he came to Edinburgh in 1854. Its relaxed atmosphere (pungent with pipe smoke) was evidently congenial. It was probably to some Raleigh members he began circulating early drafts of a long epic poem on the introduction of Christianity into Northumbria during the time of the Seven Kingdoms, after the Roman occupation. Another member was John Skelton, also a lawyer, who contributed critical essays under the protective pseudonym 'Shirley'. A sparkling conversationalist and a brilliant advocate, he possessed considerable administrative gifts which later led to various state posts and a knighthood. Skelton's article in Fraser's Magazine ('Northern Lights', January 1858) had reviewed Smith's first two collections, persuasively demolishing the plagiarism charges but advising the poet to "cease from writing dramatic and to write didactic poems in their place." In one sense this was just what Smith was doing with his new epic *Edwin of Deira*. In his review of it in the North British Review Skelton once again has to defend Smith from charges of imitation, this time of *Idylls of the King*. He puts on record what he knew from personal observation: "the fact that Mr Smith had planned and well-nigh executed his poem before the appearance of the Laureate's masterpiece..."[140]

By 1858 at the latest, then, Smith was already engrossed in the new epic, no doubt finding useful source material in the College and the nearby Advocates' Library before beginning to write. According to Pat Alexander it was to be the labour of nearly four years, undertaken at a time when his official duties greatly increased due to legislative reform of all Scottish universities. The working day, from 10 to 4, was by now less than ever a sinecure as extra responsibilities crowded in upon the Secretary. A large part of this can be laid at the door of Scottish university reform which culminated in the 1858 Act. The intention was to raise the standard of teaching and by implication the status of a degree awarded by each of the five Scottish Universities (up until 1858 only strictly speaking Colleges). With insufficient space here to list the changes to university constitutions, financing and academic syllabuses, it is still important to note the introduction of the General Council which gave each institution, now freed from the purse strings of the Town Council, wide-ranging powers and autonomy in its own affairs.

Before 1858 few students bothered to incur the extra expense of graduating: for example, just twelve Edinburgh MAs were awarded in 1856 out of nearly 800 qualifying students. After the Act the proportion of graduates increased rapidly. This can be partly ascribed to the peculiar voting rights that Scottish graduates have on the General Council, along with the Senatus Academicus, the University Court (a watchdog to regulate the Senatus), the other professors and the University Chancellor (elected by the General Council for life). The Council provided a system of constitutional checks and balances by which the various parts of each university are represented. It was remarkably democratic for its time, providing staff and students with the chance to put forward and elect a Rector every three years, a right still jealously guarded. Although no longer the main funder of the new University, Edinburgh Town Council (Smith's current employer) was still able to establish its influence through a unique Court of Curators where they had the casting vote. One might have thought that these radical changes would have meant the end of the Secretary's current role. But Smith was now taken on as Registrar and Secretary to the General Council, as well as continuing his duties with matriculation and other student affairs. For this the salary was raised to £200 per annum, a point at which (according to domestic economy pundits of the time) a thrifty household could properly engage two living-in servants. They would have been ill-advised, however, to incur the expense of running their own carriage.

The Act did not come into force until the following October, and in the intervening months a Commission was set up to see that the changes were carried out as programmed. From then on the Secretary may well have acted as something of a messenger between the University Act commissioners and the Town Council on points of practical detail. Then Principal Lee died early in 1859, so the last piece of College business undertaken by the Town Council was the choice of Sir David Brewster as the first Principal under the new constitution. He was also the first in the Edinburgh College's history who was not an ordained minister of the church. A greater contrast to Dr John Lee (described by a visitor an "an old wife") could scarcely be imagined. Whereas Lee hardly set pen to paper, Brewster had published his first scientific paper in his early twenties and went on to produce three hundred more, usually on various branches of optics. He became editor of numerous scientific journals, a founding spirit of the British Association and an adviser to the Great Exhibition. When he came to Edinburgh he was at the height of his fame, having recently demonstrated to sceptical colleagues the efficiency of polyzonal lenses in producing a lighthouse beam. Through a genius for devising appropriate experiments rather than for abstract deductions, he improved the efficiency of the telescope and invented the stereoscope as well as the kaleidoscope. Treatises were written on all these. What Smith thought of this human dynamo he never recorded.

There was hardly time, though, to reflect on this. In late October 1859 the first meeting of the General Council, numbering more than a thousand souls, took place in the Music Hall and elected Lord Brougham as Chancellor. A fortnight later polling was conducted among the students to elect a Rector. Gladstone, at the time a Whig, was elected for the first of two three-year terms. From the outset he enjoyed laying down the law on how the new Constitution should operate. Smith seems to have been less than over-awed by the arrival of these political superstars. His critical essay in The Argosy in 1866 recalls that one of Gladstone's rectorials lasted for nearly three hours:

His addresses were carefully composed beforehand, and if recited as only Mr Gladstone could recite them, they were recitations all the same. On the occasions referred to he was master of the situation just as a preacher is on Sundays. There was no interruption to chafe, no opposition to excite, no heat of debate to energise and spur the intellect to an activity more than normal. Mr Gladstone, speaking to the Metropolitan Scottish University about the old Greek poets and Mr Gladstone on a grand field night in the Commons, carrying fire and terror into the ranks of the Opposition, are conceivably very different. There is the same difference between rhetoric hot and rhetoric cold as between the red-flowing lava and porous pumice-stone.[141]

In between his official duties and the evenings spent on his Northumbrian epic Smith incredibly appears to have found time to do literary hackwork as well. He had already researched and written literary biographies for *Britannica*. Now he was to be extensively occupied writing shorter pieces for the new *Chambers Encyclopaedia*. This was a ten-year project by the Chambers brothers, to create a whole encyclopaedia in 520 weekly parts at a penny ha'penny each. The Caledonian Mercury described it as "a library in itself, wondrously full and thoroughly reliable." The first payment ledger for contributors exists, showing that in 1859 Smith received £14 for three pilot articles on Matthew Arnold, Professor Aytoun and P.J.Bailey.[142] By comparison his friend Maclennan was paid less than a pound for nearly three thousand lines. The following year, however, the Chambers brothers seem to have realised their mistake and Smith was paid only four guineas for 625 lines. This work could have hardly been rewarding in any sense, but he made a good job of boiling down a mass of biographical and critical material into very readable articles. His assessment of Arnold is probably the most interesting, showing that he could be fair towards a poet for whom he probably had little taste:

The strain of his mind is calm and thoughtful; his style is the reverse of florid; deep culture and a certain severity of taste has submerged every tendency to a gay or a passionate exuberance. As a poet he has little sympathy with the present; his Muse has hitherto delighted in the remoteness and repose of the Ancient World.

Smith must have been staggered by the almost universal warmth of the critical reception that greeted *Edwin of Deira* in August 1861. The Dublin University Journal, which had enjoyed sneering at his first two books, welcomed the new work with a sigh of relief. Its review went wildly over the top:

Improving on the partial success of his former essays [attempts, i.e. *Poems* and *City Poems*] he has written the best epic poem which the age of Tennyson, Longfellow and Mrs Browning has yet seen.... A noble subject here meets with noble treatment, and the author's skill lures on the reader from page to page, as it were by the lightest of silken cords.[143]

Others were more severe, but most of the metropolitan weekly periodicals (including The Athenaeum, The Spectator and The Saturday Post), which previously agreed that there was no more room on a pedestal that already supported Tennyson, the Brownings and Arnold, now tossed him critical scraps. The Saturday Review approached enthusiasm: "at times he rises so near the level of a first-class poet that on every new occasion of his coming before us we are tempted to anticipate something really excellent and lasting from his pen."[144] In The Athenaeum Gerald Massey applauded the ex-Spasmodic for coming to his senses:

By the aid of history, he has got out of a morbid consciousness of self, and, by looking outwardly on the realities of life, has seen more than he would have perceived by continually looking within.[145]

The story of *Edwin of Deira* follows more or less the narrative given by Bede in his *History* (Book II Chs 9-14). Hume's *History of England* has the succinct version:

Adelfrid, king of Bernicia, having married Acca, the daughter of Aella, king of Deira, and expelled her infant brother Edwin, had united all the counties north of Humber into one monarchy and acquired a great ascendant in the heptarchy: he also spread the terror of the Saxon arms to the neighbouring people; and by his victories over the Scots and Picts, as well as the Welch, extended on all sides the bounds of his dominions... Notwithstanding Adelfrid's success in war, he lived in inquietude on account of young Edwin whom he had unjustly dispossessed of the crown of Deira. This prince, now grown to man's estate, wandered from place to place in continual danger from the attempts of Adelfrid, and received at last protection in the court of Redwald, king of the East Angles, where his engaging and gallant deportment procured him general esteem and affection. Redwald, however, was strongly solicited by the king of Northumberland to kill or deliver up his guest: rich presents were promised him if he would comply, and war denounced against him in case of refusal.

After rejecting several messages of this kind, his generosity began to yield to the motives of interest; and he retained the last ambassador till he should come to a resolution in a case of such importance. Edwin, informed of his friend's perplexity, was yet determined at all hazards to remain in East Anglia and thought that, if the protection of that court failed him, it were better to die than to prolong a life so much exposed to the persecutions of his powerful rival. This confidence in Redwald's honour and friendship, with his other accomplishments, engaged the queen on his side; and she effectually represented to her husband the infamy of delivering up to certain destruction their royal guest who had fled to them for protection against his cruel and jealous enemies.

The result was that Redwald was persuaded to attack and defeat Adelfrid then hand the throne of Northumbria (or Deira) to Edwin who became a model monarch and, through Paulinus bishop of York, spread Christianity through the kingdom. In 627 AD there was a mass conversion by missionaries steeped in the Augustinian monastic tradition. Edinburgh, the northernmost settlement of Northumbria, was named after Edwin.

Smith made a few alterations to the Bede narrative, introducing a touch of Hamlet by making Edwin's mother marry Adelfrid (Ethelbert in the poem), and Edwin to woo Redwald's daughter Bertha. Edwin was killed in 633 and thirty years later the Roman Church was in the ascendant, a situation formalised by the Synod of Whitby.

As Masson's review in Macmillan's suggested, the narration flags in the last two parts when Edwin ascends the throne, marries Bertha, is wounded by an assassin after he has defeated a band of robber brigands, then is converted by Paulinus. In the descriptions of feasting, hunting and fighting the poetry is remarkable for its figurative power:

> So all the land around the Palace glowed
> With upward-striking fires when fell the night,
> And shapes of men went flitting through the glare,
> Gigantic. From the ruddy distance came
> The hum of thousands, and steed neighed to steed:
> The minstrels sang great battles to the lords,
> But, in his hand the reins of all the host,
> The Prince, with Redwald, Regner and the rest,
> Sat half the night discoursing, grave and sad,
> For in the presence of the war each heart
> Was clear and naked as a sword unsheathed.
> The minstrels ceased, the Palace lights burned low,
> The circle round the King arose at last.
> Beside a thousand fires the army slept,
> Except the watcher leaning on his spear,
> Or when, affrighted by a falling brand,
> A war-horse reared and snorted at the stake.[146]

There were some anachronisms in this passage, as one critic pointed out. Plate armour and brass trumpets did not yet exist in Anglo-Saxon times, and the rearing "war-horse" would have been no larger than an Exmoor pony. More significantly critics pointed to the four-stressed line of *Edwin* having metrical similarities to Tennyson's *Idylls of the King*, the first four books of which had appeared two years previously. This is not the place for detailed metrical analysis. But it is reasonable to assert that Smith's verse has a distinctive fingerprint: the mid-line caesura and the clustering together of stressed syllables in one half of the line owe more to Shakespeare than Tennyson's evenly-paced lines. By the end of the nineteenth century the verse epic was out of favour and only the most devoted mid-Victorian specialist would now work their way through *Edwin*. But in the 1860s it was still the fashion (ideal for reading in domestic settings after dinner by the new gas lighting) and Smith must have been expecting a reasonable sale.

The rewards of four years' graft were, however, meagre. On the basis of a profit-sharing agreement with his publisher Macmillan he ended up with precisely £15 five shillings and threepence. One possible reason was the loss of the American market. Although an edition was shipped to Ticknor and Fields in Boston, anti-English feeling was high after the *HMS Trent* affair. And with the outbreak of the Civil War no copies could be distributed beyond the blockade. Macmillan's initial print-run barely covered costs, it appears, but it was reprinted within a few months. The book also contained two Skye poems – the anthologised 'Blaavin' (with its reference to the birth of daughter Flora) and the legend of 'Torquil and Oona' which had been first printed in *Macmillan's* the previous November. However sales were sluggish, possibly because the reading public was suffering from indigestion. They had swallowed Arnold's *Sohrab and Rustum*, they had struggled through *Aurora Leigh*, they had tapped their fingers to Longfellow and they had swooned to the Arthurian moods of Tennyson. For the time being they had probably had enough. Tennyson sensibly waited ten years before publishing the second part *of Idylls of the King*.

Around this time Smith's literary disappointment was compounded by the deaths of two writers who had influenced him. First, in December 1859, was De Quincey, still occupying the garret just behind the New College complex. His daughters lived in much more comfort out at Polton, a good hour's walk to the south of the city, but one that he regularly completed often at night. Then, in March the following year, Hugh Macdonald died from gastric fever at the age of forty-three. Smith and he had much in common, both having Highland ancestry despite being brought up in Glasgow's east end. Both were also largely self-taught writers. That said, Macdonald's lyrics were lightweight, at their best diluted Burns. Smith's affectionate memoir (in Macmillan's the next year) stressed the perhaps uncongenial environment in which they both strove to be poets:

And then, to complete a poetic education, there was Glasgow herself – noble river and dark groves of masts, begirt by miles of stony streets; grand cathedral, filled once with popish shrines and rolling incense, on one side of the ravine and on the other the statue of John Knox, impeaching it with outstretched arm that clasps a Bible. And ever as the darkness came, the district north-east and south of the city was filled with shifting glare and gloom of furnace fires; instead of night and its privacy the keen splendour of towering flame brought to the inhabitants of the eastern streets a fluctuating scarlet day, piercing nook and cranny more searchingly than any sunlight.[147]

The echoes of 'Glasgow' are unmistakable here. The imagery – the stone-paved streets, the ships at the quayside and the light from the foundry fires – is common to both, but the effect is more sensational in prose, the contrasts more forced. He also wrote another tribute for the Paisley & Renfrewshire Gazette (24 March 1860) which reveals the existence of the obituary pact that he made with Macdonald before parting for Edinburgh. They both took biographical notes on the other and, whoever died first, the other was to write his obituary. If Smith had predeceased Macdonald we would surely have had a more satisfactory account of Smith's early years as a writer than we possess from Brisbane's *Early Years*.

A tight-built, modest youth of middle stature, or nearer the short than the tall, with lightish-brown hair worn close, a round but nowise singular head, a placid and shrewd expression of face, and a distinct but not disagreeable cast in one of his eyes – such was the Alexander Smith one saw just after he had become famous. Latterly he had become stouter about the shoulders and more manly-looking, with a tendency to baldness over the forehead, which gave a better impression of mental power. But the most remarkable thing about him was his wonderful quietness of demeanour. There was never a quieter man, one who could sit longer with others and obtrude himself less. People meeting him casually complained of this, and wanted more conversation, more of the poet. They might try him on this tack and that, but he foiled them, listening pleasantly to what was said but keeping his own contributions to a minimum.[148]

This is one of the most detailed descriptions of Smith in print and, inevitably, comes from an obituary – this time by David Masson who succeeded Aytoun as professor at Edinburgh in 1865. We have to rely on these verbal portraits because other kinds are almost non-existent. As we have seen Smith sat for a portrait in oils because Flora wanted it, but apart from that there are only two known photographs (one of which probably comes from around this period and is the original for a number of engravings used in frontispieces and to accompany obituaries). Could it have been that he was averse to sitting for long periods under intense observation? Maybe it activated his snail-like ability to draw in his horns and fade into the background that some observers found exasperating. Masson's sketch also mentions this:

When he was really known one came to like his quietness as but the social form of a mind of the most perfect good sense, incapable of flummery or pretence, and sagacious in taking the measure of persons and things around it, but kindly-humorous rather than explosive or aggressive. There was something even formidable in this power of at least never, in the midst of other people's rubbish, saying anything that was silly or untrue.

Masson also refers to the equanimity with which Smith treated the plagiarism campaign of 1857. This philosophic attitude was no doubt the right strategy for keeping things in perspective, but he also had to face the fact that he was no longer 'bankable' as a poet. The only option, if he were to continue to make an income from writing, was an awesome one. He must start all over again and build a new reputation as a prose writer. In 1858 his piece on Macdonald's *Rambles Round Glasgow* had been accepted by Blackwoods and the following year saw the appearance of 'How We Went to Skye', a brilliant article aimed at a readership relishing discomfort and danger in outlandish places from the comfort of an armchair. It was widely supposed that he was encouraged to write for Blackwoods by Aytoun who was now supreme on the editorial board. In fact, these were the only two pieces offered.

In 1860 Smith moved smartly to the new Macmillan's which, priced at only one shilling (against Blackwoods half a crown) was soon selling 10,000 copies per issue and paying its contributors more generously.

The account of an eventful journey from Inverness before the opening of the railway to Kyle appeared in the Blackwoods of February 1859. Retitled 'Skye at Last' when later used in *A Summer in Skye*, it includes the profiles of Father McCrimmon and Captain Fitz-Tartan (changed to McIan). After just two August holidays at Ord we can see Smith experimenting with how he might deploy some of the weapons in his poet's armoury in the service of prose. These were the first of eight annual visits. In 1858 Flora's father, the irascible Captain Charles Macdonald, might have mellowed a touch at being presented with his first grandchild (five-month-old Flora) at the age of eighty.

The character of McIan ("He was quick and hasty of temper, and contradiction brought fire from him like steel from flint") must have been written with some trepidation by his new son-in-law. As a kind of palliative Smith mingled details from the rather more distinguished military career of Charles Macdonald's predecessor at Ord, Captain Donald Macdonald. Whereas Captain Donald had served with gallantry during the Peninsular War, Captain Charles had only been involved skirmishing with the Irish rebels at Vinegar Hill. Smith admitted that he did this "to gain more picturesqueness of individuality." He also had to tread warily when using another of Flora's relatives, this time an uncle on her mother's side, Kenneth McLeod of Gesto (pronounced Gay-sto). He had acquired Greshornish (pronounced Grish-nish) House in 1851 and had settled down to being a Skye landlord. McLeod was a man of real abilities who had made his mark in the Empire. As a young man he left for India to grow indigo and soon owned an estate and a processing factory near Calcutta. Still in his early forties, he decided to return to Skye and make things happen on the lands he had purchased from the Macleod estates around the shores of Loch Greshornish.

Within five years he had achieved a near miracle. This is the description of the main village, Edinbain, from *A Summer in Skye*:

On the hill-side, on my left as I drove, stretched a long street of huts covered with smoky wreaths, and in front of each a strip of cultivated ground ran down to the road which skirted the shore. Potatoes grew in one strip or lot, turnips in a second, corn in a third, and as these crops were in different stages of advancement, the entire hill-side from the street of huts downwards resembled one of those counterpanes which thrifty housewives manufacture by sewing together patches of different patterns.[149]

Kenneth McLeod represented a rare species on Skye: the incumbent landlord with cash to spare and his tenants' welfare at heart.

With the fall in the demand for kelp (made from seaweed tangle collected by cart from the Atlantic-facing beaches) and then the potato failures of the 1840s the islanders needed more of his kind. Although he was the epitome of enlightened social regeneration (even endowing a small hospital at Edinbain) McLeod ranked high in Smith's esteem for other reasons. The basement flat in Northumberland Place, while conveniently situated for the College, was increasingly oppressive to Flora. Also, by Spring 1860 Jessie, their second child would have been on the way. If the family was to grow a larger house was required, preferably a villa in one of Edinburgh's desirable suburbs. But it was quite clear that such a dream property was well beyond the reach of the Secretary to the University on £200 per annum. Flora must have brought up the topic. McLeod was after all her mother's brother and godparent to her first daughter Flora. Most importantly he was a bachelor and likely to remain so. Kenneth McLeod's portrait shows prematurely grey hair and flashing blue eyes, a man of great dynamism but probably not readily given to compromise. By the end of the year they had made a successful bid for a substantial semi-detached villa in the newly-developed Wardie area right on the shores of the Firth of Forth overlooking Granton Harbour. A £600 deposit was paid immediately thanks to Kenneth McLeod and the couple moved in the following Spring. It was a house of five bedrooms and three public rooms, allowing the provision of a nursery and a study without strain. At the back, steps led down to a laundry and storage in the basement, giving access to a long garden. The two adjoining houses, built in 1854 and known as Peel Place, were almost mirror-images. The name on the left-hand one was smartly changed to Gesto Villa as a tribute to their benefactor. Later the same year Charles Kenneth McLeod Smith, their son, was born here. Gratitude was fully acknowledged in the naming of both property and progeny.

The cleaner greener world of Wardie and its adjacent suburb Trinity must have lifted their spirits considerably and helped to cushion the disappointment over the reception given to *Edwin*. From the top floor of the house were breathtaking views: to the north straight across the Firth of Forth to the hills of Fife, to the south over the city's distant landmarks to the Castle and to Arthur's Seat, jutting above the smoke pall. In between was a *cordon sanitaire* of fields, cultivation and hedgerows. The following year (1862) his poem 'Wardie – Springtime' was published, written in the wake of Prince Albert's death but registering the poet's own deep contentment at his new surroundings. His delight in the local birdlife is infectious:

> The crocus gleams along the garden walk,
> And from the tree-tops sings the speckled thrush;

> Within the flying sunlights, twinkling troops
> Of chaffinches jerk here and there; beneath
> The shrubbery the blackbird runs, then flits
> With chattering cry, and at the ploughman's heel
> Within the red-drawn furrow stalks the rook.[150]

This was almost his last completed poem, for it was exclusively to prose that Smith now turned in order to supplement his income. The weekly and monthly periodicals were his chosen market. For one of these, the North British Review (a strange title to our ears, but to most Victorian Scots 'NB' was a badge of pride), he wrote a round-up review 'Novels and Novelists of the Day'. This begins surprisingly as a quasi-sociological investigation into the growing popularity of current fiction. Victorian men and women lived in an increasingly complex urban society. Simpler, deeper feelings were traditionally set forth in verse, according to Smith. But the novel, he concludes, "is the mirror in which society looks in order that she may become acquainted with her own countenance." The novel serves a variety of functions, sometimes seizing on areas previously the province of poets, breathing life into past history (as in *Edwin*), airing a contemporary social issue (as Dickens and Thackeray, later George Eliot) or inventing an ideal picture of the future. Increasingly poetry was to relinquish its epic role to the novelists, despite Tennyson and Arnold.

By Smith's prognosis the scale and range of fiction were boundless and increasingly appeared attractive to a society strongly influenced by the idea of progress, if not always by its practical implications. The North British article, in hindsight, is an announcement of his own conversion to writing prose (making a parallel to his 1853 letter to Brisbane, announcing "I do not wish to fill a pulpit" which announced that his vocation was to be poetry):

Prose is more Protean than verse, and can make itself at home anywhere – in the rare passionate and imaginative regions, in the severities of logical statement, in the even flow of narrative. It can do all that verse can, and it has no pride: it can concern itself with trifles; it can paint Dutch pictures; it can analyse proverbs. And it is curious too that the wider intellectual region over which prose dominates almost inevitably attracts to itself, sooner or later, writers whose minds are of the purest poetic type. Men who begin with poetry feel, as time passes on and experience widens, a strange propulsion to prose or to the drama. They weary of abstractions, of the beautiful masks and shadows of things, and long to feel the earth beneath their feet, and to assure themselves by human fellowship. Verse takes the cream off their thoughts, so to speak; but much remains behind on which the shaping instinct cannot help exercising itself, and which seeks a prose outlet.

From semi-rural Wardie the smokey centre of Edinburgh was no more than three miles away. The Secretary, making his way to his College office every morning, could either walk it or take the train from nearby Trinity station which would have brought him in at the West End station near the Caledonian Hotel on Princes Street. From there he would have had an interesting walk or cab ride through the Grassmarket to the College. We get a glimpse of Smith at work from James Hannay, a deracinated Scot who after making his name in London as a journalist and lecturer came up to Edinburgh in 1860 to edit the Tory Edinburgh Courant. They had first met in London in 1853 when Smith had attended a lecture he gave on satire. Once again in an obituary piece, Hannay, clearly a welcome visitor, gives a vivid picture of the Secretary's daily grind:

Every visitor to Edinburgh knows the University, now chiefly famous for its medical department. Passing northward from the Register House (itself at the east end of Princes Street) you come to a large, rather dusky building with a quadrangle inside —a building blocked by rather mean streets, but not without an impressiveness of its own. Here, at the left side of it, the Secretary was to be seen during all the best hours of the day, for much of the greater part of the year. You turned in and found him in a little room, with a window opening on the street, and with an inner room to which he was constantly summoned by the banging of a door announcing that some student or some other person wanted to see him. He had endless enquiries to answer – often from rough country lads who had never heard of him and who might put idle fussy questions to him as they might have done to a porter. He had correspondence to conduct, books and accounts to keep, and was perpetually at the mercy of professors, some of whom hardly realised an Englishman's notion of what a gentleman ought to be, and treated the poet-Secretary with scant courtesy. The post was poorly paid and was reduced rather than raised during Smith's tenure of it; it was a laborious and – what is worse – a vexatious post. To any such "Spasmodic Poet" as Smith's maligners declared him to be, it would have been an intolerable post; such a man would have lost his temper, thrown it up, and relied upon literature at all risks; but the solid bard held on with a patience, nay, with a cheerfulness which said wonders for his strength of character and naturally sweet yet firm temperament. "Well, great man," he would say in his friendly manner to a visitor, and with a smile which his squint made not ugly but picturesque, and he glided into a chat, interrupted immediately by the bang of that door.[151]

The Secretary's office (now the Old College mailroom) is situated within the southernmost of three gated archways that Adam punched into the front façade of the College, sheltering from the street the large quadrangle behind. The four pairs of Doric columns make an impressive statement, one Smith had little leisure to admire during his fraught working day. He would have had a good view of everything going on the street (then known as East College Street) outside his window. And the noise of horse-drawn traffic on the cobbles must have been continuous, possibly irritating and distracting. Pat Alexander, who had close links to the College, also noted in his Memoir in *Last Leaves* how the Secretary's duties continued to increase as the extra General Council responsibilities were absorbed into a job that already contained a mass of demanding detail. The suspicion might be that the Commissioners left a lot of the practical management of reform up to the Secretary, including areas where the implications had not been entirely thought through.

A typical example of this occurred in February 1862 when under the provisions of a University benefactor a trust fund had been set up to allow any Edinburgh student the right to attend an annual concert in the Music Hall in George Street. Because of the recent explosion of student numbers Professor Donaldson had rationed the free ticket allocation to fifty and it was up to the luckless Secretary to dispense these to first-comers. The result was predictable. With nearly 400 unsuccessful applicants a group of students decided to underline their legal rights with force. As the concert was about to begin, one of those denied entrance began setting about the entrance doors with a sledge hammer despite the best efforts of the police. Once in, they found somewhere to stand and apparently behaved with perfect propriety. After the concert they retired, flushed with success, to the College quadrangle where they organised an impromptu ceilidh. At this point the constables moved in and arrested the pipers and a few others they considered ringleaders. Although the incident was reported in the Mercury there is no mention of a subsequent court appearance, so presumably the Secretary patched things up with the constabulary. Not all student demonstrations ended so happily. Two years earlier in January 1860 a heavy fall of snow had led to student violence in his back yard. 'Snowball Disturbance at the College' was the Courant's headline. It started when early in the morning two firemen were called in to disperse the heavy snow lying in the quadrangle. This was not to the liking of the students who began appearing at around 9.30 and obstructed the firemen's attempts so that they had to give up with the job only half-finished:

A scene of general disturbance took place, and the students began to pelt onlookers and passers-by with snowballs. This conduct continued with little intermission from ten till about five o'clock in the evening. The gates with one exception were closed all day; and not only had the shopkeepers opposite to close their shutters, but they dared scarcely venture to open their doors owing to the shower of snowballs instantly directed against them. An almost complete suspension of business with them was the result. A considerable body of police were from an early hour upon the spot; and about noon seven or eight students were singled out and apprehended by them.

As a result "a pretty general mêlée broke out" between the police and students, resulting in the street being closed to traffic for some hours. More arrests were made, but still the students refused to move and, barricading themselves behind the College gates, loosed a fusillade of snowballs and possibly stones at any carriage attempting to run the gauntlet. Windows on the upper storeys across East College Street were also broken. The Lord Provost paid a visit in the afternoon, but it was not until five pm that the Professors were called upon to exercise their "moral influence" and, possibly to their surprise, the unruly element called it a day. The fifteen students arrested were later defended by Alexander Nicolson who alleged provocative behaviour and brutality by the constabulary. He raised himself in the students' esteem by his fiery speeches both in court and at a prior meeting in the College. Despite witnesses testifying to some students carrying sticks and clubs, only one was given a (suspended) sentence.

It is difficult to imagine what Smith, who once again had had to call in the constables, thought of the registrar at his wedding being involved in all this. He would have probably spared some sympathy for the youthful culprits who were given more than enough rope to hang themselves, but Nicolson as populist was a totally new side to one of his closest friends. A regular visitor to the basement at Northumberland Place, he and Flora reminisced about Skye and the Western Isles. Nicolson appeared in a more familiar role in February the following year when he gave a lecture to the Young Men's Literary Association of Linlithgow on the authenticity of Ossianic Poetry. Naturally, as a Gael, he refuted Dr Johnson's slur on James Macpherson's 'translations'. A brief note of the evening, possibly by Smith, appeared in the Caledonian Mercury.[152] The disparity between Nicolson roused to a Robespierre one day and the more accustomed role of Gaelic scholar the next must have set Smith thinking. A passage from 'On the Importance of a Man to Himself' (which appeared a couple of years later in *Dreamthorp*) is relevant and insightful:

In the midst of the most amicable relationships and the best understandings, human beings are at times conscious of a cold feeling of strangeness – the friend is actuated by a feeling which never could actuate you; some hitherto unknown part of his character becomes visible, and while at one moment you stood in such close neighbourhood that you could feel his arm touch your own, in the next there is a feeling of removal, of distance, of empty space betwixt him and you in which the wind is blowing.[153]

Whatever the precise reason, the pressures of the job were getting to the Secretary. His increasing distaste led him to day-dream. According to Pat Alexander he started to make plans for setting up as a sheep-farmer on Skye, presumably once again with support from

Kenneth McLeod. Although the idea was greeted with disbelief, there is no reason why he shouldn't have acquired the tack on a reasonable house and a hundred acres or so in Sleat. Flora would have probably been happy with the idea too. In the meantime however they had to keep up appearances and this necessity was epitomised by the substantial stone façade of Gesto Villa with its five bedrooms and extensive garden. The elevated situation on Boswall Road was close to the site of a castle and later a manor house belonging to Sir Alexander Boswall. Although his house still stands today there was a much older ruined structure which seems to have been re-cycled in building a dozen or so villas in the late 1840s. By the time the Smiths moved into what was originally Peel Place (presumably named after the founder of the Metropolitan Police) the new Wardie had been inhabited by a mix of retired couples, widows and others who sought genteel seclusion but also valued good connections by railway and carriage to the shops of Princes Street.

Across the road was Wardie Lodge where the two Misses Hope got by with a staff of ten, including the coachman. Further east a row of three houses known as Wardie Villas was taken over entirely by a trio of widows. At Erneston, the atmosphere was a little more lively with the presence of six children (aged one to thirteen) belonging to the Niblets, but they were incomers from London. The Smiths' immediate neighbours (through the wall, so to speak) were William and Isabella Houy, siblings in their early fifties, who had only two servants. Although the house has since been divided into upper and lower flats (necessitating the removal of part of the main staircase) Gesto Villa still impresses with its spacious hall lit by a tall south-facing window. The main bedrooms and living room were upstairs. It was here that Smith had his study, lined with bookshelves, on one of which there was a plaster death mask of Dante. Here, on a Saturday or Sunday afternoon, bachelor friends such as Nicolson, Pat Alexander (who inherited the Dante bust), John Downes and McLennan[154] would make their way via Inverleith Row and the Botanic gardens. More often than not there was a simple evening meal provided *en famille*, recalled here by James Hannay:

There still lingered about his house ... the tradition of Edinburgh literature and Edinburgh old-fashioned and simple hospitality. Cordial suppers prevailed there, where there was no sham splendour or shabby-genteel pretension; but where the classic oyster held a position worthy of his associations and was accompanied by the fragrant hot beverage of the country; where the talk was good and hearty and lettered without pedantry; where Scotch songs and Scotch humour (free from all provincialism, however) took their turn; and bright-eyed Highland lasses, sprung from the old clans, broached obsolete but generous notions about Prince Charlie and sweetened the atmosphere with a faint odour of the white rose.[155]

Hannay also recalled Smith had little time for the Brahmins of Edinburgh society who "entertained with London literary gossip at third-hand." By putting a good three miles between himself and the New Town, the Secretary ensured that his visitors would be nearly all "the vagrant talent of the world... Men that break loose from the professions, who stray from the beaten tracks of life", as he himself expressed it in the essay 'Men of Letters'. According to Pat Alexander the talk was often pretty unliterary, a well-lubricated meeting of minds that came to be known as 'A-musement' (ie No-muse-ment). After dinner they would all retire upstairs where

Pipes would be lit; the spirit-case being on the table and, a kettle singing its siren suggestions close by, the inference of toddy is obvious; and the tumbler being duly mixed, the business of the evening would commence which was good, hearty, careless talk, frequently of a dreadfully unintellectual character.[156]

Here, amongst his cronies and yet also in the bosom of his family, the erstwhile *enfant terrible* was most at his ease, a blessed relief from the duties that awaited him in East College Street for the following five days. By introducing a streak of mild bohemianism into the ultra-respectable purlieus of Trinity, Smith could be accused of having it both ways. But it was not the self-evident propriety of these neighbours that he sought but rather the seclusion of the Boswall Road villas with their long gardens and, beyond, the farmland and belts of woodland diverting the eye from the distant urban silhouette only ten minutes away by train. His poem 'Wardie –Springtime' was accompanied by an engraving showing scenes of ploughing and shepherding with the Castle rock in the distance. To obtain this needful tranquillity the Smiths had to buy and keep up a house which in today's prices would have a six-figure price tag. They lived amongst those whose incomes must have been far greater than his. It was seclusion, therefore, at a price. At the cost of working early and late to meet editors' deadlines, once his day-time job was finished, he must now become the professional man of letters, a being who is not really part of the humdrum world of buy and sell but yet can ill afford to ignore its harsh realities:

At the outset of his career the man of letters is confronted by the fact that he must live. The obtaining of a livelihood is preliminary to everything else. Poets and cobblers are placed on the same level so far. If the writer can barter MSS for sufficient coin, he may proceed to develop himself; if he cannot so barter it, there is a speedy end of himself and of his development also.[157]

Most of Smith's remaining hours were to be dominated by this "obtaining of a livelihood" through the production of sellable copy. But merely obtaining a bare livelihood as Secretary sapped the very life force that he depended upon for literary success.

Chapter 9:
1862-63

> *What power in books!*
> *They mingle gloom and splendour, as I've oft*
> *In thund'rous sunsets seen the thunder-piles*
> *Seamed with dull fire and fiercest glory-rents.*
> ('A Life-Drama' sc.2)

WITHIN SIX MONTHS of moving into Gesto Villa Smith had applied for the new chair of English Language and Literature at Glasgow. The application was accompanied by an array of testimonials from Professors Aytoun, Masson (Professor of English Literature at University College London) and Fraser (who held the chair of Logic and Metaphysics at Edinburgh) and Shairp of St Andrew's as well as by fellow vagabonds from the Raleigh Club Hannay, Skelton and McLennan. The timing seems strange. Under the Universities Act the new chair at Glasgow attracted a government subsidy of £200 that could be made up to £300 or more depending on the fees taken each year. But success would have meant uprooting his family and selling the recently acquired Gesto Villa. Maybe the running expenses of such a large house suddenly looked daunting. About this time apparently his younger brother William was sent out to India to seek his fortune, requiring a contribution towards clothes and travel. In addition, Flora was pregnant. After eight drudging years in post as Secretary, he must have doubted that he would ever be able to make enough extra from writing to be able to live comfortably.

By the time the trunks were packed for going to Skye in August 1862 he would have been told that his application had been unsuccessful anyway. It was not to be Professor Smith but Professor Nichol. After five years at Baliol, where he had helped to create the Old Mortality Society and had formed a bond with Swinburne, John Nichol was the coming man. He had been abroad, met and championed Browning, and was publishing poetry. He possessed a vigorous intellect and was a good speaker; he was not yet thirty and had no family distractions. The new university council probably chose the right candidate. Nichol stayed at Glasgow for 37 years, building up the department and making it notable for its awareness of contemporary writing. He also pioneered extension courses, giving public lectures on literature as his father John Pringle Nichol had once done on astronomy.

Smith was still an unknown quantity to the academic world. He had a slight connection to the old Glasgow College through the Nichols and may have attended a dinner or two. Of course he had no academic background and no reputation as a public speaker, an essential part of the job. In his testimonial Aytoun foresaw these objections and tried to allay them. First he states, on slender evidence, that the self-effacing Secretary was "an able lecturer, happy in his illustrations, [who] can both excite the interest and command the attention of an audience."[158] On rather firmer ground he asserts that the candidate "is a complete master of the English language" and thoroughly conversant with the classics of the literature. Smith's lectures would have made stimulating and possibly provocative reading material, but their delivery might well have been a disappointment. No longer an enfant terrible, he had failed to learn how to display his learning in the approved fashion. And then there was the Spasmodic label, for which of course he had Aytoun to thank. His friend John Skelton wrote an essay 'People who are not Respectable' where there is a vignette that might well have been based on Smith: "where he gathers these jewelled words puzzles his well-to-do friends amazingly, seeing how shabby and threadbare the outer man always is."[159]

After eight years at Edinburgh Smith was now part of the scene. Yet he was more of an observer from the sidelines than an active player. On the main stage the professors, each enjoying his local celebrity, relished their role to the full. Smith had been befriended by one or two of them, pre-eminently John Stuart Blackie. As Professor of Greek, he was an innovative teacher who tried to instil the Classical world into raw minds by combining "the authority of a master with the familiarity of a friend", as one ex-student saw it. Some evenings his more gifted students were invited to his house in Drummond Place to consult his Greek texts or to have difficult points in the morning lecture explained in greater detail. Taking his chair around the same time as Smith arrived to become Secretary, Blackie was to spend more than 35 years at Edinburgh. His immense energy, initially directed to university reform in Scotland, was then used to some effect in other areas such as home rule, the preservation of Gaelic and the issue of Highland depopulation. A natural linguist, it was he who established the first Gaelic chair at a Scottish university. A contemporary who had observed him speaking was clearly impressed:

His mind is of a quick, bold cast, and he has at all times the fearless courage of his convictions, in consequence of which virtue he has become the most widely quoted of platform speakers. He can never possibly be dull or uninteresting in a book, or in debate, as he unites in high perfection the two popular qualities of humour and animation. As a poet, he is distinguished for sense, enthusiasm and melody.[160]

Smith's other champion was, as we have seen, William Edmonstoune Aytoun. After recovering from the loss of his first wife he had remarried and regained some of his old spirits. Certainly he was still prolific in Blackwoods, reviewing German literature, commenting on the final years of Palmerston, reporting from the Great International Exhibition and generally pouncing on particular follies which appealed to his sense of the absurd. Maybe he was not so quick to see in himself the extremes of prejudice to which his varied talents led him. James Hannay had ample opportunity to sample Aytoun's public appearances. As editor of the Courant, a Tory organ – in his 'Recollections of a Provincial Editor' re-titled *The Reekyborough Chronicle* – he might have been expected to side with a bastion of the Edinburgh establishment. But he was clearly jaded by the showy side of Aytoun (disguised here as 'Jawkins'):

He was always ready to make a speech about any other subject [than English Literature] under heaven. We had Jawkins on rope-dancing, Jawkins on the potato-disease, and he shed quite a lustre over the winter season – especially that dreadful winter when the waiters, who wait at a whole host of genteel private dinners in turns, raised their fee from five to six shillings and nearly created a revolution.[161]

There was no department of Fine Art at Edinburgh. This was the territory of the Royal Scottish Academy, founded in 1826, and their annual exhibitions provided the opportunity for discussion and debate on the latest trends. Smith was well placed to befriend prominent Edinburgh painters. These included George Harvey, the current RSA President; Joseph Noel Paton who, ten years older than Smith, also began as a textile designer in Paisley; and James Drummond, a stalwart of the historical school who is probably best remembered for *The Porteous Mob*. (Both Drummond and Paton were later behind the appeal for Smith's imposing headstone in Warriston cemetery.)

"The Scottish brush is stronger than the Scottish pen" was Smith's verdict on the creative scene around him. The national temperament was best suited to painting portraits or writing biographies, he declared in *A Summer in Skye*. He admired the work of a number of painters preeminently that of Horatio McCulloch, the landscape artist to whom Smith owed his first meeting with Flora on Skye. McCulloch was judged the leading exponent of a Scottish landscape tradition:

He is the most national of the northern landscape-painters; and although he can on occasion paint grasses and flowers, and the shimmer of reed-blades in the wind, he loves vast desolate spaces, the silence of the Highland wilderness where the wild deer roam, the shore on which subsides the last curl of the indolent wave. He loves the tall crag wet and gleaming in the sunlight, the raincloud on the moor, blotting out the distance, the setting sun raying out lances of flame from behind the stormy clouds – clouds torn into gold and flushed with brassy radiance.[162]

From 1857 he and McCulloch had been linked together through Flora's much older cousin, Marcella, who had become McCulloch's wife. In that year McCulloch painted his *View of the Cuchullin (Cuillin) Mountains*, the viewpoint being close to Ord House. Smith accompanied him on this *plein-air* expedition which took in Fort William (*Inverlochy Castle*) and Oban as well as Skye. McCulloch searched him out as soon as he arrived in Edinburgh, probably inviting him to one of those informal late dinners at his house and studio in Danube Street. In 1862, at the peak of his success, McCulloch moved to St Colm villa, overlooking the Forth, only a few minutes walk from Wardie. According to Pat Alexander, Smith enjoyed spending Saturday afternoons in the studio watching the artist at work and smoking his pipe. McCulloch's craggy features and blunt west coast manner maybe encouraged confidentiality. He was twenty-five years older than Smith: Pat Alexander saw the relationship as that between two brothers, but their closeness might possibly be explained by the fact that the McCullochs had no children.

Probably through McCulloch's influence Smith began reviewing the RSA annuals in the late 1850s and he seems to have attended every preview until 1866. These were not written for Hannay's Courant, but for the rival Caledonian Mercury, a Radical daily with only half the circulation. They appeared every February usually over three or four issues. The payment would hardly have recompensed him for the labour involved, so he must have found other rewards in doing it. His voice was a distinctive one and, although unsigned, the articles were widely known to be by him. The last RSA annual he reviewed was an important one, the fortieth in 1866. Comparing Smith's pieces for the Mercury with those reviews written by others for the Courant and The Scotsman some idea can be gained of Smith's strengths and characteristics as an art critic. He was allowed more space than his rival reviewers but even so one can still appreciate in his pieces a clarity of vision undistorted by fashionable prescripts and prejudices.

His views on art were derived partly from his father's influence and more importantly from interaction with his contemporaries, but they can be seen as a reflection of the creativity theories he elaborated on style in his essay 'Literary Work'. Above all, the artefact should reveal something of its creator. The true painter should never be a slave to fashion or rely too much on finish, even though both may be important in finding a buyer. At its simplest, Smith looked for the expression of some inner power and feeling ('soul' in modern parlance). Whereas his contemporaries mainly used neo-classical criteria focusing on correctness of form, composition, colour and even appropriate subject matter.

The Courant reviewer made a safe selection from the nine hundred works on view in 1866, amongst them work by Harvey, Fettes Douglas, McCulloch (*Loch Katrine*), E.T.Crawford, Graham Gilbert, Macleay's portrait of Prince Alfred, Noel Paton (*Fact and Fancy*) and Drummond (*The introduction of Robert Burns by his printer Smellie to Henry Erskine, one of the members of the Crochallan Club*). These were mainly well-established names and The Scotsman also awarded accolades to most of these whilst noting that there were "few works of high art" that year. Typical of the landscapes received with special favour were several painted by Sir William Fettes Douglas, a self-taught painter and art-collector, later to become Keeper of the National Gallery. He habitually wintered in Italy. The Courant singled out for praise *The Grand Canal, Venice* for its "marvellous combination of rich, quaint and varied architecture, rising from the calm waters reflecting the bright skies of Italy that still present so many charms and attractions to the artist, the antiquary and the man of taste." This demonstrates the kind of word-painting reviewers were expected to have a go at, since no illustrations accompanied the articles.

In his first piece for the Mercury (17 February) Smith judges standards to be high but fails to see "one very absorbing or commanding work" amongst the landscapes or watercolours. Journalistically, he speculates on the steady exodus of Scottish painters "hungering for the praises and the bank cheques of the south". Despite the disappearance of the Faed brothers, Orchardson, Pettie and Erskine Nichol he is not despondent: "there is a native instinct for art in the Scotch mind, and as one man goes off another springs up and takes his place". Returning to the watercolours and sketches, he is struck by some works of McCulloch. Strangely ignoring the oil painting of Loch Katrine, he pronounces them as "brilliant, true and strong as anything he has ever produced in the robuster field of oils." The second article (21 February) looks at non-Scottish paintings. Where the Courant reviewer saw only a "stiff quaint picture" (Henri Leys' *Christmas Day at Antwerp during the Spanish Occupation*) Smith admires "the vivid presentment [which] attracts just as the reality would be sure to do." Three days later Smith writes about portraits, a genre where he considered Scottish painters to excel. Together with his rival critics he singles out those by Kenneth Macleay but reserves the supreme accolade for *Portrait of Miss Caird* by John Phillip (1817-67). This picture, now in the Scottish National Gallery under the title *Mrs Mary McKay Glen*, he compares to Gainsborough and rates as "the high water mark of British portrait painting for the last 20 or 30 years at least." The Scotsman agreed.

His final piece on 1 March looks at figurative painting, mentioning a number without enthusiasm, more frequently giving flashes of the subject matter:

> We have perhaps more than a sufficiency of pictures which can be classed under no head of art – a monk, candle in hand, descending a stair; a solitary knight in armour, the crescent moon shining through the castle lattice; a pretty haymaker, the sun full in her face, leaning on a rustic gate and reading a love letter; an old woman peeling potatoes, the clock on the wall pointing to half past twelve, the scarlet runners and Indian cresses shining outside the cottage window. Of all this kind of thing which may, however, be delightful enough, but which makes a greater demand on the hand and eye than on the brain, we have a superabundance. Whether this arises from want of time, from greed of immediate returns, from want of patience and courage, or from lack of what Coleridge used to call "the sleeping imagination", the "flashing in on the inward eye" of the ancient beauty or terror, it may be heedless to enquire.

He concludes this review by predicting the imminent demise of the history painters. Rather like a present-day art director, dressing the set and cast for a costume drama, the artist needed to assemble all the attendant detail of interior décor, costume and bric à brac. In Drummond's *The Massacre of Glencoe*, widely admired elsewhere, he dismisses the Macdonald harper as "deficient in intensity". The RSA reviewing was valuable in giving him some practice in writing to deadlines, an experience he hadn't had since the Glasgow Miscellany in 1854. Soon it would stand him in good stead in his struggle to live gracefully by the pen.

It must have been an intense relief to discover, so soon after the disappointment of *Edwin*, a publisher who would pay generously for both poems and prose. This was Alexander Strahan (pronounced 'Strakun') who had set up a religious publishing business in Edinburgh's George Street while still in his twenties. He had a gift for finding bestsellers (*Aids to Prayer* and *Beecher's Life Thoughts* were early successes) and soon people were comparing the young man from Tain with Archibald Constable who had fifty years earlier created waves by outbidding rivals for writers like Scott.

By 1860 Strahan was ready to take on the periodical market, and with Good Words he hoped to bridge the gap between secular and religious reading matter. "To convey the wisest instruction in the pleasantest manner" he succeeded in persuading Dr Norman Macleod to become part-time editor. Macleod's name was worth thousands in readership. As a Church of Scotland minister for the sprawling Barony parish in Glasgow, his reputation as preacher and social reformer had spread far. After being invited to preach at Crathie church he was appointed Queen Victoria's personal chaplain but remained mostly in Glasgow, at 204 Bath Street, where his home contained a small room over an outside laundry which he used as his editorial study. Even so, for nearly three years Good Words did not earn its outlay. The first issues bore the hallmark of shrewd editorial judgement (whether Macleod's or Strahan's) in the mix of material. In one Macleod advocated a self-imposed tax of 10% on what he called "free income" to go to poor relatives, poor Christians and the Church in general. In another there was a doctrinal essay on Messianic Prophecies, together with the start of a series 'God's Glory in the Heavens (The Moon – Is it Inhabited?)'. To counterbalance the religion and metaphysics Good Words from the start serialised new fiction (Sarah Tytler, Dina Mulock, Mrs Oliphant and Macleod himself), published short stories, scientific essays and non-religious verse. The monthly gained a reputation also for hard-hitting reportage on subjects like the London Model Lodging Houses, the American Slave Markets, prison conditions, even a description of a night on the Ramsgate lifeboat.

By 1865 Good Words was selling 120,000 copies every month and Strahan could attract names like Trollope with payments that dwarfed rivals' offers. He was one of many who tried to lure Tennyson away from his publisher Moxon, and eventually succeeded by a guaranteed annual cheque for £4,000 (more than £400,000 equivalent value). However, even with Macleod at the editorial helm the broad church views advocated in Good Words were not popular with the Church of Scotland establishment. In 1863 it was attacked for including scientific articles and other items not suitable for Sabbath reading. The following year Macleod supported Dr Robert Lee of Greyfriars in his improvements to the form of worship, as well as in sanctioning baptism service and the saying of the eucharist in buildings that were not consecrated. In 1865 the Sabbatarians were further enraged by Macleod's call for trains to be allowed to run on Sundays. Despite all-round condemnation (although supported by The Scotsman and The Saturday Review) Macleod stayed on course and Good Words rapidly recovered lost sales. He dismissed his opponents as preaching "Pharisaical evangelism". He was later to be recognised as an important figure in finding a new role for the Church in an increasingly secular age and in 1869 he became Moderator of the Church of Scotland.

For Good Words in 1862 Smith wrote the two poems 'Wardie – Springtime' and 'Autumn' (both embellished with picturesque engravings) and more significantly a piece of prose. In 'An Essay on an Old Essayist – Montaigne' he struck a chord that continued echoing through subsequent writings. We do not know when Smith first read Montaigne (presumably in Florio's translation), but he must have instantly recognised that the essays of this sixteenth-century recluse provided a model that he could readily adapt. From reading the *Essais* he was able to see what was lacking in the contemporary way of writing:

In point of style the Essays [of Montaigne] are different from anything that could now be produced. Not only is the thinking different, the manner of setting forth the thinking is different also. There is a certain want of ease in the old writers which is irresistibly charming. The language flows like a stream over a pebbled bed, with propulsion, eddy and sweet recoil – the pebbles, if retarding movement, giving a dimpled surface and a natural music. There is a ceremoniousness in the mental habits of these ancients. Their intellectual garniture is picturesque, like the garniture of their bodies. Their thoughts are courtly and high-mannered. They carried gallantry (so to speak) into literature. They touched the hand of truth as they would the hand of a high-born lady in a minuet.[163]

The North British Review had begun with strong affiliations to the Free Church of Scotland. By the time Smith began to contribute it had broadened its appeal whilst still remaining a journal for the intellectual elite (modelled on the Westminster Review) particularly for dissenters. By the 1860s its influence outweighed its 3,000 circulation. It had been David Masson's thoughtful piece on 'A Life-Drama' that had bolstered Smith in the summer of 1853, as well as mortifying Arnold. For the North British Smith was now persuaded to write two long 'round-up' reviews, both prefaced with his own critical views of the genre in question. 'Novels and Novelists of the Day' has been covered in the previous chapter. In 'Essayists Old and New' he begins by considering the effects on essayists of the new periodical market which demanded a brisk pace and immediate comprehensibility to appeal to the widest readership. He compares the work of past generations of writers to the pure water of Loch Katrine in its natural setting. His contemporaries' work is more like the same water taken through the pipeline to Glasgow:

The magazines bring literature into every home, just as aqueduct and pipe bring the water of Loch Katrine into the homes of Glasgow citizens. It is quite true that the water occasionally tastes of iron and wears a rusty stain; quite true that a perfectly pure draught may always be had at the legendary lake in the shadow of the hills; but the water is flowing in every house, and that, after all, is the important matter.[164]

The irony cannot be avoided. Although he puts up a token defence for the utilitarian modern essay, his heart is not in it. Before reviewing the five collections, one by his friend John Skelton, Smith looks back to the essayists of a former age, principally Hazlitt, Leigh Hunt ("His essays are gay and cheerful as suburban villas") and Charles Lamb ("the softness and remoteness of dreams"). He even prefers essayists still living but of a previous generation such as Carlyle, emphasising his "allusion, suggestion, light touches of fancy, spurts of humour, grotesque imaginative exaggerations." Anything, in fact, is preferable to factual, unplayful prose; so he returns once more to Montaigne and the way he exploits the reader's credulity:

No other literary egotist had ever so good a subject, and then his style is peculiar as himself. In his Essays he continually piques the reader; every now and then more is meant than meets the eye; every now and then a great deal less. He plays at hide-and-seek with his reader round his images and illustrations. In reading Montaigne, we always think we are finding him out.[165]

In August 1863 Strahan published *Dreamthorp, A Book of Essays Written in the Country*. On the back of the Good Words and North British pieces Smith was propelling himself gingerly into the white water of Victorian periodical writing, but in a way that was once again distinctive. The normal practice was to gather together pieces that had already appeared in the weeklies or monthlies, bringing the essayist both the extra satisfaction of appearing in more durable hard covers and a second income stream. *Dreamthorp*'s genesis was different. Apart from the two profile pieces on Chaucer and Dunbar (which appear slightly out of place), the essays were all written specially. They were never occasional pieces: they were intended to be read sequentially.

And there was more. By adopting a persona Smith links the ten pieces stylistically and in the way they relate to the reader. In 'Essayists Old & New' we have seen how he had already revealed his misgivings about the modern methods of producing copy for the periodicals. His was to be a different way, and the parallel with Montaigne becomes crucial to understanding what he was trying to achieve. Certain titles – 'On the Writing of Essays', 'Men of Letters', 'A Shelf in My Bookcase' – contain the sort of material that would have been under discussion at The Raleigh Club or even at the A-musement evenings. They have some stylistic traits of thinking aloud: ideas still in development, much off the cuff speculation, and little attempt to impress by close exegesis or display of knowledge. Above all, the most successful pieces rely on establishing a feeling of easy intimacy with the reader.

Although they were mainly written in 1862 and early 1863, it is possible to see the gestation of some of these essays in the talks he gave in the Glasgow Addisonians fifteen years previously. Had he retained MSS or notes which he then used to work up into the mature pieces of *Dreamthorp*? 'Thoughts on Youth, Manhood and Old Age', delivered to the GALS in June 1847, may have formed the germ of 'On Death and the Fear of Dying' with its disconcerting conclusion: "probe joy to its last fibre and you will find death." 'Thoughts Anent Life' (November 1849) could have provided the starting point for 'On the Importance of a Man to Himself' which put personal achievement under the microscope with its assessment: "It is the sternest philosophy, but on the whole the truest, that in the wide arena of the world failure and success are not accidents, as we so frequently suppose, but the strictest justice."

It is the confidential, almost garrulous tone of *Dreamthorp* that has attracted critics nearer our own time. The introduction to a 1914 edition described it as the work of "a poet in undress" (is there any other kind?) whilst a feature in The London Mercury in 1925 imagined the writer as "a middle-aged philosopher living in the retirement of a small village, looking with a kindly eye upon the simple pursuits and amusements of the natives, recking nothing of the great world of cities, and discoursing with pleasant candour and humility on any subject which comes to his hand." Middle-aged, rural lifestyle, in leisured retirement: could any profile be further from the truth? In the 1930s Christopher Morley discovered the book's "delicious gift of melancholy" but began to suspect that the "pose as an old gentleman" was for some obscure purpose, since he had discovered that Smith was only thirty-four on publication. A 1970s critic discovered vividness and directness in the writing "in spite of a touch here and there of Stevensonian preciousness".

Contemporary critics almost to a man (and they all seem to have been) failed to notice that Smith the essayist had quite intentionally adopted the persona of a mild eccentric whom the world seems to have passed by. He has little taste for modern manners or values, deplores the effects of urbanisation, and is immediately suspicious of anything that appears institutionalised, including religion. He is always looking below the surface rather than being impressed by the superficial. Instead he prefers to muse sceptically on writers and other figures from history, to seclude himself in the forgotten village of Dreamthorp and to find endless preoccupation in examining his own thoughts and feelings. He is looking for "the suggestiveness of common things", as he puts it. By comparison, Montaigne retired to his chateau at the age of thirty-seven, after a life spent at court and in local politics, to do much the same for the next twenty years.

Within the essays there are, it is true, unmistakable traces of Smith's own views as he expressed them elsewhere, and even one or two autobiographical touches. In 'On The Writing of Essays' there is evident distaste for the need to keep up appearances in urban settings; 'A Lark's Flight' contains a reminiscence of the execution of two Irish navvies in 1841 that Smith witnessed as a child; in 'Christmas' there is a reference to younger sister Katy; in 'On the Importance of a Man to Himself' a passage on egotism echoes closely 'Essayists Old & New'; 'A Shelf in My Bookcase' mentions titles that he writes of approvingly elsewhere. Then there is the white death-mask of Dante "looking out with blind, majestic eyes" that was also present in Smith's own study at Wardie.

But these straws are insufficient in themselves for creating solid enough bricks to contain fully the elusive narrator. The "I" of *Dreamthorp* is a kind of Superannuated Persona, a narrator with only occasional similarities to the prematurely world-weary Secretary to the University residing in an Edinburgh garden suburb. He is by no means one and the same. Central to the book is a preoccupation with the purpose of essay-writing itself, and here we approach Smith's already professed views. The essay writer has to build a close relationship with the reader, even though it is sometimes a teasing one. Next the essayist must shun novelty of subject matter (as already outlined in 'Literary Work'):

Absolute novelty of idea - in a poem, for instance, - is felt by many as a disturbance, because it is devoid of the sweetness of acquaintanceship and association. Absolute novelty, even if it could be procured, the reader does not very much care about; what delights him is the setting of a familiar thought in a new light, the discovery of subtle links and relationships between things with which he is acquainted, but which he was in the habit of considering disconnected and remote.[166]

This theme is developed in one of the core essays in *Dreamthorp*, plainly entitled 'On the Writing of Essays'. The last thing a good essayist à la Montaigne should do is stick with his professed subject matter:

His main gift is an eye to discover the suggestiveness of common things; to find a sermon in the most unpromising texts. Beyond the vital hint, the first step, his discourses are not beholden to their titles. Let him take up the most trivial subject and it will lead him away to the great questions over which the serious imagination loves to brood, - fortune, mutability, death, - just as inevitably the runnel, trickling among the summer hills, on which sheep are bleating, leads you to the sea; or as, turning down the first street you come to in the city, you are led finally, albeit by many an intricacy, out into the open country with its waste places and its woods where you are lost in a sense of strangeness and solitariness. The world is to a meditative man what the mulberry plant is to the silkworm.[167]

It was increasingly difficult to retain an awareness of "the suggestiveness of common things" in an age when advances in communications, in industrial technology and the growth of towns all corroded a sense of individuality. The picturesqueness of human character, celebrated in 'Vagabonds', ran increasingly foul of the quicker tempo of Victorian urban life and the conformity it required. For Smith there were two possible options for the writer. One was to go with the flow, to produce consistently on demand, and the dangers of this are spelt out in 'Men of Letters':

It is the professional character which authorship has assumed which has taken individuality and personal flavour from so much of our writing, and prevented to a large extent the production of enduring books. Our writing is done too hurriedly, and to serve a purpose too immediate. Literature is not so much an art as a manufacture. There is a demand and too many crops are taken off the soil; it is never allowed to lie fallow and to nourish itself in peacefulness and silence.[168]

The alternative is to cultivate detachment, to let the stream of life run around you rather than run with it. Here too is a danger, according to Smith. Taken to its logical conclusion this stance makes the writer a voyeur. Smith calls him "a spy in the service of literature": he enters into life around him only insofar as it will provide him with good material. Smith cites an instance from Goethe's *Letters from Italy* where the writer's craving for 'copy' gets the better of his natural humanity. The essay goes on to speculate on the paradoxical effects of this overwheening "consciousness of authorship".

The peculiar temptation which besets men of letters, the curious playing with thought and emotion, the tendency to analyse and take everything to pieces, has two results, - and neither aids his happiness nor even his literary success. On the one hand....it gives him somewhat of an icy aspect, and so breaks the spring and eagerness of affectionate response. For the best affection is shy, reticent, undemonstrative and needs to be drawn out by its like. If unrecognised, like an acquaintance on the street, it passes by, making no sign, and is for the time being a stranger. On the other hand, the desire to say a fine thing about a phenomenon, whether natural or moral, prevents a man from reaching the inmost core of the phenomenon. Entrance into these matters will never be obtained by the most sedulous seeking. The man who has found an entrance cannot tell how he came there, and he will never find his way back again by the same road.[169]

The burgeoning periodicals market was producing an unnatural superabundance of print written on demand. The effects, Smith predicted, would be dire for writers: "I am afraid that the profession of letters interferes with the elemental feelings of life; and I am afraid, too, that in the majority of cases this interference is not justified by the results." This would not have been a popular view with those who saw such things as part of an Age of Progress and Plenty; there was really no useful role here for "curious playing with thought and emotion".

As already indicated, Smith's use of the Superannuated Persona was based on his admiration for Montaigne's essays and the persona that emerges. In *Dreamthorp* the Persona is a solitary man, choosing to live among rustics where his only intellectual acquaintances are the doctor and the minister (whose sermons cause his mind to drift away from the present). His favourite summer occupation, when not in his library or garden, is to take his umbrella and go "floating about the lake" in his rowing boat. Even in a place so cut off from the mainstream, the Superannuated Persona contrives to remain as detached as possible. Of himself he says: "I am not an actor, I am a spectator only" and his house "sees everything but is itself unseen." Many of the essays are contrived in such a way to make the reader continually conscious that the Persona's inky fingers are on the pen. Sometimes there is an over-fussiness and the inclusion of material which is at best tangential. The Persona can assume greater or less transparency, his role being to act as a filter between the essay's exposition and the reader's comprehension. In a moment of exquisite paradox the Persona declares that he has nothing to conceal about himself:

Of the essayist, when his mood is communicative, you obtain a full picture. You are made his contemporary and familiar friend. You enter into his humours and his seriousness. You are made heir of his whims, prejudices and playfulness.[170]

A similar profession is made in Montaigne's famous Preface to the *Essais* which begins: "Here, Reader, is an honest book". He goes on to justify this by saying that they were written only for immediate friends or relatives who know the writer well. However, within the "honest book" many scholars have pointed to dissimulation and abuse of the reader's credulity. Margaret McGowan (in *Montaigne's Deceits*) demonstrates how the reader's sympathies are often manipulated through Montaigne's knowledge of forensic rhetoric. She cites a number of instances of evasiveness, where he is apparently unwilling to pronounce a definite opinion on a person or to counter an argument. At other times he will apologise for the weakness of his exposition and appear to have genuine self-doubt. But McGowan argues that this is just a device to obtain the reader's sympathy in advance, often used by barristers in the law courts where Montaigne briefly practised. Again she points to his apparently simple style – the use of staccato statements interspersed with long, rambling sentences as if the essayist is thinking aloud – as further ways of getting the reader's attention. He also cultivates a cautious attitude to introducing anything controversial so that the reader is well primed beforehand; he will sometimes leave out a piece of information that the reader has to deduce for himself, drawing him/her into the role of collaborator; another device is to repeat a key word in contexts which can change its meaning, leaving the reader a little uncertain as to exactly what point is being made.

In *Dreamthorp* Smith is not so blatant a manipulator as Montaigne because he fears destroying that sense of intimacy with the reader. One can also discern something similar going on in the much earlier work of Goldsmith, Hazlitt and Lamb. By the mid-century, however, the role of the essayist had changed to become more of a public spokesman, dealing in hard facts and communicating with the mass. Smith, and a few others, attempted to find a new way of communicating using a more confidential tone and relying often on personal anecdote. Nowadays this approach is a commonplace; hundreds of newspaper columnists adopt it every week.

The most memorable piece in the collection, and unusual in containing an extended narrative, is 'A Lark's Flight'. It is a piece that has often been misunderstood. The central section describes a public hanging, or rather the Persona avoids describing it by panning away at the final moment. The scene-setting is strangely cinematic as well as being sparely written, the description of the lark ascending taking barely half a page. This dispassionateness makes the episode much more disturbing:

Be it remembered that the season was early May, that the day was fine, that the wheat-fields were clothing themselves in the green of the young crop, and that around the scaffold, standing on a sunny mound, a wide space was kept clear. When the men appeared beneath the beam, each under his proper halter, there was a dead silence, - everyone was gazing too intently to whisper to his neighbour even. Just then, out of the grassy space at the foot of the scaffold, in the dead silence audible to all, a lark rose from the side of its nest, and went singing upwards in its happy flight. O heaven! How did that song translate itself into dying ears? Did it bring in one wild-burning moment father and mother, and poor Irish cabin, and prayers said at bedtime, and the smell of turf fires, and innocent sweethearting, and rising and setting suns? Did it – but the dragoon's horse has become restive, and his brass helmet bobs up and down and blots everything; and there is a sharp sound, and I feel the great crowd heave and swing, and hear it torn by a sharp shiver of pity, and the men whom I saw so near but a moment ago are at immeasurable distance, and have solved the great enigma – and the lark has not yet finished his flight: you can see and hear him yonder in the fringe of a white May cloud.[171]

The whole section on the execution forms barely a quarter of the essay. It is framed by a prelude and postscript which have led some to compare it to De Quincey's 'Murder Considered as one of the Fine Arts'. This was a gory and almost gloating description of a succession of murders in the East End under the pretext that the essay was an objective assessment of whether a murder could be argued to possess aesthetic features. There the reader is led from the discursive to the descriptive with barely a word of warning. In Smith's essay the Persona starts his essay by giving the reader a few of his usual quaint observations, only this time they are a little more contentious.

First he concedes that public hangings are a painful spectacle but that people make too much of their instinctive aversion to watching, which he puts down not to increased refinement but to "debilitation of public nerve". He then disputes the view that the onlookers are there out of morbid curiosity, claiming that there is something of more psychological significance that compels their presence: "they would pluck if they could some little knowledge of what death is; that imaginatively they attempt to reach to it, to touch and handle it through an experience which is not their own." He then claims that the event often brings out the best of the condemned man's character, allowing him to depart from the world in some style.

Whilst the reader is digesting the moral implications of this, and possibly becoming wary, the Persona takes his hand and leads him gently to where the gallows stands and two figures, accompanied by their priests, are waiting in the cart. It is only here that we reach the essay's philosophical heart, an issue that was revisited by Smith in poetry and prose: the cruel paradox that arises from the mutual dependence of beauty and finiteness. If those onlookers were struck to the core by the lark's song, Smith suggests, how much more intense was the sensation for the condemned men with mere seconds of life remaining? (Pretty much the same point is made with two larks in von Eichendorff's poem 'Im Abendrot' used subsequently as the text for the last of Richard Strauss's *Four Last Songs*.)

The ending of 'A Lark's Flight' is a study in anticlimax. There follow three folktales, each more pointless than the next, but they restore the easy-going tone of the early pages before the account of the hanging ("It is Nature's fashion: she never quite goes along with us.") The reader has been tricked into becoming an unsuspecting collaborator, probably a quisling to his professed beliefs. He has indeed taken the part of a witness to the event just as the Persona had said he would.

In 'Men of Letters' the Persona calls himself "a spy in the service of literature" suggesting his manner of operation is possibly a little underhand. (The late Muriel Spark made a similar point with her tongue-in-cheek job description 'loitering with intent'.) It might also have meant that Smith was aware that some of his views would be regarded as subversive if they were not disguised by some literary ventriloquy. This essay investigates the demands that an increasingly materialistic society places on its writers. Similarly the Persona has little time for modern religion and its teachings about the after-life. 'Of Death and Dying' is an almost Stoic assertion of the divine purpose behind human mortality, and both Montaigne and Bacon are quoted to support his case. Any attempt to make death a more comfortable concept is rejected by analogy ("The atmosphere is always cold around an iceberg")[172] and by observation ("Recognition of death may exist almost constantly in a man's mind and give to his life keener zest and relish")[173]. Death can be viewed as a beneficial influence on leading a better life, not because of any final judgement day but purely as a result of the heightened significance our lives attain through continual awareness of mortality and finiteness:

> Consider, then, how the sense of impermanence brightens beauty and elevates happiness. Melancholy is always attendant on beauty and that melancholy brings out its keenness as the dark-green corrugated leaf brings out the wan loveliness of the primrose. The spectator enjoys the beauty, but his knowledge that *it* is fleeting and that *he* is fleeting adds a pathetic something to it; and by that something the beautiful object and the gazer are alike raised.[174]

From this and other passages Smith (or his Persona) has clearly digested some of Montaigne's admiration for Aristotle and that cultivation of self-belief that is an essential element leading to increased Virtue. Smith had little interest in religious controversies: maybe as a result of the early brushes with Evangelicalism and his subsequent recoil, a deep suspicion of institutional religion seems to have taken hold. At the root of many of his views, and this comes up more often in *Dreamthorp* than elsewhere in his writings, was the abhorrence of a growing uniformity that he saw in contemporary society. Like Ruskin he sensed a new philistinism in art by those paid to produce it. His more wide-ranging concern appears most openly in the final essay which masquerades as a lecture given by the Persona to the Dreamthorp Literary Institute. 'On Vagabonds' laments the picturesqueness that he detects passing from urban societies; it castigates the lessening of humanity brought about by the more regimented lives people in towns are required to live; it points to the paradox of how those living in the most liberal European democracy still feel victims of "a petty social tyranny."

We are our own despots – we tremble at a neighbour's whisper. A man may say what he likes on a public platform – he may publish whatever opinion he chooses – but he dare not wear a peculiar fashion of hat on the street.

Eccentricity is an outlaw. Public opinion blows like the east wind, blighting bud and blossom on the human bough. As a consequence of all this, society is losing its picturesqueness and variety – we are all growing up after one pattern.[175]

Maybe Smith had in mind Professor Blackie's wide-brimmed hat and plaid, which were sometimes the object of ridicule by those who engaged him in political debate. The purveyor of unorthodox views must necessarily become a 'spy'. If his activities become suspect he will lose the confidence of his readers; to avoid this happening it is perhaps better to express himself obliquely. This obliqueness made many contemporary reviewers completely miss the point of the 'deceits' in *Dreamthorp*. The Westminster in a generally favourable review describes the tone as "musically soothing as a lullaby"; the Athenaeum noted "much genial feeling and many quaint half truths". But within these faded bouquets there was a thorn or two. Coventry Patmore in the Spectator, whilst admiring the style ("elegant, almost models of style, simple, far above the mania for fine language and the tawdry grandiloquence which some people call grace"), dismissed the writer as "a perfect type of the school, who, with second-rate minds and a great ambition, make the classical traditions of a bygone phase their fulcrum and starting-point..." [176]

Even later critics with more time to reflect have not made the correct connections with *Dreamthorp* and its preoccupations. After Strahan's edition there were six new versions up to 1914 while in the US there were numerous editions and versions into the 1970s. In 1925 J.B.Priestley included 'A Lark's Flight' in *Essayists Past & Present*. In the Introduction he seems to echo passages from 'On the Writing of Essays'. However his critical verdict on Smith is a reserved and lukewarm one: "had he lived he might possibly have become one of the major essayists of the century, but his work as it stands lacks body and personality…"

The most perceptive contemporary piece appeared in The Museum, a publication mainly for those working in education. This critic (John Nichol?) noted in Smith's prose "a synthetic or cumulative process" which he likened to stringing pearls. This had by now become a hallmark of his essays. This technique of burying a concept in an image and then elaborating it marks the essays in *Dreamthorp*. It is a hallmark of Lamb's essay-writing too, but taken to a greater degree. On originality (or "cleverness") in literature and art (from 'On the Importance of a Man to Himself'), for example, Smith brings out the issue by a double-imaged approach that seems to rejoice in its own incongruity:

It [originality] exists, but it is impossible to tell from whence it comes, - just as it is impossible to lift the shed apple-blossom of an orchard and to discover, from its bloom and odour, to what branch it belonged. Such cleverness illustrates nothing: it is an anonymous letter. Look at it ever so long, and you cannot tell its lineage. It lives in the catalogue of waifs and strays.[177]

True originality or mere whimsy from a second-rate mind?

Chapter 10:
1864-65

Our beings mellow, then they fall,
Like o'er-ripe peaches from the wall;
We ripen, drop and all is o'er;
On the cold grave weeps the rain;
I weep it should be so, old Night.
('A Life-Drama' sc.4)

TO DEFINE THE CHARM OF STYLE is as difficult as to define the charm of beauty or of fine manners. It is not one thing, it is the result of a hundred things. Everything a man has is concerned in it. It is the amalgam and issue of all his faculties, and it bears the same relation to these that light bears to the sun, or the perfume to the flower. And apart from its value as an embalmer and preserver of thought it has this other value, that it is a secret window through which we can look in on the writer.[178]

This is from the essay 'Literary Work', one of Smith's most significant attempts (the literal meaning of the French *essais*) to explain what writing style meant to him. For a writer it was an undertaking equivalent to self-dissection on living tissue. Far from being an optional adornment, adding a self-conscious rhetorical flourish to his way of writing, style is rather a linguistic analogue to his mental process. The reader is part psychoanalyst, part spy as he strives to "decipher a man by his style". The value of the final work, Smith argues, can be judged by the extent of this personal revelation. Of course, there is nothing to prevent the writer leaving false trails so only discriminating readers will pick up the clues to find him out. The conclusion is inevitable: "We read books, not so much for what they say as for what they suggest".

'Literary Work' appeared in Good Words towards the end of 1863, creating something of a sensation. Alexander Strahan saw it as audacious because it "deprecates all endeavour after originality"[179]. It is easy to see why the some of the ideas sown in this essay were adopted by the Aesthetic movement of the 1890s. A month or so later Strahan published 'Winter', a more self-conscious prose-poem which elaborates on the 'Christmas' section of *Dreamthorp* where the comfort of the indoors allows the writer to indulge in the "imaginative sense" of the icy weather outside. 'Winter' demonstrates how both town and country are affected by cold temperatures, pointing up the cruelty that is an essential ingredient of so much beauty in nature. Ironically Smith's prose imagery, at a time when he was supposed to have settled into the more comfortable guise of essayist, bears just that quirky Spasmodic quality noted ten years before in his verse:

> For an hour or so a small uninteresting sun is stuck on the murky sky, like a red wafer on a dirty letter... The tea urn purrs like a fondled cat...The white flakes are coming at last! Stretch out your hand – the meteor falls into it lighter than a rose-leaf and is in a moment a tear.[180]

'Winter' began a year which saw him employed ceaselessly at literary tasks, none of them major but still impressive in the demands they must have made on his leisure time. Fairly early in the year he was at work on the 96-page introduction to a two-volume selected *Poetical Works of Robert Burns* in Macmillan's Golden Treasury series. The title page states it was "Edited from the best printed and manuscript authorities, with glossarial index and a biographical memoir by Alexander Smith". Perhaps Smith was also responsible for the selection of poems, as well as the memoir and the glossary. If so, this was a major piece of editorial work, involving him in reading much of Burns' collected letters. He may not, however, have made the selection himself (Alexander Macmillan later claimed the credit). The Memoir made an attempt to address the issue of why an intensely nationalist poet such as Burns should appeal to readers of many other nations. Towards the end Smith returns to the same idea that had also struck him twelve years earlier when he delivered his address on Burns to the Glasgow Addisonian Literary Society. There he emphasised how "the poet's favourite period of composition was whilst holding the plough" and how his daily involvement with the Ayrshire farm was a direct stimulus to his poetry. Maybe an awareness of natural cycles and living off the land gives his writing a global resonance.

In the Golden Treasury Memoir he makes it clear that as a nature poet Burns was concerned first and foremost with the human predicament and not with "philandering after Nature". There can be little doubt that Smith saw parallels between Burns' early life and his own. An article by an American academic[181] lists some of them: "their background as 'labour-poets', their self education and wide reading, their inspired poetic vision, their self-limitation to principally Scottish subject-matter and settings as their most effective poetic material, their meteoric rise to fame and their distrust of public favour, their satiric wit (more often apparent in Smith's essays, but nonetheless present in his poetry), and the tragedy of their premature deaths". Dr Scott also points out that Smith's comment on Burns that his grave "was dug too early – and yet too late" (implying that he had not died at the height of his poetic powers) would apply equally to himself. Smith had made the same predictions about his own future as early as 1854 in 'Glasgow' with its prescient reference to "the road of toil / With my grave cut across".

His views on Burns' strengths as a poet were unorthodox for their time. It is not the mellifluous vocabulary he values so much as those shorter lines and sentences which "circulate everywhere like current coin; they have passed like iron into the blood of our common speech." As a poet Smith himself rarely tried the Burnsian mode, marking him out from the mass of his contemporaries who inevitably lapsed into it whenever they required shorthand for national identity. Smith certainly knew his Burns nevertheless. In the centenary year of 1859 he even made a speech in public, admittedly to a small audience got together by Hugh Macdonald. One of Burns' grandsons was present at the Glasgow gathering along with other notables such as William Simpson, the Crimean war artist, who noted that "it was longer than expected from him because he was not a speaker."[182] Smith later confessed that he still had in his head the words of a tribute he had just written for the press.

His edition of Burns (containing the glossarial index that apparently "bored him dreadfully" according to Pat Alexander) was still in print twenty years later. Another version, known as the Globe Edition in three volumes, went on selling until the 1920s. Smith was paid well for his editorial work but unfortunately he gained nothing from subsequent reprints. He was also much in demand as a contributor to periodicals and even to the weekly and daily press. Shortly after Smith's arrival to take up the Secretaryship in Edinburgh in 1854 Aytoun had tried to get him to contribute regularly to Blackwoods, but only received a couple of extended pieces which were later trimmed for inclusion in *A Summer in Skye*. More Skye pieces were written for Macmillan's Magazine. Smith then switched to the North British Review for two long reviews of recent essay collections and some novels (see previous chapter). After that Strahan lured him to Good Words and then to The Argosy, to which he contributed regularly until a few months before his death. Strahan's magazines, immensely popular as they were with the middle classes, were not considered serious enough fare for Literary Men. They lacked the weight of the Edinburgh Review, for example, with its oracular tradition of espousing and expounding great principles in literature and politics.

The plain truth was that Smith had no interest in taking stands and indulging in literary feuds. His major dread was to come face to face with the "prolix and wise, bore and blockhead." He just found it too difficult to cut and run, always in thrall to the diffidence that made participation in any public event such a forbidding ordeal. He occasionally ventured into print with a purpose (for example, the 'Maud' controversy) but usually anonymously and with no real axe to grind. His interest in politics, according to Pat Alexander was

"Precisely nil"; with religious disputes "he quite declined to meddle." Not even the abolition of slavery debate could engage his attention for long. Smith must have passed his time in Edinburgh almost unrecognised by the opinion-formers, the trendsetters and *belle monde*. He belonged to no clubs except the informal Raleigh, shunned balls and soirées, concerts and any other gathering except those for which the University post absolutely demanded his presence.

Once established at Wardie (by the summer of 1861) he with increasing frequency held open house to a small circle of friends whose company was a source of refreshment. As we have heard, they were characterised as evenings of "A-musement", in other words they were not for literary talk or readings aloud, more for smoking, drinking and gossip. They were intended for a group that Smith came to call Social Vagabonds. Foremost among those who attended was Pat Alexander himself. An intimate of Smith and Macdonald during the rambles along the Clyde in the early 1850s, he moved through to Edinburgh around the time the Smiths took up residence in Gesto Villa. By then, with a small inheritance, he had given up any pretence at a business career. His time was devoted to reading, sketching, fishing, writing occasional articles (the most ambitious being an entry on Golf for the Encyclopaedia Britannica) and occasional philosophy teaching.

In discussions, the contrast between Smith's measured delivery and Pat Alexander's must have been remarkable. One can imagine Smith in his study with the lights of Edinburgh in the distance, the briar pipe going full throttle, listening patiently to his friend's diatribes. Alexander's quicksilver mind jumps from one subject to another: he was knowledgeable on art, literature and philosophy but never produced anything that could be described as a major contribution to any. Through his sister Esther he was brother-in-law to Dr John Adamson, one of the pioneers of photography. Surprisingly there is no recorded photograph of him. A member of Edinburgh's Pen & Pencil Club, he played the part of bohemian to the full. A piece in the St Andrews Citizen entitled 'Patrick Proctor Alexander, Philosopher and Poet' stressed this aspect of his character:

It was nothing short of refreshing to behold him calmly threading his way among the gay lounges of Princes Street on a bright summer afternoon wrapped in the voluminous folds of an ample cloak, vastly more comfortable and picturesque than fashionable, his noble clear-cut features surmounted by the softest and most shapeless of felts.[183]

Probably Edinburgh, a magnet for academic eccentrics, would have clasped Alexander to its bosom, smiling indulgently on bachelor improprieties such as being spotted on a Sunday morning with fishing tackle under his arm. Almost everyone who made an assessment of him lamented that he made so little use of his obvious talents. Although his preferred wish was to join the army, he could surely have picked up a full-time university post had he so wished, especially with his father holding the chair of Greek at St Andrews. But beneath the nonchalance and bohemianism he was a sympathetic friend to Smith and many others who he encouraged to sustained literary effort that seems to have been beyond his powers. After jousting in print with Mill on the question of moral responsibility and causality Pat Alexander obtained the part-time job of Examiner in Moral Philosophy at St Andrews. Francis Espinasse, against his better judgement, published a string of his philosophical articles in the Edinburgh Courant, which he came up to edit in 1864. Like his predecessor Hannay he was probably another of those who attended A-musement evenings, leaving us a description of Smith's shy manner:

Silent as he was in general company, there fell from him, when the hearers were both fit and few, many a quietly incisive remark on Nature and on books. Political and theological discussion he eschewed. He was a middle-sized brown-locked man, with a squint which gave a certain *espiègle* look to one of the honestest of faces.[184]

"The most remarkable thing about him was his wonderful quietness of demeanour." Thus David Masson who came to Edinburgh to take up the Chair of English in 1865, echoing James Hedderwick's assessment when the 20-year old contributed early poems to the Glasgow Citizen: "a reserved and silent youth." Prof Blackie was even more damning, failing to "find him interesting, or succeed in melting him into geniality." Alexander Strahan echoed "reserved and silent" but found him easy to get to know. They first met in 1861 or 1862 in the offices of the radical Edinburgh Evening Telegraph where Strahan remained totally unaware of the heavily-bearded figure leaning against the mantelpiece. Dragged into the general conversation, Smith then ventured a few words. The beard, resembling one that Dickens sported at around the same time, appeared in the late 1850s, perhaps at Flora's suggestion.

From the war artist William 'Crimea' Simpson emerges a rather different picture. He returned from the Crimea in 1858 and visited the Smiths at Gillespie Street. There he met Lauchlan, Flora's eldest brother, who was home from India for a spell. Being Sunday, the three men decided on a walk out to Dalmeny. They had scarcely crossed the river at Cramond when, according to Simpson, "yearnings for refreshment" came upon them. An inn obligingly appeared on the horizon and it was Smith who knocked on the door. Obtaining a drink on the Sabbath was a legal impossibility north of the Border unless one could prove oneself a bona fide traveller (BFT for short) under the then current licensing laws. If the landlord was not totally convinced (a book for entering your name, address and point of departure was provided expressly for the purpose) neither food nor drink would be forthcoming. Everything therefore hung in the balance, according to Simpson, as Smith began his plea to the sceptical innkeeper:

Smith pointed at once to his brother-in-law as having come from India, then turning to me said I was from the Crimea. If I am not mistaken he then used some phrases highly imaginative and hyperbolised about himself which also conveyed the idea of space and travel, but which served the purpose. The incident, which in itself is unimportant, struck me at the time for its showing the poet's quick and perfect power of realising a position and of grasping what was essential to his purpose. He did this on the spur of the moment, and all so easily as if he had been answering in the most matter-of-fact manner.[185]

Maybe this was more the side that he revealed at the Gesto Villa evenings, attended by the spirits cabinet and toddy jug. Until 1864 a regular attender was James Hannay who as part of the bohemian set in London had stood as a Man of Letters candidate at the 1857 General Election. He wrote a series of articles in the Quarterly satirising the political aims of the radicals which brought him to the attention of leading lights in the Tory party. So he was dispatched north to put more beef into the Courant. Despite Scottish ancestry he had never lived there, but his four years in Edinburgh left him greatly disillusioned at "the gradual decomposition of Scottish nationality, the steady continuous transmutation of that nationality into provincialism." Instead of a vigorous, self-confident capital with a flourishing distinctive culture, Hannay encountered a coterie of lesser talents writing "insipid tales, respectable reviews or twaddling essays, precisely similar in character to those of Englishmen of the same character". Poetry (here Smith is made the sole exception) had descended to being imitations of either the traditional ballads or pastiches of Burns. Still in his early thirties, Hannay managed to cause offence in nearly every quarter as editor of Edinburgh's most read evening paper. The National Association for the Vindication of Scottish Rights (supported by Aytoun and Blackie) was dismissed with particular relish: "The provincial mind... is intensely jealous as well as feeble, and this little movement is one of its characteristic exploits."[186]

Such a loose cannon was made most welcome at Wardie where Hannay refers with particular relish to dining on oysters (a relatively cheap dish at the time). A sample of the kind of scathing contributions he made to the A-musement soirées can be found in an article he wrote in 1868 pouring scorn on the pretensions of the Edinburgh intellectual elite. Blackie (Professor Dotterel) is characterised as superannuated and more than a little eccentric. An increasingly embittered figure, Hannay himself died aged forty-seven in Barcelona where he was British consul.

Another regular was John Ferguson McLennan, the expert on tribal bride-catching who had shared accommodation with Smith and Flora in Northumberland Street (see Chapter 8). By now he had caught his own bride but still remained a sardonic figure with trenchant views on political patronage. Like Smith he contributed to the Argosy. He had dismissed those who indulged in formulaic writing in a crisp article entitled 'Concerning Easy-Writing' signed Jonathan Jones:

Easy-writer, whatever his nominal theme, goes off on every suggestion and runs it dead, unless, indeed, in the pursuit some whim seizes him, when he instantly follows his whim. And his whims, even more than other people's, are inexplicable – obey no obvious law of origination or association. They come on him all at once, as an aerolite comes to the earth.[187]

As we have seen, Alexander Nicolson, in common with Pat Alexander and McLennan, was a non-practising lawyer. He had commissioned Smith to write the piece on Scottish Ballads for *Edinburgh Essays* back in 1854. A particular friend of Flora's through his Skye lineage, he eked out a living reporting court cases for the Scottish Jurist. A large, bulky man, he lacked the energy (possibly through a heart condition) to achieve his potential. He would, however, sit and talk for hours, particular about Gaeldom issues, and Smith was to use him for the figure of Fellowes in *A Summer in Skye*.

Undoubtedly there would have been some fascinating discussions from these 'vagabonds' who gathered in the small, book-lined study under the blind stare of a death-mask of Dante. Their observations, if they had been recorded, might well have made more interesting reading than the long-winded stuff in the heavy reviews such as The Athenaeum. But the whole point of A-musement was they were not. We can get a hint of the tone and content, perhaps, by reading some of Smith's periodical writing during these years, taken on principally to make ends meet. For example, from 1862 he was a regular contributor to The Museum, a new journal devoted to Scottish educational matters.

In January there was an article on Chaucer which Smith seems to have been gestating for several years. An 1856 letter now in the National Library of Scotland suggests an article on him because "he [Chaucer] is rather a stranger nowadays to literary periodicals."[188] Sandwiched between articles on arithmetic teaching and 'Natural History in Home Education', this piece was extended and used later in *Dreamthorp*. Six months later a reassessment of Spenser compared his poetic allegories with "the modern burlesque, with its barren glitter of verbal wit, its mockery of sentiment." A later piece on Christopher

North (John Wilson, Aytoun's father-in-law), whilst complimentary on his prose style, is scathing on his plots: "more unreal than dreams, more lachrymose than a schoolgirl's tale." In 'Literary Work' he points to want of literary style as a contemporary failing and finishes with an exotic epigram that deserves surely to be better known: "There are no dishes of peacocks' brains now, but there are wholesome wheaten loaves for all."[189]

All this might well have featured at Wardie, but Smith's contributions would scarcely have displayed the same polish that, with much labour, identified his writing. His own work might have come up for discussion, probably under protest. But his interests and those of his companions ranged much wider than literature; the whole human condition pricked his curiosity and spurred him to write such observations, however uncomfortable the implications. In 'An Essay on an Old Subject' he notes that beauty in old age springs from each sex adopting similar characteristics. 'On Dreams and Dreaming' emphasises the importance to creativity of liberating the subconscious, an idea that ran contrary to contemporary medical opinion. His jaundiced view of Gladstone as a public speaker was widely considered perverse. The discussions at Wardie would certainly have been unconstrained by conventional diktats of taste, but remarks were probably more thoughtful than outlandish. There seem to have been no fallings out. The vagabonds all remained good friends and most supported in any way they could Smith's family after his death.

All told, between 1862 and 1866 Smith contributed for Strahan nine substantial essays and three poems to Good Words and The Argosy. Most of the prose was reprinted in *Last Leaves*, edited by Pat Alexander. These essays are not assertively erudite like most periodical fodder. Occasionally an image is allowed to flower, but in general there is understatement and even a certain playfulness. Paragraphs are meticulously constructed, rhythmically inventive, often ending on a cadence that keeps them in the memory. Not as strident as Hazlitt or anything like as eccentric as Lamb, Smith was developing a distinctive style that would have assured him a place in the critical canon if only there had been more of it. By 1864 he must have realised that four or five essays a year was the maximum that for him would pass as ready for publication.

But that volume of writing could not keep the wolf from the door. His post as Secretary, whilst placing him securely amongst the ranks of the new middle classes, was insufficient in salary to maintain the lifestyle. Servants and a nanny, the cost of heating and maintaining Gesto Villa with its large garden, even the entertaining of the vagabonds was clearly stretching his income to a dangerous degree. Kenneth McLeod was not to be looked to just yet after his generosity in buying the house. As became clear later, there was also a gradual falling out between him and Flora.

As Smith had written in his essay 'Men of Letters', "the finest expression will not liquidate a butcher's account." To write more speedily would be to reduce the quality of the writing. But how if he were to turn from essay writing to something else more lucrative? A solution must have occurred to him that summer when he took his growing family (including baby Marcella, barely a year old) up to Ord. Shortly after returning he put the idea to Strahan, just as they were about to part on Princes Street near North Bridge (which leads up to the Old College). The question he asked was simply "Is there an opening for a novel?" Strahan remembers encouraging Smith to talk to Norman MacLeod, the editor of Good Words which by now serialised two novels a year. No time seems to have been wasted. For a sum probably equivalent to at least twice his University salary it was agreed *Alfred Hagart's Household* would appear in the first six issues for 1865.

At some point it must have occurred to all parties that Smith had never tried his hand at fiction before, but the bargain was struck nonetheless. With one breathtaking twist the financial straitjacket appeared to be at his feet. Writing for a monthly deadline, though, was a daunting task, reminiscent of the furious pace required twelve years earlier with 'A Life Drama'. The secret was to remain one or two instalments ahead, allowing latitude for illness or writer's block whilst not getting too far ahead of your reading public. Between eight and ten thousand words were needed for each monthly instalment to make a completed novel of around 55,000 words. By March he was well past the halfway mark, but then MacLeod, presumably because of increasing sales figures for Good Words, asked him to extend *Alfred Hagart* for another six issues. The incentive was another £500 or so. Smith duly buckled down to the task of lengthening the story by the introduction of the Skye episodes, the very things which so weaken the novel's impact. In September an instalment was missed. The August and October issues contained nearly 13,000 words each, the November one 17,000 and the final instalment was a last protracted gasp at 18,500 words, making a total book length of 120,000 words. The ending was probably in MacLeod's hands just a few days before the new University year opened in October.

The expanded requirement meant that a manageable narrative with a few well-developed characters was sacrificed to a straggling plot fortified with increasing doses of personal observation and unpersuasive melodrama. The original concept is clear in the first seventeen chapters, where the interest lies in seeing Aunt Kate's flinty heart turn away from the calculating Staverts to be reconciled with the impoverished Hagarts, taking their son Jack with her to Hawkhead where he receives the best education and makes a promising start in a legal practice. The device of arranging secretly for Jack's father to be offered a partnership with the shawl merchants where he works as a designer (making him believe it is due entirely to his own creative brilliance) is an original touch and a more experienced novelist could have made even more of it.

Instead Smith rather loses sight of the Hagart parents as he wades into a romantic morass containing the Byronic figure of Henry Willoughby and the rarefied Miss Oona McQuarrie with the enchanting black eyes. Much of this stuff takes place in a remote Skye clachan not all that dissimilar to Ord. In a creditable attempt to introduce a breath of realism Jack Hagart is sent to Hawkhead (Glasgow) University, only to deliver an improbable speech in support of the Poet Laureate as a candidate for the rectorial election. Jack then falls in love with Miss Oona's younger sister Maggie; Aunt Kate dies in her sleep; finally enough loose ends are tied up to bring the narrative to a respectable close.

A closer look at the characters reveals Smith's literary debts. Miss Havisham peers out from under Aunt Kate's spinster's cap, while young Jack setting out to repair the family fortunes is clearly kin to David Copperfield. The designing Staverts, who never let slip a chance of doing some doubtful business whilst mixing with the country house set, are straight from the pages of Thackeray. Martha, the Hagarts' lifelong retainer, is reminiscent of Martha Docken in Galt's *Sir Andrew Wylie*. Nevertheless Smith made them very much his own: Dickens' characters with their broad eccentricities and unashamed recourse to sentimentality are worlds away. Smith was perhaps nearest to Galt in the affection with which he regards his characters, the domestic settings and the incidental detail. His style is, of course, nowhere as original but here for the first time Smith attempts Scots dialogue.

Alfred Hagart's Household is a creditable *Bildungsroman*. In its first half, at least, Smith demonstrates a clear grasp of the essentials: there are memorable characters, and an interest is maintained in the predicaments and progress of his young *alter ego* Jack Hagart. Jack's father is the most successful creation, obviously modeled on John Smith, still alive and well.

The novel reflected real life in a more distressing way. On February 22nd, at only seven months, Marcella died of whooping cough. The writing went on as it had to. But this blow would probably have reawakened the earlier trauma of younger sister Katy's death which happened when Smith was five or six. Sure enough, in the April issue of Good Words the fictional Katy falls ill, followed by the deathbed scene, with her funeral occupying much of the June instalment. In these chapters, written under the shadow of Marcella's death, there is a sense of holding back which, one could argue, contributes to the narrative power. In one passage Jack is wakened by his father coming into his room to tell him that Katy is on the point of death. His mind takes in a whole host of circumstantial impressions rather than confront this central fact:

The room was full of warm, brown light from the fire, which had been kindled some time before, and which had burned down now. He curiously noted chair and table; his little white bed, with the clothes partly turned down, and his night-gown on the pillow. He undressed slowly..... A light came in and Jack saw his shadow run up the wall, hit the ceiling, and disappear. Then the door closed, his father came forward, put the candle on the little table, and sat down on the chair beside the bed. Jack noticed that his father's face was grave, and that there was a solemnity in his manner which he had never witnessed before. Hagart drew the boy to his knee, and put his arm tenderly round him.

"You love your sister very much, John?"

"Yes," said Jack.

"You must be very brave. She is going to leave us – you won't go to school with her or play with her any more."

"What is it? I don't understand you. Say it again!" cried the boy, in whose ears the words had made but a confused ringing and murmuring, like water in the ears of a drowning man.

"She is going away from us. Dr Crooks says there is no hope – she is dying, John."

This time the words delivered their meaning, but not in sharp outlines, only in a bewildering way. Some deadly stupor had got into his brain. He stared at the candle, which his father had brought and laid on the table, and noticed that in the flame a tall pillar of wick was standing, like a black martyr.

"The doctor says she is dying. She is to be prayed for in the church tomorrow."

Jack, staring still at the candle, noticed that the wick had split in the centre and was overlapping and hanging over, and that one of the overlapping portions had become red; and then he noticed that the red portion had dropped off, and fell down on the tallow at the foot of the flame, and that the melted tallow had begun to run down on a great smear on the candlestick.

"God is going to take her to Himself, and we must be resigned. Pray for her tonight, John, and for yourself, and for your mother, and me – that we may all be good, and that when we come to die we may all meet her in heaven."

"Yes," said Jack, taking involuntary note that the fallen portion of the wick had become black, and that the tallow had ceased to melt and run.

"My boy!" cried Hagart impetuously, and clutching Jack to his breast, "if Katy dies you are the only thing left to us," and then Jack felt big tears dropping upon his face.

"Go to bed now, John," he said after a while and in a low voice, "go to bed, and don't forget to say your prayers – don't forget tonight, nor any other night."

Jack said he would not forget; and, standing in the same place, he saw his father take out the light with him, and his shadow come across the ceiling and down the wall to him, and then the door closed, and he was standing again in the warm brown light of the sinking fire.[190]

The physical cost of the serialisation must have taken away much of the pleasure of completing his first novel. On the other hand, his immediate financial problems had been relieved and the reception given to *Alfred Hagart* had been gratifying. A two-volume edition came out the following year, followed by a single-volume in 1867. In America Ticknor & Fields rushed out the first volume in the late summer of 1865 in order to frustrate a rival publisher pirating the text from the serialisation in Good Words. As a result the second volume (entitled *Miss Oona McQuarrie*) starts one chapter later than the British edition.

In the light of his published views on some of his most celebrated contemporaries in the world of painting (most notably the Scottish School), it is surprising that Smith begins his seminal essay 'The Minister-Painter' with a claim that Scottish artists were in the ascendant and literature in decline. The essay's main purpose was, however, to bring back to public attention the neglected work of the Rev John Thomson (1778-1840), an almost exact contemporary of the better-known painter David Wilkie. From the age of twenty-one he had been a Church of Scotland minister, first in Ayrshire then from 1805 at Duddingston, a village just to the east of the Old Town at the foot of Arthur's Seat. Smith considered him to have almost single-handedly established a distinctive Scottish school of landscape painting.

Four Thomsons had been gifted to the National Gallery upon the death of Professor Pillans in 1863. In 1866 they were to receive another three. Even though he had been dead for twenty-five years his work was still unknown outside Scotland. Smith's essay for the Argosy is a long, eloquent piece sketching in the painter's double life as cleric and artist, his friendships with better known artists like Turner, plus a penetrating assessment of his landscapes:

Although defective in drawing, he was fond of colour, and by repainting on his pictures succeeded in producing a surface which increased the richness and lustre of his tints. But his gains in this way were not entirely clear. In the hurry and excitement of the task, he often worked over his surface before the under colours were dry; and as in laying on his colours he used various kinds of medium, or vehicle, to attain brilliancy and depth of tone, many of his pictures have suffered by contraction and cracking, and are now but the dim ghosts of themselves – the battle-flag, shot-torn and smoke-stained, as compared with the original silken sheet. An incomplete draughtsman, Thomson had yet fine general ideas of form and the effect of grand lines. His works are always bold, picturesque, vigorous, and they never fail to impress the imagination. He is always great in masses, and having by that means touched the soul of the spectator he allows the spectator to supply the details. He pours himself, so to speak, on the key of the position in gloomy brigades of strength, and having won that is satisfied – he does not waste himself in skirmishes, however brilliant. There is no play in his pictures. The truth is he was always a little divided in his allegiance between Nature and the Poussins.

He was all for Nature in his sketch in the open air, he was all for Poussin while working in his studio. His pictures, with their incontestable fine qualities, are just a little too like pictures. Nature in them smells of oil, somehow. Bold and noble as was his imagination, able to cope with scenes of gloom and piled-up rocky wildness, he lacked a tender sense of beauty and an exquisiteness of colour. His picture of the Trossachs, in the Scottish National Gallery, is ugly almost; the hills are lumpy and unrelieved by the grace of twinkling birch woods, and there are no distant peaks, as in Nature, softened by miles of airy azure. Light, which laughs and plays, and sleeps smilingly when it does sleep, is sad-visaged in this work as a mute at a funeral.

In colour, again, Thomson, although often grand and imposing in a broad general way, is seldom what can be called exquisite – the world with a sun shining upon it is not cloaked in drabs, russets, dark-greens and blacks, as the artist loved to attire her. Thomson's pictures have many of them lost their pristine brilliancy and freshness but even when straight from his hand one can hardly conceive them to have been other than deficient in this respect.[191]

Some of these shortcomings might well have been applied to McCulloch, regarded by Smith as the minister-painter's natural successor. As long as he has something to express, Smith argues, the artist has the right to decide how it is to be conveyed on canvas. Technique and composition, which he could assess as well as any professional critic, he saw as secondary. (Perhaps his twelve years in the pattern studio designing leaves and sprays had made him indifferent to fine execution and artful composition.) This was an advanced view to take in the 1860s. When later in the century Impressionism began to take hold, Thomson's work was seen in an entirely new light. If Smith had lived another decade his art criticism would have made fascinating reading as McTaggart and his circle and later on the Glasgow Boys created a furore. During the 1850s and 60s there was hardly sufficient substance or novelty to critique. However, reading his writing on painting a century and a half later does reveal that he had the one essential quality of an art critic: a sharp and discerning eye whose perception he kept unclouded by the taste and fashions of his time.

But what of that other minister who had been so influential in Smith's early career, the one he might have called the Minister-Herald? The Reverend George Gilfillan's critical career had been in serious decline since *Firmilian* ten years earlier. Whereas Smith, Dobell and some of the other Spasmodic writers were able to appreciate the finer points of Aytoun's satire, Gilfillan had immediately seen that it was a deathblow to his reputation as a critic. By far the cruelest strokes of parody in the piece refer to Gilfillan as Apollodorus, and contemporary readers would have come away with a vivid picture of someone who had relied perhaps to an unhealthy degree on 'discovering' young poets whatever their quality. Within months commissions from the periodicals that had supported him in the past mysteriously dried up.

Then the knives came out. The London Quarterly referred to him as "a corrupter and misleader of youth" and muttered about profanity. Even Tait's which had accepted many of Gilfillan's latest protegés now dismissed him as a false prophet. However The Eclectic, The Critic (both of which he had used to promote Smith before the publication of *Poems*) and Hogg's Instructor (where he had published his articles on Genius) defended him. Effectively from 1854 onwards he was in decline, yet he had another twenty-five years of life as cleric and critic remaining. As a recent article in *Victorian Poetry* emphasises, although his literary reputation had been destroyed he remained active in encouraging others:

[He] worked tirelessly until his death to foster the efforts and honour the memory of little-known Scottish writers, many of them working-class, and several of them women. Had he gone south (so to speak) with Carlyle, W.E.Henley and Robert Louis Stevenson, he would have profited from the move in many ways. But he would also have forfeited his significance as a mentor, mediator, opponent of dogmatic anathemas that blighted ordinary people's lives, and preserver of the most humane currents of nineteenth-century Scottish culture.[192]

His case had not been helped by publication of the *Third Gallery of Literary Portraits* in late 1854. Instead of being a collection of in-depth biographical and critical profiles like the first two Galleries this was merely selected periodical pieces of a polemical tone repackaged between hard covers. In these he ceaselessly promotes the Spasmodics and continues the fight with Aytoun; the tone is often querulous and unbalanced and reviewers had a field day with it. For the next seven years he was occupied with editing the *Library Edition of the British Poets* series for Edinburgh publisher James Nichol. With a long list of subscribers a new volume needed to emerge every two months, and this (while bringing him £150 a year) proved to be a rod for his own back. As well as writing lengthy Introductions, Gilfillan was expected to provide accurate textual glosses and this became almost impossible given the lack of library facilities in Dundee. After he had offloaded this responsibility he still found the introductions every two months a chore. And the ripples of *Firmilian* had begun to wear away at Gilfillan's bankability. The series was prematurely brought to an end in

1860 and a projected series of modern poets was shelved. Next from his pen was a strange mixture of autobiography, fantasy and invective which he was initially unwilling to put his name to. Unusually the style of *The History of a Man* changes from excitability to relative objectivity as the Gilfillan persona ages. But as soon as one of his longtime adversaries surfaces in the narrative, the tone changes once again into stridency. Here he is writing about one 'Antony E.Will' (W.E.Aytoun) and for any knowledgeable reader one word leaps out as it was intended to:

In an evil hour he was smitten with a desire to be a great original genius... His existence since has been one long spasm of weakness determined to be strong, of clever commonplace striving to be inspired... He has set himself, in the true spirit of an ape, to rail at and caricature the true men and poets of the age.[193]

After the failure of his book and the completion of the British Poets editions Gilfillan further withdrew from public view, although locally in Dundee he was still treated as a great sage. Towards the end of 1862 he began to keep a journal, apparently not intended for publication. Here he was able to look inwards on his errors of judgement both in literary criticism and also in his religious dissent. Even this was not his final word. A few years later he must have been hard at work on *Night: A Poem*, a rambling epic in nine Books that was intended to show the world that he too was a poet. But it was in the main very prosaic indeed, often with a repeated attempt at poeticisation by inverting a key noun and its adjective ("land unseen... tune divine..., craters dim ... thy presence pure"). It showed up once again the preachy side of Gilfillan; and there is a danger of provoking unintentional humour. From Book 5 ("The Joys of Night") is a portrait of the poet at his nocturnal writing with only a shining light for inspiration:

 Above our lonely fire, a lamp as lone
 Burneth in beauty o'er our black'ning page;
 It too is loved, and lovely in its place,
 Raining light down, not darting glory up:
 It seems at times a prying angel bright,
 Stooping to see what human worms inscribe,
 And smiling with a quiet, half-scornful eye!
 Yet what a willing slave our gas-lamp is![194]

More stimulating material forms the core of Book 7 ("Poets of the Night") which, despite its title, ends apocalyptically and not very transparently. The process he describes is of Promethean poets, successors to Alastor (Shelley), the "larks of love's coming", taking over the earth with divine blessing:

> And has the meteor then found the morn?
> I cannot tell, but this I surely know
> That wiser poets like to him shall rise,
> Pouring their fiery music o'er the deep,
> The morning deep, through which the mighty sun
> Of God's last revelation labours up
> To drown in glory them and earth and heaven.
> Hearken, ye peoples, to these winged ones,
> Larks of love's coming, morning lost in day.
> Invisible to us, yet from that height
> Pouring down strains of prophet melody,
> To which we listen rapt, but see them not
> Till they fall down in death, ev'n as the lark
> Seems, sunbeam-shot, to drop upon the earth,
> *Seeming*, not real, her death by daylight's shaft;[195]

His turgid poem was hardly noticed when it appeared in mid-1867. It is tempting to consider whether he had sent early drafts to Smith for comment, in a dramatic reversal of their previous roles. The truth is by the late 1850s they were probably not communicating any more. By the time *Night* appeared Smith was dead. If Gilfillan had pre-deceased him Smith would probably have provided a generous obituary article (as he had done for Macdonald and Dobell) and this would have given us his retrospective take on it all. There must have been times when the minister-herald recalled those halcyon days when 'A Life-Drama' was being serialised and he was hailed as the new Leigh Hunt discovering his Keats. It had taken just a year, thanks to Aytoun, to complete his fall from grace. Was the mid-Victorian readership merely taken on an ego trip by Gilfillan or did he really possess some real critical insight that enabled him to find qualities in young writers dismissed by the establishment? Francis Fennell, an American who has written comprehensively on Gilfillan and the Spasmodic poets, comes to this recent estimate of his effect on his contemporaries: "Gilfillan was widely read, and there were undoubtedly thousands who in recalling their youth could say with Nicoll that "they cannot think of what [Gilfillan] was without remembering what he was to them." But when we consider the quality of the audience, when we try to measure his direct impact on those who either then or later were counted among the leaders of Victorian literature, I think we have to come to a more modest assessment of his true influence. Gilfillan inspired a remarkable enthusiasm among young men like Smith and Dobell who came from a similar background to his own and who were already receptive to the theories which he propounded. But for many others he must have seemed too obsessed with his *eigenen grosse erfindungen* ["the greatness of his own discoveries"] ever to achieve more than a temporary notoriety. His influence was felt, but only indirectly, through the work of those poets who owed their success to his precepts and his generosity."[196]

Chapter 11:
1865-67

I've drunk 'mong slain deer in a lone mountain shieling,
  I've drunk till delirious.
  While rain beat imperious,
And rang roof and rafter with bagpipes and reeling.
('A Life-Drama' sc.7)

IN A PALL MALL MEMOIR of Robert Louis Stevenson his erstwhile friend W.E.Henley expressed surprise, even contempt, at those who wondered how RLS managed to write some of his best work knowing that his death was near. Henley called this "writing in the shadow of the Shade" and argued that despite this no allowances could be made for extenuating circumstances. The urge to write was stronger:

For writing his best was very life to him. Why then all this crawling astonishment – this voluble admiration? If it meant anything, it would mean that we had forgotten how to live, and that none of us is prepared to die...[197]

Convinced that something was badly wrong with his health, and guilt-ridden after baby Marcella's death, Smith was by Henley's argument doubly motivated to write. He did not pause for rest after *Alfred Hagart*. He was determined that he would leave his family with some durable literary asset that could pay the butcher's bills in the future. He had talked to Strahan about it only a few weeks after the final instalment of serialisation in November 1864. This time he was not going to take on the creative workload involved in composing another novel. It was to be something rather less labour-intensive, so he believed, which would involve the use of material already mostly written over several years for the monthly periodicals, material over which Smith believed he still retained copyright. There were a few linking passages and an introductory chapter to be written and possibly a closing section to be added. It could all be done in no time at all. This unusual genesis goes some way to explain the peculiar character of the work that was to become his best known, *A Summer in Skye*.

The book's admirers – and there have been many since it was first published in a 2-volume edition in late summer 1865 – often point to a discursive narration and the lack of any perceptible structure as part of the book's great charm. The underlying belief was that Smith is from the outset determined to write an anti-guidebook. In fact he does succeed in covering most of the island by a series of criss-cross journeys, but these are no mere itineraries. Drama and incident intervene and often take over from the author's role as pedestrian guide. Who can forget the otter hunt, for example, or the unique characters from McIan's extended family of herds, gamekeepers, cottars, and the priest? Whatever are they doing here if *A Summer in Skye* is intended to be an introduction to the panoramic delights of the island? Then there are the stories of second sight and other local superstitions, continual flashbacks to the past, particularly incidents illustrating rivalry between Macleod and Macdonald, and – last but far from least – a long diversion on Macpherson's Ossianic translations.

Smith must have foreseen objections to his apparently chaotic approach. By the February following publication he had received a letter from the Rev. John Macrae of Glenelg, a "sincere admirer of your genius", despite taking issue with Smith's rendering of some Gaelic proverbs. To this native West Highlander Smith tries to explain his purpose in writing the book:

> I did not wish to be statistical, or historical, or geological but simply to record the impression which the Island, with its weather, its scenery, its people and its peculiar spiritual atmosphere had, during many visits, made on my own mind. There is something more in the Island than heather and cattle, and it was this something more I wished to get at and describe.[198]

Although Smith had first set foot on Skye with Horatio McCulloch in the 1850s, leading to his first meeting with Flora, it was a true Skyeman (and another of the A-musement set) who quickened Smith's interest in the island's lore and legend. After an unsatisfactory year as editor of the radical Daily Express (merged in 1859 with the Caledonian Mercury) it was Alexander Nicolson who had invited Smith to contribute his Scottish Ballads piece to *Edinburgh Essays*. As we have seen, he was a large, imposing man with a languidness partly physical, partly cultural, Nicolson was one of those unfortunate Victorians who lacked the Smilesian qualities summed up in *Application*. After eventually qualifying for the Faculty of Advocates and receiving next to no work, he was offered the post of Assistant Commissioner on the Scottish Education Commission, involving a year visiting and reporting on schools in the Western Isles. His one qualification seems to have been a scholarly command of Gaelic.

Whether his reports to the Commissioner made any strong plea for improvements or change is questionable. A contemporary noted that he talked mainly about "sailing from island to island, and watching the mists and sunsets"[199], and in due course some poems came from the experience, collected in 1893 with a Memoir. His understanding of the island way of life was never in dispute and it is significant that he was the only non-landowning native Skyeman on the Napier Commission which looked into crofting law in 1883. In the creation of *A Summer in*

Skye he was the spark for Smith's creative tinderbox. As a confirmed procrastinator Nicolson would drop in on the Secretary at his office on South Bridge, as well as attending the Raleigh Club and the evenings at Gesto Villa. The one thing he could certainly do was talk. It was nearly always of the island of Skye: his boyhood spent among the crags of the Cuillins (Sgurr Alasdair is named after him), the stories told him by shepherds and speywives around Husabost where he grew up, and of memorable evenings in smokey crofthouses and inns on return visits to the island that he always regretted leaving.

If anyone was ideally qualified to write the Skye book it was Nicolson, but he willingly encouraged his more industrious friend to do it instead. Although he lived on into his sixties, and did eventually make some progress in the legal world, he never wrote more than a few articles about his native Eden. As a tribute he appears briefly in *A Summer in Skye* as Fellowes. This was only just, as he had been feeding Smith with material on Skye for the previous five years or more, supplementing Smith's own material gathered every year during the August holidays. Around half the material in the published book had already appeared in monthly journals like Blackwoods. Five chapters had been published there (including the long reminiscence on Glasgow) and two more had appeared in Temple Bar in 1862, containing the Ossian translations essay. Two more had appeared in Macmillan's Magazine ('In A Skye Bothy' in 1859 and 'The Fair at Keady' in 1860).

So the material was mostly there, already in print for more than five years in some cases, and now waiting for some literary nip and tuck. This method of composition had been famously adopted by De Quincey when he used four articles written for Tait's Magazine twenty years previously as the basis for his *Recollections of the Lakes* with its acid portraits of Coleridge, Wordsworth and Southey. Smith's new material, written at top speed in the first half of 1865, is generally the most factual: the route to Oban via Stirling and Callander; the description of Ord House and the way McIan (his ageing father-in-law Charles MacDonald) runs his 'tack' contrasted with the new methods of The Landlord (Flora's uncle Kenneth McLeod of Gesto); the journeys up the Trotternish and Vaternish peninsulas; that short, enigmatic chapter 'The Emigrants' and the description of the three-day return journey on SS *Clansman* where he ruminates on what the visits to Skye mean to him.

A Summer in Skye would be considerably poorer without this material. But the writing has a different quality, produced with less polishing and perhaps content to be more transparently travelogue, but embroidered with that quirky observation that still marked out the writer as an erstwhile enfant terrible. At Orbost the Cuillins reminded him of "some stranded iceberg, splintered, riven, many-ridged, which the sun in all his centuries had been unable to melt", while Ben Idrigill is "dappled brown and olive like a seal's back." Maybe notes were taken at Ord during the August stay in 1864, but the extra text was produced nightly after working his daily stint as Secretary. This leaves only the opening chapter on Edinburgh, a totally independent piece, weaving into contemporary scene-painting some flashes from the capital's eventful past. Did Smith write this specially to Strahan's suggestion? It almost defies commonsense to think he would have composed it to bulk out a book already about 300,000 words in length. Who would have expected to be faced with thirty pages on smokey, overcrowded, insanitary Edinburgh as introduction to a book about Skye? But having read those first paragraphs, who would regret the decision?

Summer has leapt suddenly on Edinburgh like a tiger. The air is still and hot above the houses; but every now and then a breath of east wind startles you through the warm sunshine – like a sudden sarcasm felt through a strain of flattery – and passes on detested of every organism. But with this exception, the atmosphere is so close, so laden with a body of heat, that a thunderstorm would be almost welcomed as a relief.[200]

The Skye chapters, however, are the heart of the book; it is on their ability to conjure up the special spiritual atmosphere of remote Gaeldom (to the Victorian reader who would have only the image promoted for the purposes of railway and steamer tourism) that the book needs to be judged. His approach may be contrasted with the standard collection of Highland impressions, exemplified by *Two Months in the Highlands, Orcadia and Skye* which had come out in 1860. Written by noted alpinist Charles Weld, who had recently experienced a week on the island, it amasses an impressive amount of venom directed at the weather, the inhabitants, the food, all of which do appear to have been exceptionally unwelcoming. The Contents page gives an overview:

Bad Inns in Skye – Want of Fish – James VI and the Goose – Paucity of Books – Dr Johnson and Cocker – Nocturnal Companions – Rain again…A Second Expedition to the Cuchullins – Start for Sgor-na-Strith – Wet Mosses – Ignorant Guide – Smallpox Rock – Enter the Mists

Smith's picture of the island, based on month-long annual visits since 1857, is an amalgam of skies both blue and grey. Even when the rain is all-pervasive Smith can make use of it. In a nocturnal boat trip made from Plockton, described in the chapter 'Skye at Last', he and

Fellowes persuade two unwilling boatmen to take them over to Broadford before the arrival of the Sabbath. Inevitably they are overtaken by a squall:

> Suddenly a strange sighing sound is heard behind. One of the crew springs up, hauls down the sail, and the next moment the squall is upon us. The boatmen hang on their oars, and you hear the rushing rain. Whew! How it hisses down on us, crushing everything in its passion. The long dim stretch of coast, the dark islands, are in a moment shut out; the world shrinks into a circumference of twenty yards; and within that space the sea is churned into a pale illumination – a light of misty gold. In a moment we are wet to the skin.[201]

On Skye Smith became super-sensitive to sense impressions as the manacles of professional drudgery and urban routine fell away. It is just this awareness he attempts to explore and explain in parts of the book. The Skye experience contributed "this something more" to the process of rediscovering a mental balance. Having no Gaelic himself, although he had no shortage of interpreters, Smith has been accused of idealising the conditions in which the Skye cottars lived. But he had seen far worse conditions in the city environment, already painted in 'Glasgow' and other city poems. On Skye he saw things as clear-sightedly as his situation allowed, allowing for some peat smoke. He believed that his octogenarian father-in-law was a good man at heart even though the feudal system gave him the rights of a despot over his tenants. Issues of land reform, the economics of marginal small-holdings or even the emigration debate are not on his agenda. The Glasgow journalist Robert Somers had been on Skye in the wake of the 1840s potato famine. His detailed reports showed *inter alia* how the emigration societies and the Highland Relief Boards, although well-intentioned, were actually saving the landlords the expense of making as little as five acres of land available to each cottar household. There were no long-term benefits for the cottars on their unsustainable smallholdings. Smith watches a small group of young emigrants about to leave for Canada where The Landlord has purchased and prepared farmland for them. He can only see the benefits.

> The deported villagers may have been cumberers of the ground, they may have been unable to pay rent, they may have been slowly but surely sinking into pauperism, the prospect of securing a comfortable subsistence in the colonies may be considerable, while in their own glens it may be nil – all this may be true; but to have your house unroofed before your eyes, and made to go on board a ship bound for Canada, even though the passage-money be paid for you, is not pleasant. An obscure sense of wrong is kindled in heart and brain. It is just possible that what is for the landlord's interest may be for yours also in the long run; but you feel that the landlord has looked after his own interest in

the first place. He wished you away and he has got you away; whether you will succeed in Canada is a matter of dubiety.[202]

This comes from a chapter called 'The Emigrants' which some present-day readers find hard to swallow. By the 1860s attitudes to emigration had changed considerably from the atmosphere of intimidation that for example Johnson and Boswell encountered almost a hundred years previously. When Smith was writing, some two thousand people had already approached the Skye Emigration Society for help in the passage to Australia. Even the unpredictable McIan was not unwilling to encourage his tenants to emigrate. An Ord shepherd was lent five pounds to help him go to New Zealand on the understanding he sent back seeds of any indigenous trees he saw. A palm growing in the garden of Ord House still stands as proof that he did honour the agreement.

In some parts of Skye it is true that at this time creditors who had acquired lands previously owned by the Macdonalds and Macleods had again cleared some crofts and offered emigration as the only alternative to starvation. Smith's approach is to concentrate on the most common occurrence rather than seek out and highlight particular instances of inhuman conduct. He uses the words of Kenneth McLeod, Flora's uncle: "the people could no more prosper than trees that have been too closely planted… He maintained that force should never be used, but advice and persuasion only; that when consent was obtained, there should be held out a helping hand."[203] Smith was certainly not alone in the belief that well-planned emigration to the New World was a reasonable and humane solution to the problem of endemic poverty and unproductive farming and fishing. But principally he is concerned to see the Skye people as individuals rather than pieces in a jigsaw. It is the human peculiarity of Lachlan Roy and Angus-with-the-Dogs that he seeks to convey; that they were also the victims of a pernicious (to our eyes) feudal system adds another dimension to their lives that Smith chooses not to go into. If he has a model in this, genre painters like Wilkie provided it. Look at his 'Village Politicians' or 'The Blind Fiddler' and put them beside the description of McIan's kitchen at Ord. In many cases verbal detail and painted image mirror each other, down to the detail of the hound licking the discarded plates.

A Summer in Skye has two dominant 'characters'. It is best to call them this since Smith took the precaution of disguising real names, even though the originals (one of whom had been a major benefactor to him and his wife) would have been well aware that they featured in the book. It must have been tricky at times in his depiction of McIan to know what to include and what to gloss over with this prickly red-haired military character who had farmed at Ord since the 1830s.

Charles MacDonald was brought up on the mainland in Morvern where his father Alexander had been a doctor. His mother was a daughter of Anne MacDonald of Kingsburgh who was, in turn, the daughter of Flora MacDonald the saviour of Bonnie Prince Charlie and a heroine of the 1745 rising. As with McIan, pedigree was important to Charles MacDonald and it is no accident that his eldest daughter was named Flora.

There are surviving portraits of both Flora's parents. Her father's face is long with prominent cheekbones and shrewd blue eyes. Her mother Anne McLeod was nearly thirty when she married the retired Major and began to produce a family of eight. She had the much rounder face and long nose that Flora Smith inherited, features that did not sit well with fashionable ringlets of the early Victorian period. Anne was the oldest daughter of Captain Neil McLeod. After a more distinguished spell on the battlefield he had also taken an army pension and purchased a small farm at Gesto (pronounced Gaysto) between Dunvegan and Sligachan, with superb views to the west across Loch Bracadale. (A striking photograph of it by Cailean Maclean adorns the jacket of James Hunter's *Skye:The Island*.)

Although he was only the tenant or tacksman of land and property, Captain Neil had a long lease and after sharing the tack with a relative they decided to divide up the land. Unfortunately the boundary line or 'march' between the two portions was immediately in dispute and had to be settled in court. By now there were thirteen McLeod children and the farmholding would not provide them all with a living. The twelfth in line was Kenneth (born 1809). A year or so before his elder sister married Charles MacDonald and went to Ord, Kenneth had boarded an East India ship for Calcutta. Still no more than fifteen, the most valuable of his possessions (according to family legend) was a silver guinea given by an aunt and safely sewn into the lining of his waistcoat.

It is not entirely clear how he amassed his fortune over the next twenty-five years or so. With no qualifications beyond native acumen, at some point he became a partner in a sugar refinery and then the owner of an indigo factory "up country" in central Bengal. The silver guinea was supposed to have been profitably used at an auction of industrial machinery, but it is unlikely that he would have established himself without making some important connections in the British colony. Maybe there were army friends of his father's to tap, if not there would be no shortage of Highland Scots in the vicinity whether as merchants, doctors, surveyors, engineers, planters or even as Church of Scotland missionaries. We do know that the Lieutenant Governor of Bengal (naturally another Scot) had his work cut out trying to regulate the activities of the factory owners who drove hard bargains with the native indigo and sugar growers and in some cases were accused of using slave labour.

Kenneth McLeod returned to Skye more or less permanently in the early 1850s. He had become a 'nabob', a sterling example of the younger son forced to seek a fortune in the farthest corners of the empire, returning with his wealth to spend back home. This was how he could buy outright an estate of three thousand acres (twelve hundred hectares) from the Macdonalds, driving a hard bargain with that noble but bankrupt family who had quickly exhausted the fortune they had made from kelp. As well as the land he acquired four sizeable houses at Cushletter, Edinbain and Greshornish (overlooking Loch Snizort) and also at Orbost, further south looking across Loch Bracadale back towards Gesto, his birthplace. Kenneth McLeod was frustrated in his wish to buy back the family house, but he still insisted on being known as McLeod of Gesto.

This was the original for The Landlord in *A Summer in Skye*. As we have seen, McLeod had already put up most of the money for the Smiths' villa at Wardie, so he was not the one for Smith to risk upsetting by some ill-judged fanciful touches. That Smith manages to paint a multi-faceted portrait, suggesting fairly openly that McLeod was not immune to flattery whilst acknowledging the extraordinary improvements that his money had brought about, is no mean achievement. Surviving estate records show that as well as the four houses on Skye McLeod had two more farms in Wester Ross where cattle were fattened, and by the 1860s he had effectively monopolised the hotel trade in Portree, foreseeing the impact of the soon to be completed Dingwall to Strome railway line.

He spent most of his time at Greshornish, a house at the end of a long track following the loch shore. From the front lawn there is a fine view across the narrow loch to the crofting villages of Edenbain and Blackhall. All was his as far as the eye could see, and he had almost feudal rights over his tenants, including their free labour at harvest time. However, this landlord was giving something back. Experiments in farming and self-sufficiency were already well under way by the time Smith visited McLeod, and he felt sufficiently confident to write up an encounter between him and a group of tenants who were in difficulties. The cottars, their heads uncovered, waited at a respectable distance while The Landlord finished his breakfast cheroot on the front porch at Greshornish. As usual he was surrounded by a group of favourite dogs with a parrot and several peacocks adding an exotic touch:

The Landlord threw away the end of his cheroot and went forward to learn their message. The conversation was in Gaelic: slow and gradual at first, it quickened anon and broke into gusts of altercation; and on these occasions I noticed that the Landlord would turn impatiently on his heel, march a pace or two back to the house and then, wheeling round, return to the charge. He argued in the unknown tongue, gesticulated, was evidently impressing something on his auditors which they were unwilling to receive, for at intervals they would look in one another's faces – a look plainly implying 'Did you ever hear the like?' and give utterance to a murmured *chit chit chit* of dissent and humble protestation. At last the matter got itself amicably settled, the deputation – each man making a short sudden duck before putting on his bonnet – withdrew, and the Landlord came back to the parrot which, now with one eye now with another, had been watching the proceeding. He sat down with a slight air of annoyance.

"These fellows are wanting more meal," he said, "and one or two are pretty deep in my books already."[204]

"Do you keep regular accounts with them?"

"Of course. I give nothing for nothing. I wish to do them as much good as I can. They are a good deal like my old ryots, only the ryot was more supple and obsequious."

The comparison with the Bengali peasant farmers, who brought the indigo crop to McLeod's factory, is revealing. Although a native, Kenneth McLeod's acquired wealth makes him an incomer, almost a colonialist. As Smith acknowledges, in the chapter where he visits the empty castle at Dunvegan, the feudal owners of the island are no longer able to regulate local markets and provide a living to more than a handful of retainers. Large parts of their estates were effectively in the hands of creditors. Resourceful men such as McLeod brought in new money to invest in new enterprises. For the time being he was also earning a fortune from Bengal, as there was an insatiable demand from Europe for block indigo. Within a few years the discovery of aniline dyes produced nearer home would make a dent in the trade and eventually kill it off. Smith notes with approval the improvements to the life of the cottars brought about through this expenditure. At Edenbain he could visit the local store, the smithy and the watermill, all thriving concerns, and the new school. Later there was to be a hospital (still in existence) which was endowed with £10,000 on McLeod's death in 1869. Such personal largesse no doubt added to the value of his estate but the crofters in other parts of the island, some living perilously close to starvation and with little in the way of a secure future, would have looked on enviously.

The final chapter of *A Summer in Skye* is 'Glasgow', a long piece made from articles originally written for Blackwoods. But the last Skye chapter is 'Homewards', a description of the return journey on *SS Clansman* together with a more introspective section on the benefits of the Skye visits. Smith draws up two categories of benefits. Amongst the 'practical' benefits are the stimulating effects of a change of scenery and people, the peacefulness of existence at Ord (despite sharing a house with twenty others) and the landscapes impressed on his visual memory. More significant are the 'ideal' benefits (in the sense of belonging to the world of ideas and the imagination). Here he includes the experience of "being brought into contact with the songs, stories and superstitions; for, through means of these, one obtains access into the awe and terror that lay at the heart of the ancient Celtic life which is fast disappearing now."[205] Skye was the place where he could personally unwind for a month, but as a writer the process was longer-lasting and deeper. It would not be too much to claim it restored his sanity for another year. Assailed from an early age by a merciless urban environment and fragile health, Smith had fought to preserve his inner vision and sensibilities. The city reduced the individual to one part of the mass, a process of corrosion and attrition that was difficult to resist. Sections of 'Glasgow' underline this idea: "From terrace proud to alley base / I know thee as my mother's face … Of me thou hast become a part / Some kindred with my human heart / Lives in thy streets of stone…"

Once in Skye he could lower the defensive barriers. But in giving his senses full play once again there were dangers that he could go too far. These are that his unconscious might admit more than his mind can accept and make sense of. There are several passages in the book which reveal Smith, sponge-like, soaking up the conflicting ambience of Skye, its surrealist mountain outlines, its unpredictable contrasts of calm and storm, the irrational beliefs of the people and their strange inner knowledge. All this, impossible to rationalise and compartmentalise, fed the creative Dionysian side of his psyche that was so starved in a world increasingly well organised and more predictable, but stifling to what in *Dreamthorp* he had called "the wild and vagrant feelings of human nature." On occasions he felt his mind invaded by these experiences, once terrifyingly so.

Weary with travel, worn out with want of sleep, yet at the same time far from drowsy, with every faculty and sense rather in a condition of wide and intense wakefulness, everything around became invested with a singular and frightful feeling. Why I know not, for I have had no second experience of the kind. But, on this occasion, to my overstrained vision, every object became instinct with a hideous and multitudinous life. The clouds congealed into faces and human forms. Figures started out upon me from the mountain sides. The rugged surfaces, seamed with torrent lines, grew into monstrous figures, and arms with clutching fingers. The sweet and gracious shows of nature became, under the magic of lassitude, a phantasmagoria hateful and abominable.[206]

Smith rated De Quincey the greatest prose stylist of his time, and it is not difficult to find echoes of the Opium-Eater in this and other passages in *A Summer in Skye*. Just as the older man found the bliss and terror of opium dreams preferable to his waking life, so Smith found himself – rather as a medium entering a 'sensitive' state – becoming increasingly aware of another order of existence, almost against his will crossing a border into territory claimed by the bizarre and supernatural. He felt this particularly in McIan's company ("there is a certain awfulness about very old men"), someone who appeared to be cheating the very concept of time and ageing, maybe due to indomitable willpower. This elemental terror creeps back when he surveys the pillar of rock known as the Storr, a freak of Nature particularly when its top disappears into swirling mists. The present-day viewer can still capture something of the experience by ascending to its base and visiting the crag-bound Witches' Cauldron.

When he writes about the Second Sight and predicting the future Smith directly compares the roles of poet and seer, emphasising that while both need extra-sensory gifts it is the poet who "is more open to beauty than other men, and whose duty and delight it is to set forth that beauty anew."[207] Landscapes and man-made structures also have the power to evoke emotions and to tug at the subconscious. At Duntulm, where there is a prominent ruined castle, he encounters "a pleasant feeling of strangeness, of removal from all customary conditions of thought and locality"[208]. Perhaps most of all he felt his unconscious powers nourished and his intense delight in observation gratified when standing on the rocky promontory of Ord with the Cuillins a perpetual jagged horizon.

Fortunately today it remains a place of extraordinary tranquillity where seals and otters are sometimes to be seen. It is approached by a precipitous single-track road that poses problems for present-day drivers during an icy spell. There is still a makeshift slipway onto the beach. Ord House remains much as he described it, down to the many rabbits with their innocent faces. A walk through the birch woods to Dunsciach Castle is little different from the same journey taken 150 years ago. The 'huts' on the seashore are now configurations of broken stones. Apart from a few later houses, well-hidden behind wooded gardens, more recent development is hidden over the brow of the hill, including wooden chalets originally intended as a holiday development but now sold to local owners and others. As elsewhere on the island the population is once again on the increase.

At the beginning of September 1865 Smith, Flora and their three children (Flora was four months pregnant with Isabella, their last) left Ord House, using a pony and trap to ascend the steep track to join the Parliamentary Road that would lead them to Armadale. From the deck of the *SS Clansman* he would take his last view of Skye and regret, as always, that he had to leave.

Three days later, back in Edinburgh, Smith would have discovered that the recently published book was already proving a bestseller. There are no surviving sales figures, but it was quickly reprinted by Strahan. Possibly regarded as a good holiday read, *A Summer in Skye* sold well both sides of the border, with competition coming from *Alice's Adventures in Wonderland*. A one-volume edition came out the following May and there were at least six other UK editions over the next half century, and it cannot have been out of print for many years since. There is now a condensed edition which trims some of the historical references and the Ossian material. Smith appears to have sold the copyrights to both *Dreamthorp* and *A Summer in Skye* to Strahan. John Lane, founder of the Bodley Head Press, was blocked in his attempt to reprint them in 1896[209], by which time the copyright was held by the Edinburgh printers and publishers W.P.Nimmo who brought out an illustrated edition of *A Summer in Skye* a few years later.

News may have already reached Skye that W.E.Aytoun had died three weeks previously whilst on holiday at Elgin. This meant that the Chair of Rhetoric and English Literature (formerly Belles-Lettres) which he had held for twenty years was now vacant. Although he had remarried he lived a more secluded life and entertained less. To the Smiths he had been "the silky voiced man", and he half-mockingly called Flora "the chieftainess" in reference to her father's status. After the publication of *Firmilian,* shortly after Smith first moved to Edinburgh to take up the Secretaryship, there must have been some wariness between them. But apart from Smith's "throat-slitting" letter there is no evidence of any bad blood on his part. They may have represented opposing positions in the mid-Victorian debate about taste and culture but both seem to have maintained for the succeeding ten years a respectful relationship. A task perhaps made easier because their social circles rarely overlapped.

Aytoun had built up the Rhetoric classes to the 150 mark, making the annual income worth around £350, almost twice what the Secretary was paid. Smith clearly had to try again for a Chair, even if it meant a rebuff like the one he had suffered when he applied for Glasgow in 1862. Since then he had written three substantial books, a mass of essays and reviews, not to mention the scholarly work on Burns. But once again he was passed over in favour of the candidate with a sound academic track record, this time David Masson who was already a friend as editor of Macmillan's. Acknowledged as a Milton expert and already Professor at University College London, Masson came north to take the Chair presumably in time for the opening of the new academic year a few weeks later. For Smith there would have been little leisure for savouring his disappointment: his office had again been moved, this time into an annexe of the Natural History collection on the first floor[210], matriculation was already under way in the Old College and on top of this there was another rectorial election to be organised. Gladstone had to stand down and a new contest between Disraeli and Carlyle led to almost a thousand votes being cast by the student body in classes on the morning of Saturday 12 November. Carlyle, adopted by the Liberal faction, was elected by a 2 to1 majority.

Later in the year Sydney Dobell returned to Edinburgh for a brief visit. Having depleted energy and finances on a workers co-operative venture in Gloucestershire, he was now on his way to winter in Italy. He had a great regard for Edinburgh doctors, hence the fleeting visit. It was the last time he and Smith were to meet, and almost immediately Smith must have started writing his essay on him for Good Words. With Aytoun's death it gave him some intellectual space to look back at the Spasmodic affair. He takes the opportunity to consider the longer-term impact of literary criticism on reputation. He goes on to try and pin down the main reasons why a writer of Dobell's obvious gifts was so overlooked. This was a good time to print a tribute to the contemporary who more than thirteen years before had most influenced him. It is an honest look at the man who to some was an object of ridicule, but for Smith there was a stubborn integrity he still admired and perhaps paid tribute to in his choice of adjective for the violin string:

He stands apart from his fellow, and wraps himself up in the mantle of his own thoughts. He is terribly self-conscious; he is the slave of ideas; he writes with a purpose and as if under a certain compulsion. There is nothing he hates so intensely as commonplace; nothing he loves so intensely as beauty – the more ideal the better; and in his fine music a quick ear will not unfrequently detect a stridulous tone, as if the string from which it is drawn were a trifle too tightly strung.[211]

Not content with the phenomenal success of Good Words, the ever-ambitious Alexander Strahan had launched another magazine in time for Christmas 1865. The first issue of The Argosy (A Magazine of Tales, Travel, Essays and Poems) contained the opening chapters of a new Charles Reade novel and a short story by George MacDonald, a popular precursor to the Kailyard writers. Smith was represented by his 'An Essay on an Old Subject', confronting the prospect of old age and extinction. The piece is an anecdotal string onto which are threaded a series of concepts with an almost proverbial quality to them. His theme is that age lends a breadth of vision and a willingness to forgive. The older man "would not be satirical for the world. He has no finger of scorn to point at anything under the sun."[212] Interestingly this somewhat rose-tinted view of the effects of ageing is rebutted almost point by point in Stevenson's 'Crabbed Age and Youth'.

By now Smith believed that death was stalking him. Towards the end of 1865 he complained to close friends of certain symptoms. In the Homewards chapter of *A Summer in Skye* he reported "I put spots in the sun, I flecked the loveliest blue of summer sky with bars of darkness... I was nervous, apprehensive of evil, irritable..."[213] Few believed him. With his beefy build and dark complexion he looked in resolute health, an impression borne out by the *Last Leaves* portrait which showed the full beard he adopted around 1860. Here he is solemn but hardly delicate looking. Masson compared him to the figure he had met in his twenties: "Latterly he had become stouter about the shoulders and more manly-looking, with a tendency to baldness over the forehead which gave a better impression of mental power. But the most remarkable thing about him was his wonderful quietness of demeanour."

Stress is regarded as a twentieth-century phenomenon, but almost certainly Smith was by now suffering a great mental strain that probably caused hallucinations. "Strange nervous distemperatures – unaccountable panic", "a feeling that the ground was melting away, requiring him to dart into a cab" were reported by Pat Alexander. The "brain fever" at the age of ten suggests something radical had happened, and there may have been other complications such as a weak heart. The effects of that devastating dip in Loch Awe in 1851 suggest some inflammatory heart condition such as angina. Whatever the diagnosis, a period of rest followed by some relatively undemanding occupation might have kept recurrent symptoms at bay.

But none of this was he to have, whether as writer, householder, University Registrar or Secretary. And the costs of running Gesto Villa continued to rise as the children grew. Flora, now seven, would soon need a governess, and Jessie and Charles were close behind. In January another girl baby had arrived, named Isabella after Flora's younger sister on Skye. (She had married a John Robertson and brought him twelve children, so when Kenneth McLeod died they moved into Greshornish House). Meeting the household expenses might have been helped by the arrival of Flora's brother Keith who had trained as a doctor at Erlangen. He was practising for a time in Edinburgh and stayed with them at Wardie. He must have quickly made the acquaintance of Eliza Niblet who lived next door with her parents. They were to marry in 1872 after which Keith and his bride left and he became the superintendent of the new Gesto Hospital at Edenbain.

Isabella's arrival might have helped to erase the memory of little Marcella's death two years previously. It was in poetry Smith chose to express something close to a former serenity. In May The Argosy printed his 'A Spring Chanson' where the return of growth is greeted by the reappearance of a blackbird ('merle' in Scots) but there is still the memory of "the newly-mounded grave". And the lark makes a re-appearance. For the last time Smith regained something like his full powers as a nature poet, inevitably calling to mind John Clare, his near-contemporary who had been consigned to an asylum until his death in 1864.

> In the Spring-time's lovely thronging
> Lurk a sacred thirst and longing.
> Every deep earth-hidden root
> Yearns to turn to flower and fruit;
> Every hen-bird east and west
> Pines for eggs beneath her breast;
> On all harmless creeping things
> Comes desire of painted wings;
> And the brightest vision hovers
> In the eyes of happy lovers;
> The burst of apple-blossom brave
> Hides the newly-mounded grave;
> The voice of happy bird in brake
> Soothes the oft-recurring ache.
> Spring is breathing through my hair,
> Spring is smiling in the air;
> And in her deep delight I share
>   With far-removed things—
> The solitary mining mole.
> The lark, a disembodied soul
>   That, lost in heaven, sings.[214]

With its underlying awareness of evanescence ("Men live and die, the song remains") 'A Spring Chanson' provides Smith's poetic swansong. It was a reminder that, had he lived longer, a formidable technical mastery only rarely exercised over the preceding ten years might have again been displayed. But to pay the butcher's bill he needed to write prose and Strahan was expecting more serialised fiction from him. A "Scotch novel" was projected. But right now Smith had to turn his hand to a piece of work already commissioned by Frederick Warne. This was an extensive introduction to an anthology of more than a hundred American writers published in April 1866 and entitled *Golden Leaves from the American Poets*.

In his essay Smith reveals his awareness of writers such as Longfellow, William Cullen Bryant, Wendell Holmes, John Russell Lowell, not to mention Edgar Allan Poe and Hawthorne. He is fascinated by the telling differences that distinguished transatlantic poetry. His conclusion ("American poetry is simply a little exquisite oratory in the great cathedral of English song") may seem unduly parochial today. But remember Smith was writing within months of Lee's surrender and the capitulation of the Southern states. In the newly created United States the majority were still first-generation immigrants and links with their homelands were strong. In Hawthorne's New England many would have felt Britain to be their true home. The best-known poets also travelled in Europe and used European settings and themes for their work. The names Smith highlights have stood the test of time and his assessments are perceptive. Once again he suggests climate and environment as important factors in explaining the productivity and vitality of the American literary scene. As in Skye the awareness of nature, whether consciously or not, provides the inhabitants with "an unusual cerebral activity, a sense of beauty developed into keenness by a brighter air and a more excitable climate..."[215]

Meanwhile the periodical work was unceasing. The Quiver had been launched in 1862, the title being a reference to God's Word as an arrow to the human heart. After an unpromising start it dropped its original strapline ("Designed for the Defence and Promotion of Biblical Truth...") and rearranged its priorities ("An Illustrated Magazine of Social, Intellectual and Religious Progress") with a new editor. Such was the demand from Strahan's editors, Smith had not needed to write for anyone else. It must have taken a considerable inducement, then, to get him to produce *The McGillowies of McGillowie*, a three-part supernatural chiller which was clearly written at great speed. It is essentially an after-dinner story which could have succeeded brilliantly in the hands of a skilled raconteur but on the page it is thin indeed.

In the closing of 'A Lark's Flight' (from *Dreamthorp*) Smith had introduced the story of the Irishman's banshee and now he chose to elaborate on it. It becomes a predictable Gothic tale involving an ancestral curse, an artless English rose due to be married to a young Scottish nobleman who inhabits a very dreary castle (based on Dunvegan), plus a beaten drum foretelling his death. What little life this piece possesses lies in the Scots dialogue used by the fisherfolk of Halycross who comment drily on their betters' goings-on. This was the first time Smith had employed rural Scots in an extended way.

In April 1866 The Argosy published 'On Dreams and Dreaming'. This short essay is remarkable for going against the prevailing opinion that dreaming was an entirely physiological process, a kind of subjective counterpart to the necessary business of sleep. A variety of observations are made on the significance of dreams, the relation between waking and sleeping mental processes, their prophetic nature and their purpose. He was probably the first to propose the notion of the suspended will allowing free reign to the unconscious. This was, of course, the basis of Freud's *Die Traumdeutung* almost forty years later. In one passage the essayist considers the ability of the unconscious to store away experience and reproduce events, people, sensations in a manner far more arresting than in waking life:

Memory deals with these things as a photographer deals with his negatives; she does not destroy them, she simply places them aside, for future use mayhap. If you are a dreamer you will know this. And in dreams the imagination does not always deal with experience; it frequently goes beyond that, and guesses at matters of which it cannot have any positive knowledge. There is no more common terror in dreams than that of falling over a precipice; and most dreamers are aware that in so dreaming they have felt the air *cold* as they cut through it, in their swift rush earthwards. This, of course, cannot be a matter of experience, as those who have been so precipitated are placed conclusively out of court. But it is curious that the dreamer should so feel; that the swift imagination should not only vividly realise the descent itself, but an important accessory of the descent – the chilliness of the swiftly-severed air – as well.[216]

In August the Smiths took their family holiday at Dingwall, a market town north of Inverness, more easily reached by train than Skye. Perhaps for a summer retreat it was a little too accessible. According to Pat Alexander "even in the wilds, his inevitable Devil (the Printer's) more or less continued to haunt him; and he returned not much renovated". By October 1866 preparations for the new university term were under way and, with the increased demands on his attention and energy, he was once again subject to hallucinations and panic attacks. Around this time he visited his lawyer friend John McLennan whose book on primitive marriage customs had eventually been published the previous year. (It created a mild sensation in the newly-formed Anthropological Institute after he had given a foretaste to readers of The Argosy in a piece enticingly headed 'Bride-Catching'.) Apparently he told MacLennan he felt "death was in him" and wanted to make a will. It was put off to a later date, but in early November Smith witnessed the will of his friend Horatio McCulloch. Perhaps this was enough to induce further panic at the prospect of making his own.

A week later, by which time student matriculation was almost complete, Smith took to his bed with what was rumoured to be bronchitis. It was in fact diphtheria and after a few weeks, when it was safe for friends to visit, he was seen to be very weak. He rallied slightly at the turn of the year and acknowledged his 36th birthday. New year 1867 began with a week of dense fog punctuated by sudden blizzards. The Secretary was not seen about when term recommenced and it was assumed that he was on the mend. But his defences were down and he now contracted a fever which left him delirious for hours on end, babbling about those minutiae which had latterly made the Secretary's job such a plague to him.

By now Dr Malcolm had called in Prof. Christison and it was then confirmed that typhus was evident. The evening before his death Smith appeared calm once more and hopes revived. But as the night wore on he became weaker, passing away as the first streaks of dawn appeared over Salisbury Crags on January 5th. No dying words were recorded, but those present tried to calm his anxiety over the young family he was leaving behind.

The funeral took place on a day of hard, brilliant sunshine that flashed on newly fallen snow. As was customary, at 2pm a short address was delivered over the coffin in the dining room at Wardie before the cortege made its way to Inverleith Row and Warriston Cemetery. For those who had come over from Glasgow carriages were waiting outside Register House in Princes Street opposite Waverley Station. Altogether there were twenty carriages and the mourners included most of his close friends and relatives. Women were at that time not expected to be at the graveside, so leading the procession were Smith's father, John, now sixty-four, and his eldest son Charles Kenneth, just five.

There is no record of what tribute was offered over the grave, or by whom. On the death certificate, made out ten days later, under his name is written "Author of Life-Drama etc". First it was Alexander Smith the man they mourned. Only later did speculation turn to what he might have achieved if as a writer he had been allowed a longer span.

Chapter 12:
1867-73

His death did not disturb that ancient Night.
Scornfullest Night! Over the dead there hung
Great gulfs of silence, blue, and strewn with stars –
No sound – no motion – in the eternal depths.
('A Life-Drama' sc.7)

NOT FOR THE LAST TIME the Glasgow Herald was caught unprepared. Its obituary piece relied on a contemporary handbook called *Men of the Time*, but Smith's entry in this went no further than 1855, only the year after he had moved to Edinburgh. His already short productive span was now cut even shorter. The Scotsman (7 January), clearly better prepared, was more generous in space but still cautious in assessing the poetic output. "He had yet two or three steps to take to reach the first rank" was the verdict, but the obituary writer also pointed out that work published during 1865 and 1866 would, if collected, have filled seven volumes. Of the literary reviews the Pall Mall Gazette's was the fullest, containing in its opening paragraph a veiled reproach to Smith's inveterate critics:

It was amidst general consent... that Mr Smith attained a definite rank as a poet, and whatever he wrote afterwards was examined with a curiosity not awakened by an unknown man. This of itself is sufficient to endow his name with permanent interest and to make it the duty of those who watch over letters to describe what is distinctive about him amongst the writers of his age.[217]

This was written by James Hannay, who also did a lengthy appreciation for the February Cassell's Magazine. David Masson wrote a long piece for Macmillan's[218] that has already been quoted from. The assessment in The Athenaeum (12 January) was always going to be interesting. After allowing considerable merit to both *A Summer in Skye* and *Dreamthorp* (somehow succeeding in getting both titles wrong), it continues in more familiar vein:

Unhappily for his chances of any lasting fame, Mr Smith began his career by writing spasmodic poetry of a daring kind, which had a certain success until the trick of composition was exposed. After that exposure the public very quickly dropped the "new poet" in favour of his originals. Mr Smith had to begin his literary life again; but, being a man of some natural gifts, he was gradually making his way to a really independent style.

This reference to 'exposure' was about as close to a *mea culpa* as Chorley would ever offer. The following year *Last Leaves*, Pat Alexander's collection of Smith's essays plus the two final poems 'A Spring Chanson' and the unfinished 'Edinburgh', was published containing a long prefatory *Memoir*. Bursting with anecdote and reminiscences that illustrate an intriguing dichotomy in Smith's character (for example, his "extreme amiability" masking "a thrill of irritable fibre"), this is self-evidently written by someone who knew on a daily basis the living man. By contrast, Brisbane's *The Early Years of Alexander Smith* (1869) was composed of memories that related to the late 1840s and early 1850s. It would have been so neat if the two could be put side by side as a complete life, but as we have already seen Brisbane is always trying to portray the young poet as a lapsed Evangelical. This notion is sufficiently misleading to make the alert reader wary of Brisbane's other assertions. The detailed account of the Glasgow Addisonian Literary Society years is valuable but contains a number of inaccuracies. Finally there is the unavoidable issue of Brisbane's intense relationship with his subject which came to such an abrupt end around 1854.

By the 1870s Smith's quarter century of oblivion was beginning. Most of the Spasmodics had died, and so had Gilfillan, their opinionated herald. The two that were left were poets only in name: P.J.Bailey, secure on a Civil List pension, went on adding to *Festus* until the third edition (1889) weighed in at nearly a thousand pages. Gerald Massey abandoned poetry altogether in the 1860s in favour of Egyptology and American lecture tours on spiritualism. The taste for their kind of poetry must have lingered on in America, for in 1879 the New York publisher James Miller brought out *Poems by Alexander Smith,* an ingenious yoking together of the 1853 *Poems* and the 1857 *City Poems*. It contains an unusual frontispiece portrait (by 'Schoff') and also the text of Pat Alexander's long letter to the Athenaeum refuting the plagiarism charges. This letter had also been published in *Last Leaves* which went through three editions.

The Edinburgh publishers, Nimmo Hay & Mitchell, issued *The Poetical Works of Alexander Smith* (which includes *Edwin of Deira'*) more than thirty years later. Alexander Strahan sold the copyright of *Dreamthorp* to Mitchell in 1881. When Strahan was liquidated in the 1890s Nimmo Hay & Mitchell got their hands on *A Summer in Skye* and probably *Alfred Hagart's Household*. The first was regularly reprinted in the early years of the twentieth century, most notably Routledge's pocket edition in 1907 and the illustrated Sampson Low version of 1919.

In America, where copyright laws were not so prescriptive, *Dreamthorp* was frequently re-issued, once under the alluring title *Good Company*. After that there was a 20-year gap until the influential Doubleday Doran edition with Christopher Morley's introduction which praised it as a thoughtful book "with the delicious gift of melancholy." After this Smith seems to have become a favourite of the small press publishers: individual essays from *Dreamthorp* were issued, often with accompanying woodcuts. The book's admirers grew, and some even sought out this Lowland Scotland ruritania . The word got out that the 'real' Dreamthorp was Linlithgow, a market town near Falkirk on the route of the Edinburgh-Glasgow railway which Smith used fairly frequently. During the 1930s the town clerk was apparently overwhelmed with transatlantic summer visitors expecting a *Dreamthorp* trail. Linlithgow has the trademark features – the partly ruined castle overlooking a splendid loch, a historic high street and some atmospheric inns – but there is nothing by Smith himself to make a definite connection. And any link to the real world would surely prove fatal to the intensely introspective content of the book.

In Britain there was an edition in the Routledge New Universal Library series (1906) and also in Oxford University Press World Classics series (1914). This last, including essays from *Last Leaves*, was edited by Hugh Walker, professor of English at Lampeter College. Obviously smitten by Smith, he had already written an article for the Glasgow Herald, entitled rather unimaginatively 'A Glasgow Poet', published 10 June 1909. Whilst acknowledging the obvious value of Smith's prose works, he asks: "Would not the poems too – out of print for many a year – be worth reproducing or, if not the whole, a selection of the best?" Clearly he was not well informed or he was being disingenuous as Nimmo Hay & Mitchell were just about to publish *Poetical Works*.

Walker's article did have other results. A couple of days later a certain George Umber (almost certainly a pseudonym) wrote to the Herald suggesting erecting a plaque on the wall of 12 Charlotte Street (the Smith family home in Glasgow) which was, seventy years later, miraculously still standing. In the 1930s the tenement was eventually pulled down. A letter requesting to know the whereabouts of the plaque received a businesslike answer from the demolition firm Robert G.Robb of Bridgeton: "Presuming that the tablet was there, in all probability our workmen would send it along to the coup [refuse site] along with the debris, thinking it of no value or interest to anyone." This was written to the poet's grand-daughter Dorothea Pender-Mackenzie. The site is now a landscaped car park, and the surrounding area – including a new David Dale gateway onto the Green – is once again becoming a sought-after residential location in the Merchant City area.

A slightly better outcome attended the laudable initiative by an Alexander Smith Memorial Committee to commission a bronze bust and present it to the Corporation Art Galleries. By 1910, with the support of town councillor Dr William Findlay, a subscription list was circulating and the sculptor Kellock Brown was appointed. His task could not have been easy since he had to work from portraits and possibly a surviving photograph showing only one profile (the non-squinty side of Smith's face). However, on March 11th 1911 the completed bust was unveiled and handed over in the new Kelvingrove Art Gallery. In his presentation address Dr Findlay called it "a fine poetic presentment". But he seems to have been misinformed about the date of Smith's death which (according to him) took place "39 years ago". With existing confusion over his birth date, the poet was now to have his death recorded five years prematurely. At least Glasgow had paid a belated tribute to the writer of the best poem the city has yet inspired. Unfortunately a recent enquiry has revealed that the bust is no longer part of the civic collection.

How has Smith's reputation fared in the 150 years or so since his death? One of the indispensable books for deciding who was in and who was out in the mid-Victorian critical mind was Edmund Clarence Stedman's *Victorian Poets*. It was written initially for the guidance of American readers but was then issued in Britain in 1872. His critical profiles are generally level-headed, but Stedman has very little time for innovative poets – such as Massey, George MacDonald, David Gray as well as Smith – labeled as Rhapsodists. 'A Life-Drama' was

vicious in style, loose in thought, and devoid of real vigour or beauty. In after years, though, through honest study Smith acquired better taste and worked after a more becoming purpose. His prose essays were charming and his City Poems, marked by sins of omission only, may be rated as negatively good.

Clearly a critic who wanted to have it both ways! This positively negative judgement of Smith's reputation was often echoed during the succeeding century. In 1880 Arnold's *The English Poets* set down the guidelines for judging the next decade:

For supreme poetical success more is required than the powerful application of ideas to life; it must be an application under the conditions fixed by laws of poetic truth and poetic beauty. Those laws fix as an essential condition, in the poet's treatment of such matters as are here in question, high seriousness; - the high seriousness which comes from absolute sincerity.[219]

In this atmosphere Smith's reputation, like that of Keats and other late Romantics, failed to bloom. He was dismissed as a bold opportunist. Worse, he was hardly professional, reduced to being one of Elizabeth Barrett Browning's Parenthetical Poets who only wrote in the evenings and at weekends. Tennyson, Browning, Meredith, Swinburne, secure in the possession of private incomes or patronage, were all full-time. Arnold himself, of course, served in the Department of Education, but by then he had turned to prose writing. Smith's reputation had to bide its time. By the 1890s experimentalism had become more acceptable, and his name resurfaces in the pages of The Yellow Book in a long article that quotes from *Dreamthorp* and refers to its "decorated style of poetic architecture". The poetry was also reassessed in a column in the Pall Mall Gazette entitled 'The Wares of Autolycus' in 1898. Here, by close analysis of 'Barbara' (soon to be included in *Palgrave*) the anonymous critic concludes that it was "true and yet rather thin, new and yet not important" and wonders why it stirred up so much resentment in the 1850s.

But the book that perhaps brought Smith's name once again to the forefront was not directly about him. Arthur Waugh's *Tennyson*, written and published within months of the Poet Laureate's death in 1892 revealed that Tennyson had admired 'A Life-Drama' and had indeed written to Smith to say so. The letter has disappeared. He also refers to the plagiarism campaign in The Athenaeum after the publication of *City Poems* and for the first time identifies William Allingham as the chief protagonist. Waugh's verdict was: "The sequel was an oblivion which was, it may be, an excess in reaction." Just so, but why did it take nearly forty years to admit it?

The next step in official recognition of Smith's standing was a reference in the *Cambridge History of English Literature* (1932 edition) where Hugh Walker again makes high claims for his achievements as an essayist. Around the same time American critics rediscovered *Dreamthorp*. We have already noticed Christopher Morley. A few years later John J. Reilly's 'In Praise of Dreamthorp' bracketed Smith with Lamb, Hazlitt and Thackeray. It was the more intangible qualities that this critic most admired: "his thoughts, like the sleeping Princess, awake at a touch" and the more puzzling "His essays retain no smell of the lamp."

Most reasonable literary historians have accepted Smith's wide-ranging prose output, but his poetry still provides problems of classification. The nationalists would like to lay claim, but never was there a more unlikely candidate for the mantle of Burns. He himself declared the Scottish school an irrelevance in his own time: "Ah! It is too late in the day now: it might have done fifty years ago" (as he wrote in the Scottish Athenaeum in 1853). As Pat Alexander said of him, "there was a good deal in him that almost might be held to approximate to the English rather than the Scotch type of understood character."[220]

No major critical work on Smith has yet appeared, so perhaps it is hardly surprising that biographers have fared little better. But there have been a number of contenders. In the 1940s, as a result perhaps of the new edition of *Dreamthorp*, at least one was planned. On 6 January 1945 readers of The Ross-shire Journal could read the following from a long letter entitled 'A Summer in Skye':

It is particularly necessary at this time that a really adequate presentation should be made of Smith's life story and of the place which he held in Scottish literature. No formal biography of Smith has ever been written, and brief sketches written after his death by those who knew him tell only a very small part of the story. The family and friends of Alexander Smith have been good enough to place at my disposal all the poems, letters and manuscripts now in their possession. I have been successful in discovering a large amount of new material and new information which will throw a new light on the work and achievement of this brave and gifted son of Scotland's soil.

This emotional appeal to the readership was penned by Edward Perry, self-styled Professor of English at Brandon College, Manitoba, who was doing Smith for "my research work at the University of Toronto." Inquiries have failed to turn up any record of him at either institution and it is frustrating to think of what material he might have had in his possession. Perry did call on Dorothea Pender-Mackenzie, the eldest daughter of Isabella (who was only a year old when her father died). She lent him some of the Brisbane letters which he does not seem to have returned. Dorothea was apprehensive about seeing him because twenty years before another academic had approached her mother with a similar request.

This time one Hugh Palmer went away with a manuscript which was again not returned. Worse, after this she had contracted a mild form of typhus. The other three grand-daughters became wary of having much to do with recording the life of the poet who, even though he was their grandfather, must have seemed unimaginably distant to them. He was known colloquially by them as The Boss. They all seemed to have defied the Smith jinx of dying young, since their mother Isabella was 72 at her death in 1939 and they all lived into their eighties, the youngest dying as recently as the mid 1990s.

Neither Palmer nor Perry completed their biographies, or at best they failed to find a publisher. Maybe they were defeated by the apparently uneventful nature of the poet's life after he married and moved to Gesto Villa. And there is the problem that he lived only half a normal lifespan, with a writing career spanning at the most fifteen years. Tantalising to the present biographer is the mention of poems, letters and manuscripts which appear to have been readily available to earlier researchers. Apart from two or three sheets in Smith's hand bearing fair copies of early poems, the few remaining letters to Brisbane in the Dick Institute and the letters in the NLS, there is practically no holograph material that could be traced through conventional channels. A year before she died Isabella wrote to her eldest daughter Dorothea, expressing regret over giving a "scrap of MS to the Cambridge (Mass.) scholar Hugh Palmer". She speculates on the fate of other material:

Nearly all the MSS were lost at the time of my father's death; a maid was found lighting the library fire with some of them. The rest were lost when my brother [Charles] died in India. If they came back I never got them.[221]

If Charles, who fancied he had inherited something of his father's literary gift, took material to Calcutta in his luggage (where he died from TB at the age of thirty) clearly not everything went into the fire at Wardie. From Pat Alexander's reminiscences it is evident that the maid was not the only one destroying the poet's papers. He noted a vein of destructive procrastination in the poet himself, particularly when it came to answering letters. During the plagiarism controversy of 1857 he apparently received many letters of support from amongst others the essayist Arthur Helps, from Aubrey de Vere and even apparently from Tennyson. Few were acknowledged:

The document would thus be allowed to crumble indefinitely about in his pockets, his intentions being all the while the most virtuous; finally with a certain *insouciance* natural to him he would some day light his pipe with it, in defect of non-literary material, and the *corpus delicti* (so to call it) being thus vanished, all hope in the matter was over. His dereliction would continue, however, to distress him not a little so that he especially detested reference to it by any friend aware of the facts, and disposed, for his good, to rally him on the subject.[222]

The only surviving letter in the dead poet's desk was from Mr Rarey, the famous horse-tamer in Boston, enclosing complimentary tickets to his rodeo show and expressing "in the name of the great American people" his unbounded gratitude and admiration.

Apart from the essay on Scottish Ballads which was originally written for *Edinburgh Essays* in 1856, all the pieces in *Last Leaves* date from the last three or four years of Smith's life. They are "the spray of the writer's mind" according to Pat Alexander, although at least one

('Literary Work') contains observations central to his personal creativity. Other material, such as some pedestrian verse for Good Words and long reviews for the Edinburgh papers, was excluded. For his best work Smith needed time to ruminate, to release then collect his thoughts, time that was in increasingly short supply. 'The Norse Princess' is exceptional as a late attempt at using the ballad quatrain, but the language is too contrived to achieve the intended doom-laden atmosphere. Much more successful is 'A Spring Chanson', rightly included *in Last Leaves*. There is perhaps a wish to return to the experimentalism of his twenties but within a more disciplined metrical framework (an excerpt is included in Chapter 11). Although Smith wrote knowledgeably about Burns, Scottish history and the Border Ballads, to these his poetry owes few debts.

Of Smith's periodical essays the best have been included in *Last Leaves*, although it is a pity there was no space for the tribute to Hugh MacDonald written for Cassell's Magazine. Here in places the hidden emotion flashes through, startling the writing out of its easy jog-trot. Close to MacDonald, he is also clear-eyed, showing how the older man (in the early 1850s his mentor along with James Hedderwick and Gilfillan) was adept at writing within those limitations of geography and empathy that he imposed on himself:

> He was the most uncosmopolitan of mortals. He had the strongest local attachments. In his eyes Scotland was the fairest portion of the planet, Glasgow the fairest portion of Scotland, and Bridgeton – the district of the city in which he was born and in which he dwelt – the fairest portion of Glasgow. He would have shrieked like a mandrake at uprootal. He would never pass a night away from home. But he was a passionate lover of nature; and the snowdrop called him out of the smoke to Castlemilk; the sleepy lucken-gowan to Kenmure, the crawflower to Gleniffer. His heart clung to every ruin in the neighbourhood like the shrouding ivy; he was deeply learned in epitaphs, and spent many a sunny hour in village churchyards, extracting sweet and bitter thoughts from the half-obliterated inscriptions.[223]

Smith had a genuine gift for scene setting and dialogue. There are passages in both *Alfred Hagart's Household* and *A Summer in Skye* which contain skilful character vignettes. Unfortunately he did not write with sufficient speed to make regular journalism a feasibility. The gift appears to have been shared with his younger brother David who called himself Murray-Smith. He went to London and started a family, apparently living happily and successfully. But only a few years after Smith's death the parents received news that he had died from an overdose of sleeping powder. The details are unclear, but the two children (the elder aged five, presumably with their mother) came back to stay with their grandparents now in Paisley.

John and Christina, by now well into their seventies, were sufficiently hale to welcome grandchildren around the house. Christina died in the 1880s but John was to outlive all his children except the youngest, also Christina. William, their youngest son, went to India and died young. Of Marion, the eldest daughter (ten years younger than the poet) nothing is known. Katy, the first daughter, had died while the family were still living in Paisley for the first time. The result of this early elimination of one generation is that the surviving offspring had an intimate recollection of John and Christina, but of the poet's generation they knew next to nothing, relying entirely on their grandparents' memory. Then there was the poet's sister Christina who had emigrated to America. After her mother's death she returned briefly to Scotland and then took her father back with her to Chicago. He died shortly afterwards, still believing that things would turn out for the best, an unshakeable belief that stood him in good stead for almost ninety years as his offspring (with one exception) barely made it to middle age.

In early 1867, in the immediate aftermath of her husband's funeral, Flora MacDonald Smith found herself a widow at the age of thirty-six with four young children. To the trauma of her husband's death has to be added the news, just a few days later, that her father Charles Macdonald of Ord, had also passed away at the age of eighty-eight. His funeral was to be on the same day as the poet's but in Skye. By the beginning of March she had gone to Peebles for a few days to stay with friends. There her oldest daughter Flora, nine years old, fell ill with gastric fever. Within a month she too was dead.

Flora's worldly prospects, once her grief gave her leisure to consider them, were not far short of desperate. In 1869, after two years of trying to manage on her own, she wrote to the Royal Literary Fund for assistance, her referees being Monckton Milnes, John McLennan and John Brown, the author of *Rab and His Friends*. She stated her case succinctly to the RLF:

At the death of my husband I was left with four children (the eldest I had three months later the grief to lose), our sole provision being £600 which remained from a life policy after all due claims were settled. My husband dying intestate, this sum is the property of my children, of whom I am trustee, so to the interest only I am entitled.[224]

With this insubstantial income and the family and a large house to run, she must have been plunged immediately into an impossible situation. The death of her father may have provided a small inheritance, but it would have been divided amongst eight offspring. A more continuing source of support should have been Kenneth McLeod of Gesto, the uncle who gave them Gesto Villa as a wedding present. Since he had no children of his own, he might well have been looked to but Flora's brothers and sisters had families too. On the Smith side there was John's brother Alexander (the poet's uncle) who had by now built up a thriving engineering business in the Kingston area of Glasgow making machinery for sugar processing. He and his family, which included two daughters Mary and Marion, lived at Parkgrove, a large villa on the Paisley road.

Correspondence survives between Flora and Mary Smith. The black border shows it dates from soon after the deaths of her husband and father and probably after her child's death. There are eight letters, mostly undated and written from Wardie and from Skye. In what was probably the first she ends: "Call me no longer Mrs Smith; let me be Flora to you all", suggesting that the relationship is of recent origin. Initially Flora depended heavily on her Catholic faith, but it seems to have been insufficient:

As for me you need not ask, for my life is weary, weary and very wretched. God might make my burden heavier tho' I find it very heavy to bear up under it. My nights are so terrible to me, and every morning I take heisteria but that is of small moment. I can't think of leaving the house just at present for I think the return would be terrible, but if your Mama wants to visit next week when I have had the house well cleaned, I would be very happy to see her.[225]

There are two more letters from Gesto Villa – one of which refers to a further bereavement on the Smith side – before Flora and the three children leave Edinburgh to stay with her sister at Ord. One dated 28 August gives a specimen of what Flora called her "forced gaiety". She writes to Mary wishing her good luck for an important social event she was due to attend in the west end of Glasgow. It shows (despite unfathomable references to brown paper and lodging houses) that Flora in happier times would have been an amusing correspondent:

I can't allow this day of trains and tiaras to pass without writing to tell you that I am thinking of you all at this time. Mrs W. is the happy mother of a Mrs Duncan! Success attend brown paper. I have an interest in its future. I hope Mrs W. will have the same in lodging houses!!!

Putting all trash aside, I shall so enjoy a description of the "gay and festive scene", pray give it to me. I just fancy you at this moment with my lady sailing up to you – train over her left arm!! - to be cross-questioned in the "farm-house". Mary in dignified disgust can scarcely suppress her rage at the patronising West End swell, which being lost on my lady.

I do hope you will drink Champ[agne] at her expense, to do honour to the occasion.

Brown paper for ever.

There is a later reference to Horatio McCulloch's widow also being on Skye to see "about taking the cottage at Dunvegan" over the summer and returning to Trinity for the winter months. The painter had died on 24 June and is buried at Warriston Cemetery within sight of Smith's grave marked by its runic cross. The next letter is from Wardie, presumably later in the year, because Mrs McCulloch ("a poor helpless woman") has now turned up without warning to stay at a nearby house called St John. She was determined to find a smaller house and Flora accompanied her on many an exhausting afternoon to search all over Edinburgh. There is also a delightful passage on the three remaining children:

I can't not [sic] really get one half hour since I got your letter to write to you. Baby [Isabella] is quite well thank God. Dr Malcolm of course laughed at me – he said how had I, after all I had seen, so very little knowledge as not to see it was just a sickness caused by her eye teeth beginning. He said her gums were not even inflamed. She is now trotting about as brisk as a bee. Charlie and Jessie are feeling the good of the change of home. I think they look even better than they did on Skye. Charlie has got a new dress – of which he has much need – and he looks like a little man. He struts about with his hands in his pockets.

Despite the note of brave optimism in these sad letters, clearly the books at GestoVilla were not balancing. There was light-hearted talk of taking in lodgers and doing laundry, then in January 1869 an application to the Royal Literary Fund brought a life-raft of £100. Her brother Keith came to stay, studying for membership of the Royal College of Physicians, and probably paid for board and lodging. But as Flora turned her fortieth year it was becoming abundantly clear that she would never regain that emotional stability that ten years of marriage had provided. She had lost so much so suddenly. Now daily living was conducted on the edge of a financial and emotional precipice, with the need to keep the bailiffs at bay a continuous feature, necessitating discreet begging from comfortably-off friends and Skye family members. Long, long ago it must have seemed that the poet wrote of her, that sunny morning in May, as "the patientest knitter" in the garden surrounded by fallen blossom.

Neither was her health strong. The weak eye continually irked her and she was having trouble with her legs, latterly spending much of the day in a bathchair. Unfortunately there was another way, damaging to both health and finances, that Flora found to console herself in the darkest hours of her loss and pain. Coming from the western isles she would have seen plenty of spirit drinking, but she must surely have realised it was risky for a woman with any reputation. When she visited

Skye she seems to have stayed in one of Kenneth McLeod's houses near Edinbane. Here, in 1868, she managed to fall out with him, ostensibly over stealing a servant, but her drinking seems to have been the real cause. The following year Kenneth McLeod died. The will (dated 24 October 1868) instructs that all his Indian property should be liquidated and the proceeds (less £10,000 which was to be used for the new hospital at Edinbane) were to be divided amongst Flora's brothers, sisters and cousins. All his servants were to be left a year's extra pay. But "To Flora MacDonald Smith I bequeath the sum of one penny sterling, in remembrance of her services inducing my servants to leave me."

Although he had been generous to Flora and Alexander in the past this was a mean-spirited gesture and reflects badly on a man who did so much good to the community where he had been born and had returned to live. Of course, it was the final blow for Flora's hopes of economic independence. By 1872 things had deteriorated so much that her brother Lachlan was made legal guardian of the two youngest children: Charles, now twelve and back at boarding school after "an accident by which he had been seriously disabled and confined to bed", and Isabella, aged eight and also boarding at a local convent school. Jessie, who was now sixteen, no longer seems to have lived at home.

Lachlan was also granted powers to sell Gesto Villa (in which only the children had an interest) to redeem its value and invest it. Towards the end of 1872 Flora again wrote to the RLF. Her living-in brother Keith, by now having qualified, was engaged to Eliza Mary Niblet, the girl next door, and Flora must have been thinking of the forthcoming wedding. When he left (to go to Edinbane) she would be alone for most of the time, and where was she to live? There is no surviving reply in the RLF files, but the rules of the Fund state clearly that all payments, unless pensions, are not repeatable. After she had received a reply from the Secretary, Flora saw fit to write twice more, each time in a state of more abject desperation. On 25 June she asked:

Is there no hope for me that the Committee will some day put me on a yearly pension? I am so poor and all the shocks my nervous system got has affected my health. I have lost the use of my feet. I can't move out of the spot in which I am placed, so my life is a very lonely and sad one. My rich uncle who was expected to look to me did not leave me a penny. [Not, as we have seen strictly true] With many thanks for your kind enquiries,
        I am yours v.sinc.
        Flora MacDonald Smith
I can do nothing for myself with my hands save write and turn the leaves of a book. I have come through a sea of sorrow.

Poor Flora had only one more year of suffering. She died at 11.30 am on Monday 21 July 1873 at 33 Lauriston Gardens near the Meadows in Edinburgh. At that address, according to the PO Directory, was Miss Campbell's School for Young Ladies. So why was Flora there? Perhaps Isabella had moved from the St Margaret's Convent, or perhaps her eldest daughter Jessie was working there. There can be little doubt over what had caused her death. The death certificate is succinct: "Cardiac disease, apoplexy, alcoholism".

July 21st, according to the Edinburgh papers, was when the warm, oppressive weather that had engulfed the city ("Summer has leapt suddenly on Edinburgh like a tiger") gave way to severe thunderstorms. The Courant likened them to the roar of heavy artillery. It made no mention, however, of the death of Flora. A brief mention in The Scotsman gives no idea of the circumstances. The funeral was held on the following Thursday and her brothers Lachlan and Alexander, journeying down from Skye, discovered debts of more than £300 (£30,000 equivalent value). As beneficiaries of Kenneth McLeod's will they could easily afford to pay off the creditors between them. So that trifling matter was easily settled. Despite Flora's fears, Gesto Villa was not sold until another two years had passed, and it fetched £1450. Of this sum Charlie got half, while the two girls shared the rest. Soon afterwards the family began to disperse. In the west John and Christina had somehow kept body and soul together with the Murray-Smith grandchildren. As we have seen, after Christina died, John in his eighties went off with his youngest daughter to Chicago.

What happened to the children of the poet? With his inheritance Charles left in the late 1870s to learn flax-growing in India, but by 1890 he had died and the mysterious manuscripts saved from the fire at Wardie seemed to have perished with him. Jessie emigrated to Sydney, presumably having married first. She took with her Bonnie Prince Charlie's signet ring, supposedly handed down from the original Flora. Isabella, the youngest, only a year old when the poet died, finished her education then went to live with MacDonald relatives at Ord. A family photograph shows her standing outside the porch at Ord House in a nurse's uniform: maybe she trained or worked at the Edinbane hospital endowed by her great uncle. Anyway, Isabella eventually married Dr Pender-Mackenzie, spending most of her life in the Highlands near Dingwall. From this marriage there were four daughters (grandchildren of the poet), three of whom survived into the 1980s and one of whom the writer met a few years before her death.

Chapter 13
(postscript)

And whether crowned or crownless, when I fall
It matters not, so as God's work is done.
I've learned to prize the quiet lightning-deed
Not the applauding thunder at its heels
Which men call Fame.
('A Life-Drama' sc.13)

SMITH'S POETRY HAS BEEN CLAIMED by those who champion a more socially-conscious, documentary role for the genre, particularly by the critical label that has been applied to him of 'city poet'. Think how flat our picture of Victorian London would have been without Dickens, Gustav Doré or Mayhew. Smith gives us equally striking images of the urban experience but his response to the city was more oblique. Certainly in 'A Life-Drama' there are references to its blighting effects and the crushing of dearest hopes and dreams. However there is no truly political dimension, such as can be found in the Chartist writers and Ebenezer Elliot. By the time *City Poems* appeared Smith has discerned a transforming power in the city that makes his moral stance ambivalent, with abrupt switches (in 'Glasgow') from the sardonic to the ecstatic:

> When sunset bathes thee in his gold.
> In wreaths of bronze thy sides are roll'd,
> > Thy smoke is dusky fire;
> And, from the glory round thee pour'd
> A sunbeam, like an angel's sword
> > Shivers upon a spire.
> Thus have I watched thee, Terror! Dream!
> While the blue Night* crept up the stream.
> [* *see Appendix: The Gestation of 'Glasgow'*]

Nor was he a poet that could easily be labeled Scottish School. We have already seen how averse Smith was to dusting down old forms such as the ballad, despite the arguments of Blackie and the nationalists. A modern parallel could be made with Edwin Muir who was accused of cultural defeatism by Grieve and others in the Scottish Renaissance movement of the 1930s. As Carla Sassi's recent critique on Scottish literature shows, Muir's inability to find common cause with a nationalistic dogma led to a degree of sidelining by later critics:

Muir's analysis of the anomalous predicament of the Scottish writer, even though imbued with pessimism, is in many ways more lucid and often more accessible than that offered by MacDiarmid himself. Scotland's 'isolation' and the lack of adequate interpretative models for its predicament are central issues in many of his writings. Scotland – he explained – was living in a condition of "unchanging suspended potentiality", "half within the world of life and half outside it."[226]

Smith makes a similar point in his journalistic pieces on writers and painters. Within Smith's poetry, although there is plenty of unusual vocabulary and Jacobean coinings, hardly a word can be labeled as Scots. Despite his Ayrshire roots there were to be no imitations of Burnsian lyricism, despite his Hebridean links no Ossianic ballads. The influences were all from mainstream 'southron' sources. This was a feature noted by David Masson in his piece on 'A Life-Drama' in 1853 and nothing changed over the succeeding dozen or so years that marked the span of his literary career:

Scotland is, of course, pleased at being able to reckon so promising a new poet as hers by right of birth – the more so as it is some time since her last celebrated poet, Campbell, died; and as, notwithstanding some high names on her list, she has not during the last two centuries been so prolific as England in considerable poets. This is very natural; but it ought at the same time to be distinctly recognised that, whatever he is by birth, Mr Smith is not a Scottish poet, if we understand by that a poet of a certain supposed national type.[227]

A modern critic explains the dilemma like this. Although Smith was aware of his literary heritage (and well-read in it) he is no longer interested in emulating it. He even praises colleagues like Hugh Macdonald who produced near-pastiche of Burns:

He looks kindly on the modesty of their ambition and relishes their modest achievement. But as a young man his own ambitions were quite other. His dream is Walter's:
>   to hew his name out upon time
> As on a rock, then in immortalness
> To stand on time as on a pedestal.

He dreams of standing like Scott on some lofty column, freed from all merely local circumstances. But Scotland can no longer support such ambitions...[228]

Being brought up in Glasgow, Smith did use biographical elements in some of his work, most notably 'A Boy's Poem', but this was not his principal aim. He was more concerned with absorbing a vast range of input, including his own extensive reading, to produce a new kind of kaleidoscopic poetry that was dynamic, resonant even febrile in its attempt to escape from mundane usage. His aim was poetry aspiring to the condition of music (Walter's repeated claim that he would "set this Age to music" in 'A Life-Drama') where the word was paramount in all its dimensions. Poetry was to be a verbal fuse linking image and emotion, a synaptic assault on the subconscious. The effects are often weird, surreal even, but this was all part of a new approach to poetry that came to bear the label (at first, as we have seen, intended derisively) Spasmodic School. However it is achieved, to the responsive reader the effects can be almost hallucinogenic. Maybe transfer of meaning can be realised by more physiological means. In a recent study of how the image of the heart and the circulatory system was featured in Victorian poetry we may see the Spasmodics more through the eyes of their contemporary readers. Writing about Pat Alexander's assessment in *Last Leaves* Kirstie Blair characterises their view of sickness and perversion in such writing:

The perverted heart indicates a turn towards dangerous passion and sensuality, besides suggesting that the roots of Spasmodic poetry lie not in the mind but in the body, the heart and the blood. In 'irregular' and 'unrest' Alexander's analysis also points towards the characteristic formal irregularities of these poems in which rhythmic unevenness becomes a virtue and the looseness of a poem's structure might signify an adherence to poetry as organic and unpredictable.[229]

Blair considers that through technical and educational shortcomings many of the Spasmodics failed to communicate fully the existential shock that they harboured, but that their influence has been far-reaching nonetheless:

If Spasmodic poems are less unsettling and less novel than they proclaim (and than their poets may have hoped) it is partly because they are seldom truly innovative in form. Through their outspoken depiction of shocks, throbs, palpitations and spasms taking place both within and outwith the body, however, and in their association of these motions with the practice of poetry itself, Spasmodic writers set an agenda for other poets in this decade and beyond, and advanced the increasing interest in poetry and prosody as organic, affective powers.[230]

Inspiration was important too. After the huge effort of producing *Edwin of Deira* Smith seemed able to recapture that inner creativity only occasionally. He likens the process to the growth of a tree:

In order that the tree shall leaf, and blossom, and bear fruit, it is necessary that the root should be hidden away under-ground, deep-sunk in life-giving soil; so, in like manner, if the poet would go on prosperously with his work, it is essential that his belief and theories concerning himself and his art should be buried in the silent depths of his nature; that he should quietly draw spiritual sustenance from these, and in no wise obtrude them on the world.[231]

In his own time Smith and fellow Spasmodics like Dobell were undoubtedly influential. It was unfortunate that the figure linking them should have been such an obvious target as George Gilfillan. Aytoun's parody had deftly caught the anarchic nature of the New Poets' style; but there was a deeper concern with the wider implication of all this jettisoning of the rules. The argument has been made that Smith's early work (and by implication the other Spasmodics) was a literary analogue to the revolutionary temper and accelerating tempo of urban life in the 1840s and 1850s. Only a few contemporary critics, like Clough, could see past the sensationalism and the extravagance to the wider dissent beneath. Aytoun, a Blackwoodsman to the marrow, certainly did and took immediate counter-measures with *Firmilian*.

Kirstie Blair concludes that Spasmodic poetry "by celebrating or at least drawing attention to the spasms and irregularities of verse, in terms both of subject matter and form, …opened the way for a general theory of the place of 'Spasmodism' in poetics."[232] Despite this claim for their significance barely anyone outside the realm of Vic-Lit specialists has heard of them. Being forgotten, it might be supposed that their influence on writers of their own time and later would be negligible. But that is to subscribe to a view of literary history as only being written by the successful.

Current literary scholars are increasingly hot on the Spasmodic scent, finding traces both strong and faint on the pages of many mainstream Victorians and Edwardians. Professor Florence Boos of the University of Iowa has listed a selection: Arnold's *Empedocles on Etna* (subject to later withdrawal when the reaction to A Life-Drama created a bad attack of cold feet), EBB's *Aurora Leigh*, many of Browning's "madhouse" monologues, Carlyle's *Sartor Resartus*, Clough's *Amours de Voyage*, Morris' *The Defence of Guenevere* and 'The Wind', all from the 1850s. But, the cold feet affliction spread quite rapidly:

Aytoun's and Arnold's terrible swift words gave pause to several of these writers, of course, but they cut their deepest swathes in the hopes of the less well-connected. Others found it sufficient to furnish their works with better-defined generic boundaries or more abstruse classical or medieval plots. Tennyson, for example, took refuge in the elaborate patriotic historicist architectonic of the *Idylls of the King*; Browning buried his villains and miscreants in the learnedly displaced Renaissance scaffolding of *The Ring and the Book*; Morris invoked Chaucer as the patron saint of his twenty-four exquisitely counterbalanced classical and medieval verse narratives in *The Earthly Paradise*.[233]

Of course, a Spasmodic poem no longer appears astounding or threatening to a 21st century reader already exposed to Symbolists, Vorticists, Surrealism or even one who had experienced Dylan Thomas and his imitators.[234] Back in the Arnoldian high noon readers expected poetry to be About Something (and maybe the majority still do), so from 'A Life-Drama' onwards Smith was always going to be an object of suspicion. It was not until experimental writers emerged later on in the century that Smith's true poetic heirs become apparent: names like Meredith, Swinburne, Hopkins, W.B.Yeats. In the case of Swinburne his initial admiration for Smith, fostered by his friendship with John Nichol, turned to distaste. The Rossettis again expressed initial admiration but neither really formed their true style until several years later. In our own times Glaswegian poet Edwin Morgan could be claimed as an heir. (He knew Smith's work well and wrote perceptively on him in *The History of Scottish Literature* vol.3[235]) It is tempting to see a tribute to Smith the city poet in poems such as 'Night Pillion' and 'Northern Nocturnal' where the same urban motifs were picked by the poet and similar effects of light and dark are achieved in evoking the same scenes a hundred years on:

> The gloomy river lay in a glory, the bridge
> In its mists as we rode over it slowly sighed.
> We lost the shining tramlines in the slums
> As we kept south; the shining trolley-wires
> Glinted through Gorbals; on your helmet a glint hung

So much for Alexander Smith the poet; after all his intense literary labour it would be only just if more of his poetry were still in print. Justice is, however, seldom poetic. It is as a prose writer that he is now remembered. In particular one might claim that the quirky originality of *A Summer in Skye* affected the way subsequent writers approached the genre. Historians of travel literature make the point that succeeding generations of tourists set out with different preconceptions of the Highlands and to a large extent discovered just what they wanted to experience. The new mythology that Smith's book created about a remote area with an already considerable literature attached to it was an indication of what middle-class, urbanised Victorians felt was missing from their increasingly comfortable and secure existences. A twenty-first century historian puts the case persuasively:

Tourists were not empty vessels who absorbed whatever tourist literature offered them. They responded out of their own cultural anxieties to particular ways of viewing Scotland's past. The late eighteenth and nineteenth-century fascination with Scotland is a window through which to study the middle-class world view, considering such topics as anxieties over industrialisation, urbanisation and political change; attitudes towards nature; nostalgia for the past; and racial and gendered constructions of Gaels.... As the pace of economic, social and political transformations intensified in England in the nineteenth century, English tourists came to envision the north as a place immune to change, and understood journeys there to be antidotes to the uncertainties of modern life.[236]

In hindsight one can see that Smith's work ended the kind of condescending approach that earlier travellers had adopted in their writing, to which even Boswell (an anglified lowlander) was not totally immune. Another of those who rediscovered Smith's work was novelist and journalist Frederick Niven who returned from Chile to Scotland to attend Glasgow School of Art in the early 1900s and seems to have been keen to find literary sources to fill up the missing Scottish years of childhood. After World War I he emigrated to Canada. It was 'A Boy's Poem' that apparently drove him to both work in and later set his best-known novel *The Staff at Simson's* (1937) in a fabric wholesale warehouse (with a character loosely based on young Sandie). In his autobiography he refers to Smith's works and their effect on him as an exile. On a visit to Edinburgh he makes a journey to see Smith's headstone in Warriston cemetery after reading *A Summer in Skye*:

When they asked Socrates how he would be buried, he said, "You will have to catch me first." Alexander Smith may be caught in his books, a lovable spirit. It is usual, I believe, to class him as a minor essayist but the French phrase *petit maitre* seems more fitting – and for the Scot in exile, Alexander Smith is assuredly a classic.... For the Scot abroad, perhaps not Sir Walter Scott can himself more surely, by the magic of words, conjure home to their dreaming eyes. Alexander Smith gives it all, from the old jougs hanging on the wall at Duddingston to the odour of peat-smoke and of seaweed and the weaving of gulls along the Hebrides.[237]

But if one is looking for an immediate heir to Smith the essayist, it is on the spare figure of RLS that his mantle can be judged to have most precisely fallen. There is no proof that they ever met in person (Stevenson started his law degree at Edinburgh the year of Smith's death), but affinities of style and subject matter are readily discernible. Smith, as we have seen, acknowledged his debt to Montaigne's essays, and it is possible to see the same features in RLS's early contributions to *Longman's Magazine* in the 1870s. In 1862 Smith had written his 'An Essay on an Old Essayist – Montaigne'. Clearly he found the reclusiveness of the French writer the perfect foil for unwrapping the sometimes unfashionable thoughts and propositions that feature in *Dreamthorp*. He eventually calls himself "the affectionate spy". Even the persona of the solitary man who goes out with an umbrella for the summer heat to float about the lake in his rowing boat somehow recalls

Stevenson in the Cévennes or at Grez in 1877. We have already noted similarities (see Chapter 9) in how Smith occasionally borrowed themes from Montaigne in conscious homage and, more importantly, how he adopted a similar mindset and oblique expression to view the values of his own society. One can also see the same process at work in early RLS, certainly at the level of theme and style.

The similarity between 'An Apology for Idlers' and Smith's 'On Vagabonds' is readily apparent, but 'Ordered South' also reveals an influence. There is the same mellifluous phrase-making, the antithetical epigrams, the dying fall to end an important sentence. Certainly there are differences: RLS thrusts himself more into his writing and, as a young man had to, strives with visible effort for a dramatic effect. It is a fair wager that he had read *Dreamthorp* by 1874 (when 'Ordered South' was written). An anonymous article in *The Academy* in 1901 asserted that RLS had "somewhere left on record his indebtedness to *A Summer in Skye*". It is tempting to make the parallels between Louis' Samoa and Smith's Hebridean retreat, allowing for the somewhat vital distinction that for RLS the South Seas were to prolong his life for five years, whereas for AS a month a year was hardly enough spiritual refreshment to have achieved the same result. Both suffered fatal illnesses that they might have survived if their general health had been more robust. Whether by Bluidy Jack or nervous exhaustion each was assisted in working himself into an early grave. And both had premonitions of it.

Early Stevenson as the self-styled "sedulous ape" bore the marks of many influences, but Smith's is one that hasn't ever featured in his literary lineage. Even now (the early 21st century) few academics will admit to there being any Scottish literary talent worth consideration in the fifty years after the death of Scott. There has been some special pleading but Smith's case has been rarely taken up, partly because of the unavailability of his work. Otherwise the influences would have already become apparent. There is a similarity of tone and structure in their essays at least. To press the point, a paragraph of either could be produced at random to conduct a stylistic paternity test.

So let's try it. Which of these four passages is Alexander Smith and which RLS? (Note no allegations of plagiarism are being made.)

Life imposes by brute energy, like inarticulate thunder; art catches the ear, among the far louder noises of experience, like an air artificially made by a discreet musician. A proposition of geometry does not compete with life; and a proposition of geometry is a fair and luminous parallel for a work of art. Both are reasonable, both untrue to the crude facts; both in here in Nature, neither represents it.[238]

Or this?

A work of art is not designed to prove anything, nor yet to disseminate information useless or useful. If harshly questioned, it can frequently give no very satisfactory reason for its existence. It is something above and beyond mere use, like the colour and breath of a flower, or the burning breast of a humming-bird... Its primary office is to please; at all events if it fail in that, it fails in everything.[239]

Or this?

It is no use to write a book and put it by for nine even ninety years; for in the writing you will have partly convinced yourself; the delay must precede any beginning; and if you meditate a work of art, you should first long roll the subject under the tongue to make sure you like the flavour, before you brew a volume that shall taste of it from end to end...[240]

Or this?

Of the essayist, when his mood is communicative, you obtain a full picture. You are made his contemporary and familiar friend. You enter into his humours and his seriousness. You are made heir of his whims, prejudices and playfulness. You walk through the whole nature of him, as you walk through the streets of Pompeii, looking into the interior of stately mansions, reading the satirical scribblings on the walls. And the essayist's habit of not only giving you his thoughts but telling you how he came by them is interesting, because it shows you by what alchemy the ruder world becomes transmuted into the finer. We like to know the lineage of ideas, just as we like to know the pedigree of great earls and swift race-horses.[241]

Appendix
The Gestation of 'Glasgow'

'GLASGOW', Smith's most celebrated poem, first appeared between hard covers in *City Poems* (August 1857) along with several other poems including the semi-autobiographical, much longer 'A Boy's Poem'. It was until recently believed that this was the first time both poems had appeared in print. Contemporary reviewers of *City Poems* pointed out, however, that several of the poems (or extracts from them) had already appeared in periodicals. 'Horton' (containing 'Barbara'), 'The Night Before the Wedding' and 'The Change' had previously appeared in the National Magazine (see Ch. 6) the same year. Brisbane suggests that sections of 'A Boy's Poem' might have been written much earlier, possibly in part before Smith moved to Edinburgh to take up the Secretary post. But now it is known that 'Glasgow' had appeared in an early version three whole years before the publication of *City Poems*.

'To A City' first appeared in *The Glasgow University Album for 1854 (edited by the students)*, a mixture of prose and poetry compiled by Smith's friend John Nichol. Although published in mid-summer it was, as the editor's introduction points out, gathered in from contributors the previous December. 'To A City' is an early version of 'Glasgow', or more accurately it comprises nine stanzas which Smith later incorporated, lightly edited except in one case, into the 14-stanza 'Glasgow'. For interest, on a facing page is printed the text of 'To A City' with Smith's later changes (as incorporated into 'Glasgow') marked in bold. The text of 'Glasgow' is available in a number of anthologies, most notably in *Noise and Smoky Breath* ed. Hamish Whyte (Glasgow 1986) and *Mungo's Tongues: Glasgow Poems 1630-1990* ed. Hamish Whyte (Mainstream 1993), the first of which is a selection of poems about Glasgow, taking its title from Smith's final couplet.

The existence of 'To A City' is crucial in a number of ways. First, it provides rare evidence of Smith revising his work. The editorial changes to the core nine stanzas are fairly cosmetic (see below, where the RH column indicates the subsequent changes made for 'Glasgow'). What is striking is that even though they were written mere months after publication of 'A Life-Drama' they bear only very occasional traces of the Spasmodic style as parodied in *Firmilian*. In other words it would seem (without knowing precise timings) that, just as Aytoun was composing his clever put-down of Spasm, the arch-Spasmodic was writing a poem that stylistically owes most to Blake and Cowper.

Also the timing is interesting. Some later admirers of 'Glasgow' have tended to see it as Smith's farewell to the city of his upbringing, written after the insulating experience of living in Edinburgh for two years or so (1854 to 1856) during which time they assumed the poem was written. It is now clear that the most of the writing took place whilst he was still living in Glasgow, maybe with the recent London visit (with Nichol) freshly imprinted on his visual memory. Setting aside the biographical background, it is possible to read this as a poem embracing "the tragic heart of towns" whilst resisting the temptation to paint every scene with a lurid palette against a dark background. This poet has not retreated from the industrialised urban experience in a state of shellshock. He could more appropriately be accused of looking at the manifestations of the city's inhumane influence – the fire and smoke of foundries, smouldering sunsets, the roar of anvils and machinery, the press of people, the dark river with its forest of masts – and finding there, perhaps uncritically, "another beauty".

It is significant that his only change to the original order of stanzas in 'To A City' was to bring forward the one beginning "City! I am true child of thine.... Instead of shores where ocean beats I hear the ebb and flow of streets" from mid-poem to the second stanza of 'Glasgow'. Its prominence is thus greatly increased. This runs counter to the reading given by Prof Robert Crawford ('Smith, Macfarlan and City Poetry') where he sees evidence in the poem that the poet's heart and humanity has been compromised by the city experience and

> The poem ends with the poet in the city, but he stays there not because he has got the better of it but because he has failed, and the city's "terror" and "dream" have got the better of him. The tired conclusion, looking towards winter, death and the grave shows this clearly. [242]

The result is (according to Crawford) that the poet, hankering for the world of nature, can only summon up a vision of "an unreal city" often conveyed in a tone of "glum pride". Other critics have pounced on the sometimes surreal quality of the descriptions in the poem (and in 'A Boy's Poem') as a sign that the Spasmodic poet was still at large. The imagery sometimes tends towards the visionary: "from the glory round thee pour'd A sunbeam like an angel's sword Shivers upon a spire; Thus have I watched thee. Terror! Dream!" In a biographical approach to the poem (indeed this would apply to most poetry) who can tell where reality ends and unreality begins?

As already stated, five stanzas were written post-1853, probably during his first few months in the Secretary's post at Edinburgh. These, inserted in the final part of 'Glasgow', are interesting in that they do add some support to Crawford's view of the poet as the de-sensitised seer whose flesh has become as stone. So it is at a safe distance from the baleful influence of the city that the poet (Smith?) now writes of himself: "Of me thou has become a part – Some kindred with my human heart Lives in thy streets of stone; For we have become familiar more Than galley-slave and weary oar." Then there are the two references to the "unforgotten" grave of his lost beloved (see Chapter 4). It is almost as if she were the necessary sacrifice made to enable the poet to retain his own feelings of humanity so that he can finally declare: "A sacredness of love and death / Dwells in thy noise and smoky breath." The 'sacredness' here refers to the literal meaning of things set apart so as not to be violated by their immediate surroundings.

More immediate issue must be taken with Professor Crawford over his assertion that Smith plagiarised the peddler poet James Macfarlan in writing 'Glasgow'. When he wrote the piece in 1985 Crawford was unaware of the existence of 'To a City'. In his article he discovers intriguing echoes between phrases in 'Glasgow' and those that occur in poems appearing in MacFarlan's *City Songs* (published in 1855). The parallels are striking but there is little to be gained from raising further charges of plagiarism, which (as we have seen from the 'Z' campaign) is very much a two-way street.

On this controversy, such as it is, others must adjudicate. It should not be allowed to throw a shadow over an extraordinarily accomplished poem, original in its expression, intriguing in its stance, and pioneering in its choice of subject. In 'Glasgow' a city has been immortalised. This is an honour traditionally afforded to only the world's most gracious and influential metropolises by poets, painters and composers. In the 1850s Glasgow was neither; it was grimly making its way in the world and many observers threw up their hands in horror at the phenomenon. Twenty-first century Glasgow, now enjoying the benefits of its post-industrial flowering, should be grateful to Smith for the way he captured aspects of the earlier city in a way that still appeals to contemporary taste.

Maybe this is as good an opportunity as any to point out that at publication there existed only one memorial to Smith in the streets of Glasgow. This is a bronze plaque with the final couplet of 'Glasgow' erected at the entry to South Exchange Court (Queen Street) in the 1980s to show where Smith worked as a pattern-designer. The unveiling of the plaque, witnessed by the poet's surviving granddaughter, was accompanied by a reading of the poem by the late Russell Hunter, the actor.

2007 was the unmarked 150th anniversary of the publication of 'Glasgow'. No further monument has yet materialised. The poem's power in the minds of its many readers may prove a better memorial for Alexander Smith, unfortunately just one of Scotland's many neglected writers.

* * * *

TO A CITY

Sing, poet, 'tis a merry world,
That cottage smoke is rolled and curled
In sport; that ev'ry moss
Is happy, ev'ry inch of soil –
Before me runs a road of toil
With my grave cut across.
Sing, trailing showers and breezy downs,
I know the tragic heart of towns.

['Glasgow' inserts stanza 6 here]

Black Labour draws his weary waves
Into their secret moaning caves;
But, with the morning light,
That sea again will overflow
With a long weary sound of woe
Again to faint in night.
Wave am I in that sea of woes,
That night and morning ~~comes and goes~~.   ebbs and flows

I dwelt within a gloomy court,
Wherein did never sunbeam sport,
Yet then my heart was stirred –
My very blood did dance and thrill,
When on my narrow window sill
Spring lighted like a bird.
Poor flowers, I watched them pine for weeks,
With leaves as pale as human cheeks.

~~A week was mine, one happy year –~~
Afar one summer I was borne
~~A long long week: with joyful fear~~
Through golden vapours of the ~~morn.~~
I heard the hills of sheep:
I trod, with a wild ecstacy,
~~The shores of the delighted sea;~~
The bright fringe of the living sea

And, from a ruined keep,
~~I saw a miserable plain,~~
I sat and watched an endless plain
~~Wrapt in the curtains of the rain~~
Blacken beneath the gloom of rain.

O fair the lightly sprinkled waste,
O'er which a laughing shower has raced!
O fair the ~~tender~~ shoots!   April
O fair the woods on summer days
While a blue hyacinthine haze
Is dreaming ~~'mong~~ the roots!   round
In thee, O City I discern
Another beauty sad and stern.

City! I am true ~~child~~ of thine –   son
Ne'er dwelt I where great mornings shine
Around the bleating pens;
Ne'er by the rivulets I strayed,
And ne'er upon my childhood weighed
The silence of the glens.
Instead of shores where ocean beats
I hear the ebb and flow of streets.

Draw thy fierce streams of blinding ore;
Smite on a thousand anvils; roar
Down to the harbour bars;
Smoulder in smoky sunsets; flare
On ~~dripping~~ nights. With street and square   rainy
Lie empty to the stars –
From terrace proud to alley base
I know thee as my mother's face.

When sunset bathes thee in his gold
In ~~wreathes~~ of bronze thy sides are rolled,   wreaths
Thy smoke is dusky fire;
And from the glory round thee poured,
A sunbeam like an angel's sword
Shivers upon a spire.
Thus have I watched thee, Terror! Dream!
~~While the blue~~ night crept up the stream.
Till the dark

The wild train plunges in the hills;

He shrieks across the midnight rills;
Streams through ~~a village, where~~   the shifting glare
The roar and flap of foundry fires
~~Disturb~~ with light the sleeping shires   That shake
And from the moorlands bare
He sees afar a crown of light
Hang o'er thee in the hollow night.

At midnight when thy suburbs lie
As silent as a noon-day sky
When larks with heat are mute,
I love to linger on thy bridge,
~~'Tis~~ lonely as a mountain ridge   All
Disturbed but by my foot;
While the black lazy stream beneath
Steals from its far-off wilds of heath.

And through thy heart as through a dream,
Flows on that black disdainful stream;
All scornfully it flows
Between the huddled gloom of masts,
Silent as pines ~~unswept~~ by blasts;   unvexed
'Tween ~~the~~ lamps in streaming rows –
O wondrous sight! O stream of dread!
O long dark river of the dead.

['Glasgow' has 4 extra stanzas]

The beech seems dipped in wine, the shower
Is burnished, on the swinging flower
The latest bee doth sit;
The low sun stares through the dust of gold,
And o'er the darkening health and wold
The large ghost-moth doth flit.
~~Boon autumn calls – I cannot go,~~
In every orchard Autumn stands
~~I measure here my days of woe.~~
With apples in his golden hands.

['Glasgow' has one final stanza]

Notes
(PW = Poetical Works of Alexander Smith)

---

[1] The legal requirement to notify births with a registrar in Scotland is only 150 years old. Before 1855 many people would have had no documentary proof of their birth date; they therefore had to take it on trust. In the case of Alexander Smith this is a particular problem. First there is no record in the appropriate parish register, the usual way of registering births and baptisms before the setting up of Registry offices. But also throughout his life Smith himself would use two dates twelve months apart, seemingly unable to decide which was the more likely. This is surprising given that both parents survived him and must have known the truth. In a note "taken from his own lips" in 1853 by his close friend Hugh Macdonald the time and place of birth are given as "Kilmarnock, Hogmanae 1830". The Scottish New Year is still known as Hogmanay, but this could cover December 31st 1829 or January 1st 1830. It might even be taken as meaning December 31st 1830 or January 1st 1831. New Year celebrations in Scotland have always been extensive, starting well before the close of the old year and ending a day or two after the ushering in of the new. Never a very systematic man, Smith fails to make his mind up on this personal matter throughout his life. Maybe the details just became obscured in the family celebrations both for the arrival of a first-born son and the new year.
In another brief sketch of his early years written in his own hand on one side of a sheet of notepaper (now in the NLS)[1] he confidently states: "Born in Kilmarnock 31st December 1830". But the 1851 Census, taken on April 7th, his age is given as 21, favouring December 1829 as the true date. Two personal friends who wrote memoirs also plump for this date. Most modern reference works follow this. The *Oxford Literary Guide to the British Isles*, in separate references to Smith, credits him with being born on both dates. Maybe this should be the last word on the matter.

[2] Evening News, 4 April 1911
[3] Ibid.
[4] *Alfred Hagart's Household* p.37
[5] 'A Reminiscence of Alexander Smith' in *Ayrshire Museum* (ed Wylie, W.H.)
[6] *Alfred Hagart's Household*, pp.1-3
[7] Ibid.. pp.9-10

[8] from Johnson, J. (1834) *The Recess , or Autumnal Relaxation in the Highlands and Lowlands.* (Quoted in Berry, S. and Whyte, H. eds (1987) *Glasgow Observed.*)
[9] *Rambles Round Glasgow*, p.15
[10] From 'To A City' (See Appendix: *The Gestation of 'Glasgow'*)
[11] from *Dreamthorp* (1907) pp.126-7
[12] from 'A Boy's Poem' in *The Poetical Works of Alexander Smith*, pp.364-5 [henceforth *PW*]
[13] Ibid.. pp.366-368
[14] from The Edinburgh Review 55 (July 1832)
[15] From Pagan, J. (1849) *Sketch of the History of Glasgow*
[16] *Poetical Works* p.322
[17] The following account owes much to McCarthy, M. (1969) *A Social Geography of Paisley*.
[18] *Poetical Works* p.371
[19] This account draws on Swain, M. (1982) *Ayrshire and Other Whitework*.
[20] *Poetical Works* p.370
[21] *Early Years* pp.17-18
[22] *Last Leaves* p.vii
[23] *Early Years* pp. 27-28
[24] F.Boos 'Working-Class Poetry' in *A Companion to Victorian Poetry* pp. 224, 226
[25] Quoted in F. Boos *The "Homely Muse" in her Diurnal Setting*, Victorian Poetry no.39
[26] *Poetical Works* pp. 294 & 299
[27] Hogg's Instructor 1 pp.305-306
[28] From the introduction to *A Gallery of Literary Portraits* (1909)
[29] Quoted in MacLeod, D. *Memoir of Norman MacLeod*
[30] An equestrian statue of William of Orange erected after the Battle of the Boyne at a point on the Trongate close to Glasgow Cross, and moved to a less prominent situation near the Cathedral early in the twentieth century.
[31] From *Alfred Leslie* (1855) by Frederick Arnold; quoted in *Glasgow Observed* (1987) ed. Simon Berry and Hamish Whyte
[32] This was an almost unbelievable find for a biographer of Smith starved of MSS and holograph material. Mrs Dorothea Pender-Mackenzie, a grand-daughter of the poet through his youngest child Isabella (see Ch.12), presented it to the Dick Institute in the 1960s. From accompanying correspondence it appears she was given it by Thomas Brisbane's daughter in 1934, along with the original Smith letters quoted in *The Early Years of Alexander Smith*. Much of the following material also appeared in *Scottish Book Collector* 3 no.7

(Oct/Nov 1992) in 'The Glasgow Addisonians', containing a reproduction of the list of members page.
[33] *Early Years* pp.39-40
[34] Ibid. p.vii
[35] Ibid. pp.46-47
[36] Ibid. pp.48-49
[37] Ibid. p.59
[38] *Last Leaves* pp.xiv-xv
[39] *A Summer in Skye* (1885) p.543
[40] Most recently Prof Richard Cronin in his positively provocative 'Alexander Smith and the Poetry of Displacement' in Victorian Poetry 28. Cronin seems to make the assumption he was an active Chartist from a reference to Ebenezer Elliott in *Dreamthorp* and from Brisbane's agitated account of the 1848 riots in *Early Years*. But even Brisbane (concerned at the "ferment" that he perceived in Smith) admits that he was merely a spectator.
[41] *City Poems* p.40
[42] *Early Years* p.85
[43] The original letter no longer exists. We must assume that these are other worker poets and fledgeling writers known to both AS and Brisbane.
[44] Quoted in *Early Years* pp.87-90
[45] *Chambers' Eminent Scotsmen* p.376
[46] *Poetical Works* p.392
[47] Pae, D. *The Factory Girl* (Quoted in Berry, S. and Whyte, H. eds *Glasgow Observed*.)
[48] *Last Leaves* p.xliii (note)
[49] *Early Years* p.106
[50] *Poetical Works* p.310
[51] *A Gallery of Literary Portraits* p.74
[52] The Eclectic Review (1851) p.459
[53] Ibid.
[54] The Critic (1851) pp.567-68
[55] *Memoir of Sydney Dobell* p.243
[56] *Early Years* p.152
[57] Ibid. p.146
[58] See 'Lines to a Friend' final stanza ("Beauty and Fame, twin cheats, twin idols, grow"). From the incidental details in the first stanza the likelihood is that Brisbane – highly poeticised – was the friend in the title.
[59] UK sales figures are taken from Pat Alexander's *Last Leaves* Memoir. American sales figures come from *Cost Books of Ticknor & Fields*

[60] *Early Years* p.148
[61] Quoted in Cecil Y. Lang, ed.,(1996) *The Letters of Matthew Arnold, vol. 1* Charlottesville: Univ. Press of Virginia
[62] NLS shelf mark 9395, f.87
[63] The Scotsman, 19 April 1853
[64] Various of the ideas and insights which follow I owe to conversations and correspondence held with John McClafferty who was preparing an annotated edition of 'A Life-Drama' in the late 1980s as part of a doctoral dissertation.
[65] *Poetical Works* p.71
[66] Ibid. p.138
[67] The Evening Citizen no 538
[68] The Athenaeum no 1325
[69] The Examiner (1853)
[70] The Westminster Review 59 p.522
[71] New York Daily Times (7 June 1853)
[72] North American Review (July 1853)
[73] From ed. R. H. Super (1960-77), *The Complete Prose Works of Matthew Arnold*, Univ. of Michigan Press, v9 pp206-207
[74] 'Victorian Culture Wars: Alexander Smith, Arthur Hugh Clough, and Matthew Arnold in 1853' *Victorian Poetry* (2004)
[75] North British Review 19 pp. 330-345
[76] Blackwoods 75 p.349
[77] Quoted in *Early Years*, pp.169-174
[78] Ibid.
[79] Quoted in *Thomas Woolmer: His Life and Letters* p.55
[80] The Critic 10 (1 Jan 1851)
[81] Quoted in *Last Leaves* p.xx
[82] Evening Citizen no.570 (29 October 1853)
[83] The Scotsman (13 April 1853)
[84] The Glasgow Miscellany 3 (February 1854)
[85] *Last Leaves* p.xlix
[86] The Reformer's Gazette (1853)
[87] Glasgow University Album (1854)
[88] *A Summer in Skye* (1885) pp.19-20
[89] Tait's Edinburgh Magazine 21 (1854) pp.29-33
[90] Aytoun, W.E. & Martin, T. *The Bon Gaultier Ballads*.
[91] From the letter collection in the Dick Institute (quoted in *Early Years* p.178)
[92] Blackwoods 75 (1854) p.304
[93] '"Spasm" and Class: W.E. Aytoun, George Gilfillan, Sydney Dobell, and Alexander Smith' in *Victorian Poetry* 42 (2004)

[94] *Poems of W.E.Aytoun* (1921) p. 310
[95] '"Spasm" and Class: W.E. Aytoun, George Gilfillan, Sydney Dobell, and Alexander Smith' in *Victorian Poetry* 42 (2004)
[96] Quoted in *Life and Letters of Sydney Dobell,* p.346
[97] NLS shelf mark 3218 f.144
[98] *Sonnets on the War* p.40
[99] From the letter collection in the Dick Institute (quoted in *Early Years* p.183)
[100] *Last Leaves* p.liv
[101] *Encyclopaedia Britannica* 8th ed. Vol.VII p.472
[102] *Some 19th Century Scotsmen* p.118
[103] From Special Collections, Univ of Edinburgh Library
[104] The Titan 23 p.271
[105] *Poems of W.E.Aytoun* (1921)
[106] NLS shelf mark 1003 f.140
[107] 'Z' was also used by J.G.Lockhart and John Wilson (Christopher North) to sign their swingeing attack on the Cockney School of Poets in Blackwoods in 1818
[108] *Quoted in Cruse, A. (1930)* The Englishman and his Books in the Early Nineteenth Century *London*
[109] The Athenaeum no.1523 (1857)
[110] Collected Works of De Quincey (Author's Edition) 2, p.242 (my italics)
[111] Macmillan's 4 (Sept 1861) p.407
[112] 'Recent English Poetry' in North British Review (July 1853)
[113] Marsh, J. (2005) *Dante Gabriel Rossetti Painter and Poet* London: Phoenix p.118
[114] From *Thomas Woolner, His Life & Letters.* p.55
[115] From *Letters of Dante Gabriel Rossetti (1854-70)*
[116] The Athenaeum no.1556 (22 August 1857)
[117] *Last Leaves* [Appendix]
[118] The Leader (4 February 1857)
[119] *Last Leaves* p.62
[120] Ibid. p.18
[121] Caledonian Mercury (28 February 1857)
[122] From the AS collection in the Dick Institute (also quoted incomplete in *Early Years,* p.185)
[123] *Poetical Works* p.377
[124] *A Summer in Skye* (1885) p.105
[125] *City Poems* pp.69-70
[126] Thanks to Dr Sara Stevenson for arranging for me to view this and for information on Archer
[127] *A Summer in Skye* (1885) p.56

[128] The Leader 388 (29 August 1857)
[129] *Poetical Works*, p.291
[130] National Review (October 1857)
[131] Kitchen, P. (1989) *Gerard Manley Hopkins: A Life* Manchester: Carcanet p.195
[132] *City Poems* pp.98-99
[133] Ibid. p.76
[134] Ibid. p.119
[135] Saturday Review (17 October 1857)
[136] *City Poems* p.33
[137] *A Summer in Skye* (1885) p.24
[138] Knight, W., p.68, see 18
[139] *Letters of DGR*
[140] NB Review 35 (August 1861)
[141] *Last Leaves* p.98
[142] NLS Chambers Collection shelf mark 341, 377, 379
[143] Dublin University Journal 59, p.67
[144] Saturday Review (Aug 10 1861)
[145] The Athenaeum (Aug 10 1861)
[146] *PW* p.218
[147] Macmillan's 9 (Nov. 1861)
[148] Macmillan's 15 (Feb 1867)
[149] *A Summer in Skye* (1885) p.320
[150] Good Words (May 1862)
[151] Cassell's (Feb 1867)
[152] Edinburgh Mercury (23 February 1861).
[153] *Dreamthorp* (1907) p.202
[154] Interesting reminiscences on all these can be found in W.Knight's *Some Nineteenth Century Scotsmen*
[155] Cassell's (Feb. 1867) ('Personal recollections of AS')
[156] *Last Leaves* p.lviii
[157] *Dreamthorp* p.176
[158] *Testimonials in Favour of Mr Alexander Smith (1862)*, Glasgow University Archives
[159] *Nugae Criticae* (1862)
[160] *Recent and Living Scottish Poets* (1883)
[161] Cornhill 23 (May 1868)
[162] *A Summer in Skye* p.39
[163] Good Words 3, p.364
[164] *Last Leaves* p.211
[165] Ibid. p.221
[166] Ibid. p.127
[167] *Dreamthorp* (1907) pp.31-2

[168] Ibid. pp.191-2
[169] Ibid. p.196
[170] Ibid. p.36
[171] Ibid. pp.130-1
[172] Ibid. p.65
[173] Ibid. p.66
[174] Ibid. p.70
[175] Ibid. p.350
[176] The Spectator (15 Aug 1863)
[177] *Dreamthorp* (1907) pp.213-14
[178] *Last Leaves* p.131
[179] Day of Rest 7 ('Twenty Years of a Publisher's Life')
[180] *Last Leaves* p.119
[181] Mary Jane W.Scott: 'Alexander Smith: Poet of Victorian Scotland' *Scottish Studies* 14
[182] Glasgow Herald (20 January 1900)
[183] St Andrews Citizen (1913) ('Patrick Proctor Alexander, Philosopher and Poet')
[184] *Literary Recollections* p.399
[185] Glasgow Herald (20 January 1900)
[186] Cornhill 14 ('The Scot at Home')
[187] The Argosy (March 1866)
[188] NLS shelf mark 583, f.901
[189] *Last Leaves* p.139
[190] *Alfred Hagart's Household* (1867) pp.172-174
[191] *Last Leaves,* pp.167-169
[192] from '"Spasm" and Class' *Victorian Poetry* 39
[193] Quoted in *George Gilfillan: A Biographical and Critical Study* (1968)
[194] *Night: A Poem* (1867) p.147
[195] Ibid. pp.260-1
[196] *George Gilfillan: A Biographical and Critical Study* (1968) p.210
[197] Pall Mall Magazine (1901) (Quoted in Connell, J. *W.E.Henley* London:1949, pp.365-8)
[198] *A Summer in Skye* (1907) p. xvi
[199] *Verses* (1893) (Memoir by Walter Smith)
[200] *A Summer in Skye* (1885) p.1
[201] Ibid. pp.84-5
[202] Ibid. p.xxx
[203] Ibid. p.471
[204] Ibid. p.325
[205] Ibid. p.478
[206] Ibid. p.82

[207] Ibid. p.236
[208] Ibid. p.391
[209] Letter in the Dick Institute to Isabella
[210] This can be deduced from *Artemus Ward Esq at the Edenberry Yewniversetty*, an election squib produced by the Carlyle election committee and written in the persona of a Yankee student. It allows him to make a pun on 'natural' in its contemporary meaning of 'simpleton': "On Munday Novr 6th I arove at the Yewniveresetty, and accordin' to direkshuns givn me, went strate to the Sekretery's offiss to matrikewlait. This was the Mewseum of Nateril History, therefore when I concluded that belongin' to the prefeshun I might pass free, and so went away and tuke no further steps on the matir." (Quoted in Carlyle Pamphlets 1, ed Fielding, K.J. & Henderson, H., available from Dept of English Literature, University of Edinburgh)
[211] *Last Leaves* p.179
[212] Ibid. p.75
[213] *A Summer in Skye* (1885) p.476
[214] The Argosy X (May 1868)
[215] *Golden Leaves* p. ix
[216] *Last Leaves* p.85
[217] Pall Mall Gazette (Feb 1867)
[218] Macmillan's 15 p.342 (Feb 1867)
[219] From Introduction to *Ward's English Poets* p.48
[220] *Last Leaves*, p.cxiii
[221] From the Dick Institute collection
[222] *Last Leaves* p.lxxix
[223] Cassell's (Nov. 1861)
[224] RLF file no. 1776
[225] This and the next two extracts are all from the collection in the Dick Institute, Kilmarnock which also contains the Glasgow Addisonians minute book.
[226] Carla Sassi (2005) *Why Scottish Literature Matters* Edinburgh: Saltire Press p.118
[227] NB Review 19 p.339
[228] Richard Cronin in 'Alexander Smith and the Poetry of Displacement' *Victorian Poetry* 28 p.138
[229] Kirstie Blair (2006) *Victorian Poetry & The Culture Of The Heart* pp.94-5
[230] ibid. pp..94-5
[231] *Last Leaves* p.182 ('Sydney Dobell')
[232] *Victorian Poetry & The Culture Of The Heart* p.99
[233] F.S.Boos in'"Spasm" and Class: W.E. Aytoun, George Gilfillan, Sydney Dobell, and Alexander Smith' in *Victorian Poetry* 42 (2004)

[234] A.S.Byatt's prize-winning novel *Possession* used a semi-Spasmodic poet as the research subject of the ill-fated contemporary couple who discover evidence of a secret extra-marital affair between Victorian poets. For AS, alas, nothing similar has yet turned up, nor is it likely to. There is only poor, drowned Barbara of whom we know next to nothing.
[235] pp.341-2
[236] Katherine Grenier in "Scottishness", "Britishness" and Scottish Tourism 1770-1914 (Blackwell) p.1005
[237] *Coloured Spectacles* (1938) pp. 237-8
[238] ?
[239] ?
[240] ?
[241] ?
[242] *The Glasgow Review* November 1985 p. 49

Bibliography
(works referred to in the text)

REVIEWS & PERIODICALS

The Athenaeum
The Argosy
Blackwoods Magazine
Cassell's Magazine
Chambers Journal
The Critic
Dublin University Magazine
The Eclectic Review
The Edinburgh Review
The Examiner
The Glasgow Miscellany
Glasgow University Album (1854)
Good Words
Hogg's Instructor
The Leader
Macmillan's Magazine
The Museum
The National Magazine
North American Review
North British Review
The Quiver
The Reformer's Gazette
Tait's Edinburgh Magazine
The Titan
West of Scotland Magazine
Westminster Review

SMITH -RELATED BIOGRAPHY

Bertram, J. (1893) *Some Memories of Books, Authors, and Events.* London

Brisbane, T. (1869) *The Early Years of Alexander Smith, Poet and Essayist. A Study for Young Men, Chiefly Reminiscences of Ten Years' Companionship*. London: Hodder & Stoughton

Espinasse, F. (1893) *Literary Recollections and Sketches*. London

Fennell, F.L. (1968) 'George Gilfillan: A Biographical & Critical Study'. Northwestern Univ diss.

Gilfillan, George (1854) *A Third Gallery of Portraits*. Edinburgh: James Hogg (also in Ed. Nicoll, W.R. (1909) *A Gallery of Literary Portraits*. London: Dent)

Knight, W. (1908) *Some Nineteenth Century Scotsmen, Being Personal recollections by William Knight* Edinburgh & London

Murdoch, A.G. (1883) *The Scottish Poets Recent and Living*. Glasgow: Thomas D. Morison, & London: Hamilton Adams

Sharp, W. (1890) *A Life of Robert Browning*. London: Walter Scott
Smith, A. (1885) *A Summer in Skye*. Edinburgh: Nimmo Hay & Mitchell

Srebrnik, P.T. (1986) *Alexander Strahan, Victorian Publisher*. Michigan UP

Watson, R.A. & Watson, E.S. (1892) *George Gilfillan: Letters and Journals, with Memoir*. London: Hodder & Stoughton

19thC SOCIAL/ECONOMIC HISTORY

Anderson, G. & P. (1851) *Guide to the Highlands and Islands of Scotland Descriptive of their Scenery, Statistics, Antiquities and Natural History*. Edinburgh: A.& C.Black

Berry, S. and Whyte, H. eds (1987) *Glasgow Observed*. Edinburgh: John Donald

Cooper, D. (1992) *The Road to the Islands*. Edinburgh: Chambers

Footman, B. & Young, B. (1983) *Edinburgh University: An Illustrated Memoir*. Edinburgh: University of Edinburgh

Gold, J.R. & M.M. (1995) *Imagining Scotland: Tradition, Representation and Promotion in Scottish Tourism since 1750.* Edinburgh

Grenier, K.H. (2005) *Tourism and Identity in Scotland 1770-1914: Creating Caledonia.* Aldershot: Ashgate

Horn, D.B. (xxxx) *A Short History of the University of Edinburgh 1556-1889.* Edinburgh: Edinburgh UP

Hunter, J. (1986) *Skye: The Island.* Edinburgh: Mainstream Publishing

Morgan, C. (1943) *The House of Macmillan 1843-1943.* London: Macmillan

Niven, F. (1937) *The Staff at Simpson's* and (1938) *Coloured Spectacles* both London

Swain, M. (1982) *Ayrshire and Other Whitework.* Aylesbury: Shire Publications

McCarthy, M. (1969) *A Social Geography of Paisley.* Paisley: Paisley Public Library

Teignmouth, Lord (1836) *Sketches of the Coasts and Islands of Scotland and of the Isle of Man* vol.1. London: J.W.Parker

MODERN CRITICISM

Blair, K. (2006) *Victorian Poetry and the Culture of the Heart.* OUP

Boos, F.S. ed (2001) 'The Poetics of the Working Classes'. *Victorian Poetry* 39

Boos, F.S. (2004) '"Spasm" and Class: W.E. Aytoun, George Gilfillan, Sydney Dobell, and Alexander Smith' in *Victorian Poetry* 42

Boos, F.S. (2008) *Working-Class Women Poets in Victorian Britain* Ontario: Broadview Press

Buckley, J.H. (1952) *The Victorian Temper: A Study in Literary Culture*. London: Allen & Unwin

Cronin, R., Chapman, A., Harrison, A.H. (2002) *A Companion to Victorian Poetry*. Oxford: Blackwell

Cronin, R. (1990) 'Alexander Smith and the Poetry of Displacement'. *Victorian Poetry 28*

Maclean, M. (1904) *The Literature of the Highlands*. Glasgow: Blackie

McGowan, M. (1974) *Montaigne's Deceits*. London: Hodder & Stoughton

Rudy, J.R. & LaPorte C. (2004) 'Spasmodic Poetry and Poetics' *Victorian Poetry 42*

Sassi, C. (2005) *Why Scottish Literature Matters* Edinburgh: Saltire Press

Warner, A. (1975) *William Allingham (Irish Writers series)*. Lewisburg: Bucknell UP

Weinstein, M.A. (1968) *William Edmonstoune Aytoun and the Spasmodic Controversy*. New Haven & London: Yale UP

POETRY & LETTERS (NOT SMITH)

Arnold, M (1932) *The Letters of Matthew Arnold to Arthur Hugh Clough*. (Ed Lowry, H.F.) London: Oxford UP

Aytoun, W.E. (1921) *Poems of William Edmonstoune Aytoun*. (Ed Page, F.) Oxford

Aytoun, W.E. (as 'T.Percy Jones') (1854) 'Firmilian: A Tragedy'. Blackwood's 75

Aytoun, W.E. & Martin, T. (185X) *The Bon Gaultier Ballads*. London:

Bigg, J.S. (1854) *Night and the Soul*. London

Buchanan, R. (1883) *A Poet's Sketch-Book*. London

Carlyle, T. (1896-1901) *Works.* (Ed. Traill, H.D.) London: Macmillan

Dobell, S. (1875) *The Poetical Works.* 2v. (Ed. Nichol, J.) London: Smith, Elder

Hedderwick, J. (1859) *Lays of Middle Age and Other Poems.* Cambridge: Macmillan

Hopkins, G.M. (1959) *The Journals and Papers of Gerard Manley Hopkins.* (Eds House, H. and Storey, G.) London: Oxford UP

Macdonald, H. (1863) *Poems and Songs of Hugh Macdonald.* (with Memoir by AS) Glasgow

Macdonald, H (1854) *Rambles Round Glasgow.* Glasgow

Ramsay, J. (1844) *Woodnotes of A Wanderer.* London

Rossetti, D.G. (1897) *Letters of Dante Gabriel Rossetti (1854-70)* (ed. G.B.Hill) London

Swinburne, A.C. (1925-27) *Complete Works.* (Eds Gosse, W. and Wise, T.J.) London: Wm Heinemann

A full list of Smith's works, original editions and reprints, is printed in *Scottish Book Collector* Issue 7 (1988): 'Alexander Smith: A checklist by Hamish Whyte'.
The best source of his poetry is *The Poetical Works of Alexander Smith* (1909) edited with a critical and biographical introduction by William Sinclair. Other poems are included in *Last Leaves: Sketches and Criticisms* (1868) edited with a memoir by Patrick Proctor Alexander.
Simultaneously with the publication of this book a short-run edition of *A Boy's Poem* (2013) was issued.
Of his prose works only *Dreamthorp: A book of essays written in the country* and *A Summer in Skye* have been reprinted within living memory.

S.B.

Index

A Summer in Skye see Smith, Alexander (Works)
Addisonians see GALS
Alexander, Pat 21, 40, 46, 76, 135, 160-2, 165, 188, 191, 194, 199
Alfred Leslie 30
Allingham, William 102f., 123, 197
A-musement 138, 161, 176
Apollodorus (pseud.) see Gilfillan
Archer, James 90, 114
Argosy, The see Strahan, Alexander
Argyll, 8th Duke of 75
Arnold, Matthew 60, 69, 71, 88, 196, 209
Arran, Isle of 38
Athenaeum, The 46, 61, 63, 67, 99f., 120, 164, 193, 197
Aytoun, W.E. 60, 83f., 96, 106, 122, 141, 163, 171, 186, 196

Bailey, P.J. 53, 72, 193
Barbara (lost love) 50
Berlioz, Hector 64
Bigg, J.Stanyan 52, 72, 97
Blackie, John S. 68, 79, 85, 106, 120, 141, 156, 163, 193
Blair, Dr Kirstie 195, 209f.
Blackwoods Magazine 60, 71, 84, 93, 130, 177, 183, 196, 206
Bogue, David 22, 61, 73, 92, 96
Boos, Prof Florence 23, 87f., 196, 209f.
Boswell, James 180, 198
Bread Riots (Glasgow) 42, 108
Brewster, Sir D. 124
Brisbane, Thomas (biographer) 20, 24, 29, 36f., 42, 50f., 64, 72f., 85, 94, 194
Browning, E.B. 46, 60, 62, 73, 88, 100, 209
Bunyan, John 20
Burns, Robert 33, 77, 159f., 194, 197
Byron, Lord George 38, 56, 73

Caledonian Mercury 136, 143f., 176
Carlyle, Thomas 14, 187, 209
Carmyle 38, 41, 95
Cassell's Magazine 193, 200
Chambers Edinburgh Journal 67
Chambers Encyclopaedia 125
Charlotte Street (Glasgow) 7, 42, 46, 49, 195, (endpaper)
Chartists 8, 40, 193
Chorley, H.F. 67, 100, 103, 119, 194

Christison, R. 84, 192
Citizen, The see Hedderwick, James
City poets 104f., 193
Clough, Arthur H. 46, 69, 71, 88, 99, 102, 209
Clyde steamers 109, 114, 183
Cowgate 81f.
Cowper, Thomas 116f.
Crawford, Prof Robert. 214f.
Crimean War 90f.
Critic, The 53, 56f., 61, 74,
Cronin, Prof. Richard 71, 206

De Quincey, Thomas 8, 56, 77, 83, 100, 105, 114, 129, 177, 184
Dick Institute 199
Dingwall 182, 191, 205
Dixon, William H. 61, 97
Dobell, Sydney 73, 77, 88, 90, 173, 187
Downes, John 95, 137
Drunkenness 7, 78, 85
Dunvegan 183

Early Years of Alexander Smith, The see Brisbane, Thomas
Eclectic Review, The 52, 55
Edinburgh Essays 106f.
Edinburgh Courant 135, 142f., 204
Edinburgh Town Council 79f., 93, 124,
Edinburgh Town College / University see Smith, Al;exander
Elliot, Ebeneezer, 14, 193, 206
Evangelicalism 28, 99, 146
Examiner, The 68

Fennell, Dr Francis 173
Factory Girl, The 46
Firmilian see Aytoun, Prof W.E.
Fraser's Magazine 88, 103

Gauze Street (Paisley) 72
Gesto (Skye) 181f.
Gilfillan, Rev George 25f., 51f., 76, 84, 170f. 193, 200
Gladstone, W.E. 125
Glasgow (Hawkhead) 6f., 30f., 167
Glasgow Addisonian Literary Society (GALS) 32f., 46, 57, 148f., 159, 194
Glasgow Green 15f. 40, 195
Glasgow Herald 193
Glasgow-Edinburgh railway 11, 195
Glasgow-Johnston Canal 4
Glasgow Miscellany, The 29, 76, 107
Glasgow University Album 78

Good Words see Macleod, Rev. Norman
Great Eastern, SS 98

Hamilton, Janet 23
Hannay, James 137f., 142, 163, 193
Harrison, Dr Anthony 69f.
Henley, W. E. 93, 175
Hedderwick, James 40, 47, 67, 76, 200
Highlanders 7, 30, 41, 211
Hogg, James (publisher) 25, 52, 96
Hogg, James 60
Hopkins, Gerard M. 118, 210
Hume's *History of England* 126f.
Hunter, Prof. James 181

Jacquard looms 4
Jones, T. Percy (pseud.) see *Firmilian*

Kailyard 121, 187
Keats, John 60, 69, 104, 117. 197
Kenmuir see Carmyle
Kilmarnock 2, 22
Kingsley, Charles 71

Last Leaves see Alexander, Pat
Leader, The 59, 61, 68, 115
Lewes, George H. 58, 68, 73
London Mercury 149

Macdonald, Capt. Charles (father-in-law) 111, 131, 181f., 201f.
Macdonald, Flora see Smith, Flora Macdonald
Macdonald, Hugh 3, 9f., 39, 47, 75, 116, 129, 160, 194
Macdonald, Keith (brother in law) 188
Macdonald, Lauchlan (brother-in-law) 162
Macfarlan, James 203
Macleod, Rev Norman 28, 145f.,
Macmillan, A. & D. (publishers) 96, 103, 109, 115, 128
Macmillan's Magazine 127, 131, 177
Massey, Gerald 91, 120, 193
Masson, David 70, 101, 127, 130, 147, 186, 194, 203f.
McCulloch, Horatio 93f., 142f., 170, 176, 191
McGowan, Dr Margaret 152f.
McLaren, D. (Provost) 76
McLellan, Archibald 30f.
McLennan, John F. 95, 111, 122, 125, 137, 140, 164, 191, 201
McLeod, Anne (mother-in-law) 180f.
McLeod, Kenneth (of Gesto) 131, 137, 165, 180f., 203
Miller, Hugh 97

Montaigne, M. E. de   146f., 150f.
Morgan, Edwin   210
Morley, Christopher   149
Muir, Edwin   206
Museum, The   156, 164
Muslin trade   3, 14f., 46

National Review   116
NB Review   70, 133
New College (now Old College, Edinburgh)   81, 134
Nichol, John   57, 72, 77f., 81, 140
Nichol, John Pringle   55, 67, 140
Nicolson, Alexander   94, 101, 106, 136, 164, 176f.
Nimmo Hay & Mitchell   194
Niven, Frederick   211
Noel Paton, Joseph   142

Ord (Skye)   111f., 143, 167, 177f., 184
Origin of Species   98
Ossian   136, 176, 194, 207
Paisley (Greysley)   200
Paisley & Renfrewshire Gazette   129
Pall Mall Gazette   197
Palmer, H.   198
Patmore, Coventry   117
Pender-Mackenzie, Dorothea (grand-daughter)   198
Periodical publishing   99f.
Perry, E.   198
Phillip, John   144
Port Dundas   11, 141
Priestley, J.B.   156

Quarterly Review, The   60, 99
Quiver, The see Strahan, Alexander

Raleigh Club   94f., 123
Ramsay, John   22
Rarey, J.S. (Horse Whisperer)   199
Reilly, J.J.   197
Robertson, John (muslin trader)   24, 45f., 59, 63
Rossetti, Dante Gabriel (DGR)   73, 102, 123
Ross-shire Journal, The   198
Royal Literary Fund (RLF)   203f.
Royal Scottish Academy (RSA)   142f.

Sabbatarians   31, 85, 146, 179
Sassi, Prof Carla   206f.
Saturday Review, The   5.1, 7.16, 8.5,

Scotsman, The 193
Scott, Sir Walter 8, 60, 107, 121, 199
Scott column 207
Simpson, William (Crimea) 7, 160, 162f.
Skelton, John (Shirley) 123, 140

Smith, Alexander

Birth date 1, Paisley schooling 4, move to Glasgow 6, Glasgow schooling 10, brain fever 12, early reading 14, 19f., pattern-designing 14, 16f., 45, working day 19, reads Gilfillan's 'Genius' 25, influence of religion 27f. 57, GALS 32f., friendship with Brisbane 36f., first photo 39, walks along the Clyde 40, writing poetry 43, Eclectic Review and Critic publish work 56, *Poems* published 61f. Trip to London 72f., Edinburgh College Secretaryship 79f., 114, 125f., 134f., 165, 191, *Firmilian* episode 83f., friendship with Dobell 88f., Athenaeum plagiarism charges 100f., Macmillans publish *City Poems* 114, Marriage to Flora Macdonald 110, move to Gillespie Place 113, move to New Town 122, becomes Registrar 125, move to Gesto Villa 137f., student riots 108, 136, applies for Glasgow chair 140, Strahan publishes *Dreamthorp* 148f., essays for periodicals 158f., *Alfred Hagart's Household* published in instalments 166f., publishes *A Summer in Skye* 177f., applies for Edinburgh chair 186f., ill-health 188, dies 192, headstone and memorial bust 194f., 211, 'The Boss' 198

Works: 'A Boy's Poem' 45, 50, 118, 'A Lark's Flight' 11f., 150, 153f., 190 'A Life-Drama' *(Poems)* 53f., 61f., 'A Spring Chanson' 189, *A Summer in Skye* 160, 177f., *Alfred Hagart's Household* 1, 166f., 'An Essay on an Old Essayist – Montaigne' 146f. 'An Essay on an Old Subject' 165, 187 'Autumn' 146, 'Barbara' 119f, 197., 'Burns as a National Poet' 59, *City Poems* 104f., *Dreamthorp* 148f.,. *Edwin of Deira* 123f, 'Essayists Old and New' 148, *Glasgow* 10, 42, 78f., 179, 193, 201f. *Golden Leaves from the American Poets* 189, 'Horton' 24, 50, 116, 'Lines to a friend' 47, 'Literary Work' 143, 150, 158, 'Men of Letters' 151, 166, 'Mr Tennyson and his Critics' 87, 'Novels and Novelists of the Day' 147, 'Of Death and Dying' 155, 'On Dreams and Dreaming' 165, 190, 'On the Importance of a Man to Himself' 150, 'On the Writing of Essays' 150, *Poetical Works of Robert Burns* 159, 'Scottish Ballads' 112, 'Sederunts of the Sanct Mungo Club' 29, 77 *Sonnets on the War* 94, 'Squire Maurice' 116, 'Sydney Dobell' 222, *The McGillowies of McGillowie* 190, 'The Minister-Painter' 169, 'The Night Before the Wedding' 112, 'To a City' 214, 'Torquil and Oona' 128, 'Vagabonds' 151, 'Wardie – Springtime' 132, 138, 146, 'Winter' 158,

Smith, Alexander (namesake) 63
Smith, Alexander (uncle) 202
Smith, Charles (son) 188, 192, 199, 205
Smith, Christina Murray (mother) 1, 200

Smith, Christina (sister) 2, 201
Smith, David (brother) 200
Smith, Flora (daughter) 188
Smith, Flora Macdonald (wife) 94, 111, 122, 130, 140, 142, 176, 185f., 201f.
Smith, Isabella (daughter) 188, 198, 205
Smith, Jessie (daughter) 132, 188
Smith, John (father) 1, 167, 192, 200
Smith, Katy (sister) 5, 150, 167, 201
Smith, Marcella (daughter) 166f,
Smith, Marion (sister) 2
Smith, William (brother) 140
Somers, Robert 86f.
Spasmodic School of Poets 86f., 193f., 208
Stevenson, R.L. 149, 171, 175, 188, 211f.
Strahan, Alexander (publisher) 145f., 158, 162, 187f., 190f. , 197
Swinburne, Algernon 140

Tait's Magazine 177
Tennyson, Lord Alfred 32, 46, 51, 60f., 68, 84, 88, 104, 128, 177, 196, 199
Temperance see Drunkenness
Thompson, Rev John 169f.
Ticknor & Fields 128, 169
Trossachs 170

Walker, Hugh 195
Wardie 132f., 182, 202f.
Waugh, Arthur 197
Westminster Review 60, 68, 156
Wilson, John (Christopher North) 75, 83, 165
Women readers 100
Woolmer, Thomas 73, 103
Worker poets 22

Yellow Book, The 197

'Z' (pseud.) 100

Inside cover photo shows no.12 Charlotte street (2nd entry from the left past the shop) seen from London Road.
Reproduced courtesy of the Mitchell Library